# Managing curricular innovation

# CAMBRIDGE LANGUAGE TEACHING LIBRARY

A series covering central issues in language teaching and learning, by authors who have expert knowledge in their field.

*In this series:*

# Managing Curricular Innovation

## Numa Markee

University of Illinois at
Urbana-Champaign

PUBLISHED BY THE PRESS SYNDICATE OF THE UNIVERSITY OF CAMBRIDGE
The Pitt Building, Trumpington Street, Cambridge CB2 1RP, United Kingdom

CAMBRIDGE UNIVERSITY PRESS
The Edinburgh Building, Cambridge CB2 2RU, United Kingdom
40 West 20th Street, New York, NY 10011–4211, USA
10 Stamford Road, Oakleigh, Melbourne 3166, Australia

© Cambridge University Press 1997

First published 1997

Transferred to digital printing 2002

Typeset in Sabon.

*Library of Congress Cataloguing-in-Publication Data*
Markee, Numa.
Managing curricular innovation / Numa Markee.
p.   cm. – (Cambridge language teaching library)
Includes bibliographical references
ISBN 0-521-55512-4 (hardcover). – ISBN 0-521-55524-8 (pbk.)
1.   Language and languages – Study and teaching.   2.   Curriculum change. I. Title. II. Series.
P53.295.M37 1997
418'.007 – dc20                                        96-16202
                                                                  CIP

A catalogue record for this book is available from the British Library

ISBN 0-521-555124 Hardback
ISBN 0-521-555248 Paperback

For Susan, who constantly encouraged me during the time that I was writing this book; and to past and present teaching assistants who have participated in the CATI project.

# Contents

# Contents

# Preface

This book is about the management of curricular innovation in second and foreign language education. Part I (Chapters 1–3) lays out theoretical issues in managing curricular innovation. Part II (Chapters 4–6) discusses a case study in curricular innovation – an account that exemplifies and expands on the theoretical base developed in Part I. Part III (Chapter 7) offers some general conclusions about the issues and problems that must be resolved in any effort to implement change in language education.

Chapter 1 lays out the fundamental assumptions that underpin this book, explains who the book is for, and outlines some important caveats about introducing a "diffusion-of-innovations" perspective into the language teaching literature. Chapter 2 reviews some well-known examples of innovations in second and foreign language teaching. The purpose of this chapter is to present inductively the concepts and issues that are defined and further developed in subsequent chapters. Although all these innovations were developed in very different contexts of implementation, their acceptance or rejection by potential adopters can nevertheless be analyzed in terms of a finite set of theoretical principles that govern the diffusion of all innovations.

This approach – looking first at examples of innovations – violates the normal academic practice of defining one's terms first and then exemplifying technical concepts with practical examples. However, as Cooper (1989: 2) suggests, "evaluating a definition without prior examples is a bit like trying to imagine how new clothes will look on you when you first see them on the shelf." The defining examples of innovations I discuss in Chapter 2 include the British Council's international aid activities in underdeveloped countries, the Modern Languages Project's development of notional-functional syllabuses, the Lancaster School's work on process syllabuses, Krashen and Terrell's work on the Natural Approach, Prabhu's work on the communicational or procedural syllabus (also known as the Bangalore Project), and recent developments in task-based language teaching.

Chapter 3 develops a general theoretical framework in which core concepts are defined and the main issues in the innovation literature are formally laid out. These issues include (1) the social roles that stakeholders in the adoption process play, (2) the stages of decision making that potential adopters go through as they decide whether to adopt or reject an innovation, (3) the sociocultural context of innovation, (4) the time-bound nature of change, (5) the psychological and other factors that impinge on potential adopters' decisions to adopt or reject an innovation, and (6) the insights that language teaching professionals can gain from understanding different approaches to change.

The framework developed in Chapter 3 provides the theoretical underpinnings for a case study in *curricular* and *teacher innovation* (CATI; pronounced like "Katie"), presented deductively in Part II. This project, which is located in an ESL program at a U.S. university, has been operating since 1988. The host ESL program has been used as a laboratory for curricular and teacher innovation, in which succeeding generations of teachers develop materials, methodologies, and pedagogical attitudes that they perceive to be new. In so doing, teachers develop themselves as language teaching professionals and simultaneously contribute to the development of the ESL curriculum.

The purpose of Part II is to ground our understanding of how the theories of educational change outlined in Part I may be interpreted and applied to solving real-world problems in real-world situations. Chapter 4 examines the problems involved in designing and implementing the CATI project. Chapter 5 sets out the kinds of support structures that were developed in order to implement the project. Chapter 6 discusses the evaluative feedback used to maintain the CATI project.

Part III returns to the general theoretical perspective on innovation first explored in Part I. Chapter 7 proposes nine guiding principles that language teaching professionals may draw on in order to manage curricular innovation in any educational context.

I wish to express my especial thanks to a number of friends and colleagues who have provided much appreciated support during the preparation of this manuscript: Jack Richards, Mary Vaughn, Mary Carson, Olive Collen, and Sandra Graham of Cambridge University Press; and Charles Alderson, Kathi Bailey, Larry Bouton, Susan Gonzo, Royann Hanson, Gail Hawisher, Braj Kachru, Yamuna Kachru, Jim Lee, Howard Maclay, David Nunan, Barbara O'Keefe, Fredricka Stoller, Bill VanPatten, Ron White, Chuck Whitney, and Ladislav Zgusta. I would also like to acknowledge the extent of my intellectual debt to Bob Cooper, who first introduced me to the diffusion-of-innovations literature in the field of language planning and thereby started me thinking about how the same ideas might apply to curriculum design. His influence on my work is most obviously seen in Chapter 3, where I borrow the framework developed in Cooper (1982, 1989) to analyze curricular innovation. I also wish to thank a number of individuals for allowing me to cite material from their CATI project-related work, particularly David Broersma, whose unit "The Iceman Speaks" is extensively discussed in Chapter 4, and Lori Chinitz, Jane Nicholls, Tim Noble, and Patti Watts for permission to cite material in Chapters 5 and 6. Finally, I would like to acknowledge the fact that parts of Chapters 2, 3, 4, 5, and 6 contain revised material from Markee (1993a,b, 1994b, 1996).

Numa Markee

# I  *Defining educational innovation*

# 1 Introduction

> There is nothing more difficult to plan,
> more doubtful of success, nor more
> dangerous to manage than the creation
> of a new order of things. (Niccolò Machi-
> avelli, *The Prince*, 1513; cited in Rogers
> 1983: 1)

Language teaching professionals have built up a body of theoretical and practical knowledge since the 1980s that has resulted in the formulation of various innovative approaches to language teaching. What exactly does the phrase "innovative approaches to language teaching" mean? For some readers, this phrase may suggest various "designer" methods like the Silent Way, Suggestopedia, Total Physical Response, or Community Language Learning (see Blair 1982 or Richards and Rodgers 1986). This is not the concern here, since the examples in this book are all within the mainstream of second and foreign language pedagogy: notional-functional syllabuses, the process syllabus, the Natural Approach, and various kinds of task-based language teaching. Rather, the concern of this book is why some new ideas or practices spread while others do not. More concretely, why does a new textbook succeed in the public education system of one country while identical materials fail in another? What must program directors at universities, public schools, and private sector institutions do to persuade teachers to use new ways of teaching?

All language teaching professionals doubtless ask themselves such questions often. Yet, until recently, applied linguistics, the discipline that should provide language educators with the knowledge to answer such questions, has been noticeably silent on these issues. This silence is surprising, since understanding what determines the success or failure of new pedagogical ideas and practices is surely a crucial issue, especially for teacher educators.

This book aims to provide language teaching professionals with the knowledge – both theoretical and practical – needed to answer precisely these questions. More specifically, asking such questions – which focus primarily on issues of syllabus *implementation* rather than *design* – in-

3

volves adopting a "diffusion-of-innovations" perspective on understanding educational change. This perspective leads to other questions, about what change is, what attributes innovations should possess in order to be adopted, how different kinds of individuals react to innovations, and how various systemic factors – all sociocultural in nature – interact to affect the implemention of innovations.

Two assumptions undergird this book. First, given the ubiquitousness of change in education (Baldridge and Deal 1983), the study of how to effect educational change should be part of the basic intellectual preparation of all language teaching professionals – particularly of those individuals who possess or seek to obtain advanced graduate degrees in the field. Second, although curriculum development and teacher development are often treated as separate issues, they are in fact indivisible (Stenhouse 1975). Indeed, to summarize the message of this book in one sentence, the adoption of a diffusionist perspective on educational change involves addressing the short- and long-term professionalization of teachers, on whom real, long-lasting change in the classroom always depends.

This book is written from the point of view of an ESL program director; however, it is not ESL-specific. Whether we are talking about second or foreign language education, and whether we are Spanish, Russian, or Arabic specialists, the implementation of change in language education occurs within a systemic ecology that either promotes or inhibits innovation. In other words, cultural, economic, political, and other factors always mediate the possibility of change. Thus, whatever the language being taught, the problems of effecting change can be analyzed in terms of a common sociocultural perspective on change. This perspective is valid regardless of the contexts of implementation in which language teaching professionals operate.

This book addresses a broad spectrum of language specialists, especially those who are directly involved in language teaching and teacher education and training. Although all language teaching professionals have a stake in promoting educational change, the interests and motivations that different players bring to the task of implementing change vary tremendously. To address the needs and interests of this heterogeneous audience, the discussion is couched in both theoretical and practical terms.

In order to illustrate how innovation works, I rely heavily on the CATI project. This reliance may prompt some readers to ask, "What does this project have to do with me?" Any case study is potentially open to this criticism. If the package of *solutions* developed for the CATI project is not transferable to other institutions without considerable adaptation, nevertheless the *problems* that must be solved turn out to be strikingly similar across different sociocultural contexts.

Whether the locus of change is a school or university, and whether change occurs in an Australian, a Canadian, a Hungarian, an Indian, an Indonesian, a Japanese, or a U.S. context, the same problems occur again and again. This insight is supported by a number of case studies of educational change in language teaching (see Bailey 1992; Beretta 1990; Bottomley, Dalton and Corbel 1994; Brindley and Hood 1991; Duff and Early 1996; Henrichsen 1989; Markee 1994a,b, 1996; Prabhu 1987; Ranta et al. 1996; Rounds in press; Tomlinson 1990; Young 1992).

Thus, the rationale for providing a detailed description of a single project is that this illuminates the kinds of problems of implementation that all language teaching professionals must confront. Consequently, just as language teaching professionals learned a great deal about developing, implementing, and evaluating innovative projects from the Bangalore Project, so can important lessons about the management of educational change be learned from the CATI project, which, unlike the Bangalore Project, is still evolving.

Since this book addresses a broad audience, different readers will have different reasons for reading it. Thus, not everybody will want to read it in the same way. Readers equally interested in the theory and practice of educational innovation should read all three parts of this book linearly. However, readers who have different aims or preferences may read this book like a computer hypertext. That is, they may want to begin with the sections that interest them most and refer to other chapters as needed. For example, researchers using this book as a reference on educational innovation theory may concentrate on Parts I and III. On the other hand, teachers interested in the practical aspects of effecting educational change may focus on Part II. Similarly, readers who prefer a deductive to an inductive approach may read Chapter 3 before Chapter 2.

In order to facilitate nonlinear reading, I have cross-referenced discussions of thematically related material in different parts of the book through 167 "Text Links." For example, if I were to refer to the CATI project, the reader would be directed to a series of references through a parenthetical text citation: for example, (see Text Link 1). Thus, Text Link 1 refers readers to the preface and also to Text Links 93 and 159, which reference relevant text later in the book. This text can be located by looking for the target Text Link box and reading the paragraph in which it is located. Note that, in a few instances, some of the relevant text is located in the paragraph that immediately precedes or follows the paragraph in which the target Text Link box is embedded.

> ∞ **Text Link 1**
> For more specific information pertaining to the CATI project, see the Preface and Text Link 93. Finally, see also Principle 1 and Text Link 159.

A diffusion-of-innovations perspective on curriculum work is a growth area in language teaching (see, for example, Alderson and Wall 1993; Allwright and Waters 1994; Bailey 1992; Beretta 1989, 1990, 1992a; Bottomley et al. 1994; Bowers 1987; Brindley and Hood 1991; Brumfit 1983; Burns and Brindley 1994; Burns and Hood 1995; Candlin 1984a,b; Cumming 1993; Henrichsen 1989; Holliday 1992a,b, 1994a,b, 1995a,b; Holliday and Cooke 1982; Kennedy 1982, 1987, 1988, 1994; Markee 1986a,b, 1993a,b, 1994a,b, 1996; Phillipson 1992; Savage 1996; Stoller 1992, 1994, 1995a,b; Wall and Alderson 1993; White 1987, 1988, 1993; White et al. 1991; Young, 1992). A much more comprehensive bibliography is available from the annotated bibliography of the Language in Development Forum, a World Wide Web site on the Internet. Despite the increasing numbers of publications, however, language teaching professionals are only beginning to discover innovation as an area of professional practice and academic study. Thus, critical caution is in order before wholeheartedly embracing a diffusionist perspective on language education.

If we are to avoid reinventing the wheel, we must realize that the heyday of the innovation movement in education occurred in the 1960s and 1970s, when there was widespread optimism and belief in the ability to effect important changes in educational practice. Nowadays, educators are less optimistic (Fullan 1989, 1993; MacDonald 1991; Rudduck 1991). Language teaching professionals should also know what the limitations of innovation research are. For example, Everett Rogers, one of the leading scholars in this field, notes that diffusion research has been criticized for displaying (1) a pro-innovation bias, in that it has been assumed that such research was conducted only to help promote the adoption of innovations; (2) an inequity bias, in which the socioeconomic and other consequences associated with developing innovations have been ignored or downplayed; (3) an individual-blame bias, in which individuals (rather than the larger social system) tend to be blamed for failure; and (4) a lack of methodological rigor, as when researchers rely on the subjective recollections of informants instead of using objective observational procedures to describe adoption behaviors (Rogers 1983).

Furthermore, we must remember that all innovation is risky and fraught with difficulty. For instance, Adams and Chen (1981) estimate that approximately 75% of all innovations fail to survive in the long term. Thus, it is not surprising that individuals and organizations involved in managing change have engaged in a continuing search for more effective ways of implementing and maintaining innovations. However, even relatively recent attempts to improve the effectiveness of innovation efforts have met with criticism. For example, Fullan (1989, cited by MacDonald 1991) argues that, within education at least, all the conscious strategies of innovation developed to date have failed to fully achieve desired goals.

I do not raise these issues to make language teaching professionals shy away from a diffusionist perspective. As Ron White (personal communication) notes, it is *crucial* to understand "the importance of continuous innovation as part of professional and organizational development, particularly as circumstances in the wider environment are constantly changing." Language teaching will benefit greatly if language teaching professionals develop their own *critically informed* tradition of innovation research and practice. This entails being aware of potential problems in diffusion research, borrowing ideas from disciplines that already possess such research traditions (education, management, medicine, anthropology, sociology, development planning, language planning, and urban planning), and gaining practical experience in solving innovation-related problems. Along these lines, Brindley and Hood (1991) suggest that teachers must *experience* innovations firsthand if they are to adopt and incorporate these changes into their pedagogical practice. This advice is relevant for all language teaching professionals, particularly program directors, who must reinvent themselves as change agents who know how to promote change. It is only by becoming familiar with both the practice and theory of innovation that participants develop a critical understanding of the relevant issues.

# 2 Innovations in second and foreign language teaching

Nothing endures but change. (Heraclitus, fifth century B.C.E.)

Striving to better, oft we mar what's well. (William Shakespeare, *King Lear;* both citations from Henrichsen 1989: 63)

This chapter presents six examples of innovations in language teaching to highlight issues involved in managing change. Example 1 looks at the problematics of effecting change in the cross-cultural context of international language aid programs. The remaining five examples constitute mainstream developments in curriculum design since the 1970s. They include the notional-functional syllabus (Example 2), the process syllabus (Example 3), the Natural Approach (Example 4), the procedural syllabus (Example 5), and task-based language teaching (Example 6). For the purposes of this book, task-based language teaching is a cover term for second and foreign language teaching that incorporates elements of the process syllabus and the procedural syllabus and that also applies insights from second language acquisition research to the classroom. The five innovations in Examples 2–6 were developed by different people and organizations and evolved in different geographical and institutional contexts. Therefore, they may seem quite different from each other. At a deeper level of analysis, however, the diffusion of these syllabuses is analyzable in terms of common underlying principles that affect all attempts to innovate.

Several clarifications about the examples are in order. Most of the innovations I discuss here are syllabuses that stress the importance of communication in language teaching and learning. Thus, the term *communicative language teaching (CLT)* applies to them all. However, although I use CLT to exemplify the main theme of this book – how to effect change in language education – I am not proposing yet another variation of this approach to language teaching. Nor am I arguing that CLT represents the best solution to the teaching and learning problems of language teachers and students all over the world. Language teaching professionals who operate in countries where English is a foreign, not

8

a second, language often express the concern that it is difficult or inappropriate to teach language communicatively (Medgyes 1988). This is a real concern.

At the same time, I also want to emphasize that the problem of appropriateness is not unique to CLT. For example, in the 1920s and 1930s – long before CLT was ever invented – Harold Palmer attempted to introduce his Oral Method into Japanese secondary schools (see Howatt 1984). Similarly,

∞ **Text Link 2**
See Table 5.1 and Figure 5.2. See also Text Links 37, 42, 73, 80, 104, 105, 107, 121, 139, and 157.

Charles Fries attempted to introduce the Audiolingual Method into Japan in the 1950s and 1960s (see Henrichsen 1989 for an account of Fries's attempts to diffuse the Audiolingual Method in Japan). Both attempts ultimately failed. The problems these innovations encountered are no different from those that affect CLT today. Finally, the principles I induce from this chapter go beyond the diffusion of innovative syllabuses (see Text Link 2). They are relevant to the diffusion of *all* types of educational innovations, be these new ways of using personnel resources, conducting student placement and evaluations, organizing faculty development, using new technologies, or organizing community-campus relations (Stoller 1992, 1994).

## Example 1: The British Council's international development work

### Description

The British Council is an important cultural organization and aid agency that runs a variety of language teaching programs worldwide, one of which is the English Language Teaching Officers (ELTO) program.[1] ELTO is funded by the Overseas Development Administration (ODA), the Foreign Office agency responsible for all British aid work, and is administered by the British Council, which is responsible for staffing and managing ELTO projects. ELTO personnel – typically, specialists in curriculum design, materials development, teacher training, or evaluation – operate in underdeveloped countries. They are usually based for up to five years in education ministries, universities, or teacher training institutes. Lately, ELTO projects have also been sited in secondary schools.

From a language teaching perspective, the aims of ELTO projects are

1 ELTO superseded the Key English Language Teaching (KELT) program in 1986. There are technical differences in the way these two programs are organized, which need not concern us here. For ease of reference, I use ELTO to refer to all British Council-administered language teaching projects funded by aid money.

9

quite innovative. Most "regular" language teaching professionals probably view themselves fairly narrowly as *language* specialists. The job descriptions of ELTO personnel, however, are broader: They have to train counterparts – local teachers and administrators who will take over from the ELTOs once these individuals leave – to transform imported pedagogical ideas into appropriate solutions to local problems. The hope is that counterparts will, in the course of time, influence their local colleagues to change their educational practices and values. Ensuring that this "multiplier effect" (Cracknell and Rednall 1986) occurs is crucial if the innovations promoted by ELTO personnel are to survive the end of a project (Holliday 1994a,b; Holliday and Cooke 1982; Maley 1984; Markee 1986b). The challenge ELTO personnel face, therefore, is to change how local teachers think and behave in the classroom; in addition, they must create managerial infrastructures for the development and implementation of innovations that are self-sustaining in the long term.

∞ **Text Link 3**
For other instances of this argument, see page 3 and Text Links 5, 8, 106, and 135.

ELTO projects represent classic loci for the cross-cultural development of educational innovations. If the problems – though not the solutions – of implementing change are similar in different cultural contexts, then all language teaching professionals potentially have much to learn from these projects (see Text Link 3). For example, at a time when the importance of learner-centered instruction is so often stressed in methodology textbooks, the focus of many ELTO projects on teachers as the linchpins of educational change may initially seem odd. However, this emphasis on teachers is perfectly tenable. All teachers faced with implementing learner-centered curricula – which frequently constitute the content of language aid projects – need to develop more sophisticated pedagogical and linguistic skills than teachers who implement teacher-centered curricula. They therefore need to know how to make their classes student-centered. Furthermore, this emphasis on teacher training is in line with the emphasis on human resource development that characterizes much current international aid work (Hilton and Webber 1993; Rondinelli, Middleton, and Verspoor 1990). In addition, this emphasis on the central role of teachers in educational change is also common in the education literature (Fullan 1982a,b, 1993; Stenhouse 1975). This position is beginning to find support in the field of language teaching as well (Brumfit 1991; Freeman 1992; Richards and Lockhart 1994).

At the same time, language teaching professionals potentially have much to learn from the failure of much recent aid work. This failure not only provides rich insights into the technical difficulties of implementing change; it also serves to highlight important ethical questions that affect all change efforts – such as who "owns" or has a personal stake in change. I use British Council projects to illustrate my discussion of the failure of aid because it is through this organization that I gained my own aid experience; consequently, this is the agency with which I am most familiar. Nevertheless, my critique holds for all aid work, whichever organization acts as the donor agency.

According to Phillipson (1992), aid does not promote development, but rather perpetuates the dependence of underdeveloped countries on developed countries by implementing a "center-periphery" model of development. In this view, aid has far more to do with donor governments wishing to improve trade or gain political influence with the recipients of aid than with promoting human development through language education. This model – which involves sending expatriate "experts" from "center" countries like Britain to organize language education projects in "peripheral" countries like the Sudan – can only lead to failure. This is because most aid assumes that host country personnel are unable to organize language education in their own countries. Furthermore, it conceptualizes professionalism in language teaching in narrowly technical terms. That is, what succeeds in Britain or the United States is supposed to succeed in underdeveloped countries.

Phillipson's thesis is perhaps stated too boldly. In rare cases, language aid need not necessarily promote dependence – for example, the Brazilian project described by Alderson and Scott (1992) and Celani et al. (1988) – but that is probably because newly industrialized countries like Brazil do not need expatriate experts in the first place. Nonetheless, Phillipson's general position is well-taken. Proponents of the center-periphery model of development (whether conscious or unconscious advocates) ignore the fact that language aid projects function within specific sociocultural and systemic parameters. Furthermore, recipients of aid may perceive *language* aid projects to be irrelevant to their real needs.

For example, the Sudanese official in charge of a bilateral Anglo-Sudanese aid project I worked on claimed that the language component of a technical assistance project put together by ODA and the British Council had been *imposed* by these donor agencies, despite his strenuous objections that language aid was not needed. If true, this anecdote provides a classic example of how center-periphery patterns of development work (Markee 1993b). At the time, of course, I was skeptical that my professional expertise was so superfluous. However, I was also uncomfortably aware that my activities were tainted by this official's perceptions of what had happened. In retrospect, I am now convinced that my Sudanese colleague was right: My presence contributed little to my hosts' development. I am also convinced that "my" project was ultimately unsuccessful.

∞ **Text Link 4**

The role played by these variables is taken up again in later chapters; see Text Links 47, 52, 69, 81, 82, and 150. See also Principle 1 and Text Link 159.

There were at least ten sociocultural variables responsible for this. My project was affected by complex cultural, ideological, historical, political, economic, administrative, institutional, technological, sociolinguistic, and language planning factors (Markee 1986a,b; see also Bowers 1980a,b, 1983, 1987; Holliday 1992a, 1994a,b; Holliday and Cooke 1982; Kennedy 1982, 1988; Maley 1984; Nunan 1995; Richards 1985; Swales 1980, 1989) (see Text Link 4). In this situation, my expatriate colleagues and I were linguistically, culturally, and professionally ill-equipped to devise solutions that were appropriate for (Markee 1986b) or compatible with local conditions (Rogers 1983).

The official medium of instruction at the technological university where I taught was English. Nonetheless, the students' native language, Arabic, was widely, if unofficially, used throughout the institution. Despite these ambiguous patterns of language use, students received a great deal of English input in their technical classes, which were all taught by Sudanese teachers. More specifically, students attended approximately 25 hours of technical lectures a week given by instructors who used a Sudanese variety of English. They also received 4 hours of English for specific purposes (ESP) instruction a week from language teaching specialists, of whom four were British and four were Sudanese.

Thus, students probably learned most of their English from technical teachers, not from language specialists. Furthermore, the native speakers of British English had no special competence in Sudanese English, which was the de facto target linguistic norm at Sudanese institutions; in addition, none of the expatriates was fluent in Arabic. We expatriate language teaching "experts" were therefore at a significant linguistic and cultural disadvantage vis-à-vis our Sudanese colleagues, who had a far better intuitive understanding of the learning problems that students had trying to master the target norm – in this case, Sudanese English.

Already at a linguistic and cultural disadvantage, we expatriates were in no better position professionally. For example, due to my cultural unfamiliarity with the Sudan, it took me a long time to understand the complexity of the language situation in the country and how this situation affected English instruction within the institution (Markee 1986a). Carrying out needs analyses and organizing instruction was not a simple technical matter of designing questionnaires and developing ESP course materials. Our jobs involved managing the introduction of culturally appropriate educational innovations, for which we had no prior qualifications, training, or special expertise. Whatever expertise we developed we learned through trial and error on the job. By the time I was beginning to understand how local cultural and other constraints affected English instruction in the Sudan, it was time for me to move on (Markee 1993b).

This thumbnail sketch of "my" project in the Sudan illustrates the technical and ethical problems that beset aid work. Despite our status as language teaching "experts," my expatriate colleagues and I were linguistically, culturally, and even professionally marginalized within the university. Thus, our impact on improving the quality of language education in this institution was minimal, particularly in the long term. For example, the ESP materials I developed were based on Western ideas about language education – and these ideas were quite different from the ideas my Sudanese counterparts held. They therefore had little – if any – reason to feel ownership for these materials. Like so many other artifacts of aid work, these materials soon gathered dust on some cupboard shelf after I left the Sudan.

## Some implications for educational change

Table 2.1 summarizes the ELTO Anglo-Sudanese project, from which I wish to extrapolate some general implications for educational change. First, an emphasis on teacher development in no way contradicts the importance of learner-centered instruction in language teaching; it recognizes that innovations like learner-centered instruction cannot occur without teachers' understanding and support.

> ∞ **Text Link 5**
> See Text Links 3, 8, 106, and 135. Finally, see also Principles 6 and 7 and Text Links 164 and 165.

Second, if we accept that the problems of implementing change are similar across different cultural contexts (see Text Link 5), then we can learn much from the failures of aid projects. Although language teaching professionals working in developed countries may not encounter exactly the same problems of marginalization described here, it is still true that understanding how cultural systems work – even those with which we are ostensibly quite familiar – is a surprisingly difficult task. As I argue in Chapter 6, language classrooms are essentially mysterious places: What we *think* happens and what *actually* happens in "our" classrooms are often different (see Text Link 6).

> ∞ **Text Link 6**
> See in particular Text Links 456 and 156.

Language teaching professionals must also become more sensitive to the potential impact that sociocultural factors can have on a project's success or failure. Again, the specific factors that may impact a project's success are likely to vary from place to place. In aid work, however, the cultural *appropriateness* or *compatibility* of innovations with recipients' current practices always assumes a crucial importance. Furthermore, we should understand the model(s) of change to which we subscribe or that we are implicitly involved in maintaining. Language teaching is a highly value-laden ac-

TABLE 2.1. SOME IMPLICATIONS OF ELTO FOR EDUCATIONAL CHANGE

| Innovations | Diffusion-related issues | Attributes that promoted (+) or inhibited (−) the adoption of program innovations |
|---|---|---|
| Focus on teacher development | Classic loci for the cross-cultural development of educational innovations | Its *appropriateness/ compatibility* (−) |
| | Learning from the failure of aid: <br> − role of sociocultural factors <br> − use of a center-periphery model of change | Its *relative advantages* (−) |
| | The difficulty of maintaining a process of change in the long term | |
| | The importance of ethical considerations in educational aid (e.g., who owns and benefits from change?) | |

tivity because it potentially promotes fundamental changes in the ways individuals communicate. In language aid work, a center-periphery model of change *imposes* change on end users and is essentially ethnocentric.

Of course, language teaching professionals do not consciously set out to be ethnocentric. Yet, a center-periphery model is fundamentally ethnocentric because it is based on unequal economic and political relationships that promote hosts' continuing dependence on expatriate donors. By being associated with projects that are influenced by this model, I – like many other aid workers before and after me – unwittingly participated in maintaining a system of unequal power relationships between donors and recipients of language aid – a system I intellectually reject. Similar issues and problems affect programs in "mainstream" language teaching situations. If change is imposed on teachers anywhere, they will likely resist it. Consequently, change agents must seek other ways of managing change that involve securing teachers' participation and consent (see Text Link 7).

∞ **Text Link 7**
For related discussions of these issues, see also Text Links 17, 25, 58, 64, 86, 125, and 152. Finally, see Principles 2 and 6 and Text Links 160 and 164.

Third, although issues of maintenance are particularly problematic in aid projects, they by no means occur only in the context of such projects. By their very nature, all educational organizations are transient institutions: Students graduate, and teachers and administrators move on to other jobs (Baldridge and Deal 1983).

> ∞ **Text Link 8**
> See also Text Links 3, 106, 135, and 140).

Consequently, any curriculum development project is bound to be affected by a constant turnover in staff – which is the norm, not the exception, in education. As I argue in Chapters 5 and 6, therefore, the ways I have dealt with maintenance issues in the CATI project potentially provide important insights into basic issues and problems of change that all change agents must confront (see Text Link 8).

Finally, promoting change is not just a matter of technique; it also has important ethical dimensions. In retrospect, I can see that, while the experience I gained as an aid "expert" in the Sudan has been seminal to my own professional development, my Sudanese colleagues did not learn as much from me as I did from them – a peculiar result, since aid projects are ostensibly meant to benefit recipients, not donors. This unequal exchange occurred because I did not deal with problems of ownership

> ∞ **Text Link 9**
> For a discussion of how these issues have been addressed in the CATI project, see Text Links 129, 137, 148, 154, and 156. See also Text Link 52. Finally, see Principles 5 and 7–9 and Text Links 163, 165, 166, and 167.

very well. My Sudanese counterparts and I had different ideas about what "good" educational practice was; since these differences were never resolved, my colleagues did not own the innovations I left behind. Again, these insights are highly relevant to other educational contexts. Teachers must perceive change to be *relatively advantageous* to them if they are to accept it. Furthermore, if they are to own innovations, teachers must have the opportunity to clarify their ideas about language education and engage in ideological as well as behavioral change – a difficult, though not impossible, goal to achieve (see Text Link 9).

## Example 2: The notional-functional syllabus

### Description

In the early 1970s, Europe began to experience significant economic, political, and infrastructural integration. These social changes had important linguistic consequences. Cultural organizations like the Council of Europe recognized that monolingualism was fast becoming a problem for Europeans, especially for adults who had already completed their education. In response, the council sponsored the Modern Languages

Project, which sought to develop new syllabuses to meet these learners' language needs. The result was the notional-functional syllabus.

Influenced by then-current ideas from the ESP movement, the developers of the notional-functional syllabus saw the needs of adult learners as being quite different from those of secondary school students, who study foreign languages as part of their general education. Adolescents have relatively diffuse needs, which are generally limited to passing a matriculation exam. In contrast, adults typically require foreign language instruction that is geared to specific professional and personal needs. Whereas adolescents study the target language extensively, often for several years, adults need short, intensive programs of instruction (Wilkins 1976), which are often better provided by private language schools than by formal education systems.

The notional-functional syllabus was innovative in two respects. First, it broke with previous practice in that it was based on a systematic behavioral analysis of learners' pragmatic language learning needs (Richterich and Chancerel 1977). That is, the notional-functional syllabus was one of the first syllabuses to be theoretically based on a learner-centered, communication-oriented approach to language instruction. Second, the notional-functional syllabus was claimed to be an "analytic" rather than a "synthetic" syllabus (Wilkins 1976).

In synthetic syllabuses, the content of instruction consists of the target language's lexis, syntax, morphology, phonology, and so on. This content is preselected and taught incrementally until the whole language is covered. The learners' task is to "re-synthesize the language that has been broken down into a large number of small pieces with the aim of making this learning task easier" (Wilkins 1976: 2). In analytic syllabuses, however, learning is organized in terms of the social purposes that learners have for learning the target language. This suggests that learners must interact with and analyze samples of language that are relevant to their needs. As Wilkins (1976: 2) comments, "since we are inviting the learner, directly or indirectly, to recognize the linguistic components of the language behavior he is acquiring, we are in effect basing our approach on the learner's analytic capabilities."

According to these distinctions, the structural syllabus is a synthetic construct, but what about the notional-functional syllabus? Wilkins argued that this syllabus represented an analytic approach to organizing language instruction, pointing out that notions (such as expressing time or spatial relationships) and functions (such as asking and granting permission) were meaning-based units of analysis. By organizing language instruction in semantic terms, learners had to grapple with a much larger range of language than was possible with the structural syllabus.

For example, in a unit called "Asking and Granting Permission," the following range of grammatical forms might be included for instruction at the lower-intermediate level. In addition, these forms might be glossed with appropriate information about social register (see the material marked in angle brackets):

1. Can we smoke in here? Yes, you can/may
2. May we smoke in here? ⟨more formal, polite⟩
3. Are we allowed to smoke in here?
4. Are we permitted to smoke in here? ⟨formal⟩
5. Is it all right to smoke in here? ⟨informal⟩
6. I wonder if I could/might borrow your pen. ⟨tactful⟩

A. Would you mind if I opened a window? / my opening a window?
B. No, I don't mind at all (= 'certainly you may') / not at all
(Leech and Svartvik 1975: 143)

In contrast, in a structurally based unit on question formation for learners at a similar level of competence, it is likely that the range of language forms included for presentation would be much narrower – perhaps limited to the syntactically homogeneous language shown in sentences 1, 2, and 4 – thus restricting the information about tenses, aspect, modality, and mood that was presented to students within a single pedagogical unit. Similarly, the sociolinguistic information that could be offered about register in a structurally based unit would be much less rich.

Clearly, the notional-functional syllabus makes more language available for learning than a structural syllabus does. Equally clearly, the units of analysis used to construct notional-functional syllabuses are qualitatively different from those used to construct structural syllabuses. Nonetheless, notions and functions are still *linguistic* units of analysis. Using preselected linguistic units and linguistic criteria to select, grade, and sequence pedagogical content leads us back to synthetic syllabus design solutions. For this reason, applied linguists have rejected Wilkins's claims that the notional-functional syllabus was an analytic construct (Long and Crookes 1992, 1993).

Should we dismiss the notional-functional syllabus as a failed attempt to portray an analytic syllabus? From a diffusionist perspective on language teaching, this conclusion would be premature. This syllabus has spread well beyond Europe to the United States and to Asian countries like Indonesia (Nababan 1984) and Malaysia (Abu Samah 1984). Functional syllabuses in particular have enjoyed great popularity; indeed, by the late 1970s and early 1980s, functional materials had spread all over the world. The continuing vogue of such materials is evident from a cursory look at any publisher's current catalogue.

The success of the notional-functional syllabus raises two related questions: How was this syllabus diffused? and What qualities or attributes did it have that contributed to its widespread adoption? Let us begin with the first of these questions. The notional-functional syllabus was developed by applied linguists who had the expertise to develop a new syllabus. Once these experts had finished laying out the theoretical parameters of this new syllabus, materials writers translated these parameters into pedagogically useful categories that were used to organize teaching materials. Finally, the task of implementing these new materials was handed over to teachers. Thus, in order to promote change, this research, development, and diffusion model of change relies on a careful separation of tasks. Furthermore, these tasks are sequentially carried out by different groups of specialists.

As to the second question, the history of the notional-functional syllabus shows that its success is due not only to its solid intellectual credentials but to the role of international publishing houses. Commercial interests ensured that notional-functional materials became available to teachers worldwide and added the advantages of high quality and attractive packaging. Finally – and perhaps perversely – many "notional-functional" materials were – and still are – disguised structural syllabuses. They thus in fact often *perpetuated* rather than *challenged* the status quo.[2]

∞ **Text Link 10**
See Text Links 19, 20, 25, 28, 45, and 46.

## *Some implications for educational change*

∞ **Text Link 11**
For a discussion of more recent approaches to needs analysis, see Text Link 87.

Table 2.2 summarizes the implications for educational change prompted by the notional-functional syllabus. For present purposes, the notional-functional syllabus has made two important contributions to current curriculum theory. It contributed in no small measure to the tremendous upsurge of interest in how to define the needs of learners that characterized ESP in the late 1970s and early 1980s (see, for example, Brindley 1984; Munby 1978, 1984). As I argue in Chapter 4, needs analysis is far from being a dead issue today, even though the discussion is no longer framed in its original terms (see Text Link 11). Similarly, the analytic-synthetic distinction first posited by Wilkins has largely defined the parameters used by curriculum specialists to discuss subsequent syllabus types. For this reason, I evaluate the innovativeness of the remaining syllabus types discussed in this chapter in precisely these terms.

2   This last factor is by no means unique to the notional-functional syllabus. Task-based language teaching, for example, has weaker forms that can also be covertly synthetic constructs (see Text Link 10).

18

TABLE 2.2. SOME IMPLICATIONS OF THE NOTIONAL-FUNCTIONAL SYLLABUS
FOR EDUCATIONAL CHANGE

| *Innovations* | *Diffusion-related issues* | *Attributes that promoted (+) or inhibited (−) the adoption of this innovation* |
|---|---|---|
| Based on a systematic behavioral analysis of language learners' needs<br><br>Was claimed to be an analytic, not a synthetic, construct | Implicitly relied on a top-down research, development, and diffusion model of change<br><br>Success attributable to at least three factors:<br>– its solid intellectual basis<br>– the support of publishers<br>– often a structural syllabus in disguise | The *form* it took (+)<br>Its *compatibility* (+)<br>Its *observability* (+)<br>Its *relative advantages* (+)<br>(Its *adaptability*) (−) |

The research, development, and diffusion model of change described here is different from the center-periphery model discussed in Example 1 (see Text Link 12) in that it is not based on unequal economic or political relationships between developers and adopters. Nevertheless, these two models resemble each other in some important respects. Whether they were consciously aware of this or not,

∞ **Text Link 12**
For other references to different models of change, see Table 3.2 and Text Links 58 and 60–5. See also Text Links 7, 17, 25, 32, and 84. Finally, see Principle 2 and Text Link 160.

the developers of the notional-functional syllabus were also using an expert-driven, top-down model of change (White 1988). Although arguably successful with some innovations in some cultural contexts, this model of change also potentially suffers from problems of innovation ownership – a fact that language teaching professionals should understand when they attempt to promote change.

Finally, let us further consider how the attributes of form (Richards 1984), compatibility, observability, adaptability, and relative advantage (Rogers 1983) helped spread the notional-functional syllabus. The *form* this innovation took – tangible, high quality, attractively packaged commercial materials – helped determine its ultimate success. Because many of these materials were not that different from previous structural materials, they were *compatible* with teachers' current classroom behaviors and beliefs. Thus, adopting notional-functional materials did not present teachers with unreasonable professional challenges. In addition, the involvement of international publishers gave this innovation a great deal of *observability* – that is, notional-functional materials became highly visible all over the world. Finally, although published materials suffered from a certain lack of *adaptability* when compared to their in-house notional-functional equivalents, their high quality made them *relatively advantageous* for teachers. Once teachers became accustomed to using these new materials, they could be fairly sure – at least in theory – of delivering high quality instruction to their learners. Again, these insights suggest that innovations possess certain desirable attributes and that wise change agents would do well to ensure that their proposals for change possess as many of these desirable characteristics as possible.[3]

∞ **Text Link 13**

For further discussion of these ideas, see text Links 89, 90, 96, 111, 117, 124, and 139; see also Table 2.7, Text Links 18, 55, and 56, and Principles 1 and 8 and Text Links 159 and 166.

## Example 3: The process syllabus

### *Description*

The notional-functional syllabus achieved the status of orthodoxy in the 1970s. In the 1980s, however, alternative approaches to language instruction emerged, including the process syllabus. This syllabus evolved at the University of Lancaster, where it was initially used with ESP learners (Candlin et al. 1981; Hutchinson and Waters 1987). Subsequently, it has also been used in general English situations in Europe (Breen 1984, 1987; Breen and Candlin 1980; Candlin 1984a,b, 1987) and with migrants in Australia. In this last context, this syllabus dovetailed, at least in some instances, with a decentralized curriculum reform movement (Bottomley et al. 1994; Brindley 1984; Brindley and Hood 1991; Nunan 1988a, 1990).

∞ **Text Link 14**

See Figure 2.1; however, note also the caveat signaled by Text Link 28.

The process syllabus was, and continues to be, quite innovative. First, it is a radically analytic syllabus, in that it does not preselect the linguistic content of instruction. Instead, it uses problem-solving tasks, the most important characteristics of which I discuss in Example 6 (see Text Link 14).

Second, the process syllabus is situated within a curricular approach to organizing language instruction. In order to understand how this is so, we must distinguish between a *curriculum* and a *syllabus*. These widely used terms have different meanings to British and American writ-

---

3 In the remaining examples of innovative syllabus types, I continue to analyze each innovation in terms of its positive or negative attributes. In Chapters 4 and 5, I show how this kind of analysis has informed the development of innovations diffused by the CATI project (see Text Link 13).

ers, and are thus potentially confusing. Here, I follow White's British usage, in which " 'syllabus' refers to the content or subject matter of an individual subject, whereas 'curriculum' refers to the totality of content to be taught and aims to be realized within one school or educational system" (White 1988: 4). Thus, a curriculum subsumes a syllabus. I return to this notion shortly.

Third, in its strong form at least, not only the content but the materials, methodology, and types of assessment used in a course are not predetermined. The process syllabus thus promotes innovation through a problem-solving model of change. In traditional syllabuses, syllabus writers specify content before a course begins. Thus, traditional syllabuses are predictive documents because they set out what is to be taught. In the strong form of the process syllabus, however, content, materials, methodology, and assessment are negotiated between the instructor and the learners throughout the course. That is, learners help select course content and materials and provide input on how they want to be taught and assessed. Of course, negotiation is a relative, not an absolute, process: A teacher's decision to involve learners in making choices is not negotiable. For present purposes, the most important implication of this emphasis on negotiation is that the process syllabus is not a predictive but rather a retrospective record of what is actually taught, since it emerges over time.

Returning to the idea that a curriculum subsumes a syllabus, it is helpful to differentiate between strategic and tactical levels of planning. *Strategic planning* involves program directors creating *curricular guidelines* for instruction, whereas *tactical planning* involves teachers making *syllabus* design decisions by interpreting a project director's curricular guidelines according to their own experience (Candlin 1984a). Curricular guidelines lay out a program's educational philosophy, specify purposes and course content, identify implementational constraints, and articulate assessment and evaluation criteria. They also include banks of materials that teachers can modify to meet the negotiated needs of their learners. Syllabuses, on the other hand, represent the emerging, negotiated content of an individual course and how this content is graded and sequenced. Since syllabuses also include the methodological procedures that are used to organize classroom instruction, the usual distinction between syllabus content (the "what" of instruction) and methodology (the "how" of teaching) becomes blurred (Nunan 1988b). It then becomes theoretically possible to speak of a "methodological syllabus."

From a diffusionist perspective on curricular innovation, Candlin makes some explicit claims about how change occurs, which developers of new syllabuses rarely do. More specifically, Candlin claims that pedagogical innovation is a synthesis of tensions between strategic and tactical levels of planning and notes that *"it is only from the tension between classroom action and curriculum guidelines, recorded in syllabuses, that we can expect innovation.* It is this tension which can drive curricula forward" (Candlin 1984a: 36–7, emphasis added). This perspective on the importance of tension – even conflict – as a catalyst of change is unusual, in that language teaching professionals probably tend to implement change through consensus building – a point to which I return later (see Text Link 15). However, it is doubtful that the strong form of the process syllabus has ever been implemented.

∞ Text Link 15
See Text Links 16 and 77. See also Principle 4 and Text Link 162.

In practice, most process materials (Abbs, Ayton, and Freebairn 1975) and published reports (Budd and Wright 1992; Candlin 1984b; Nunan 1990) illustrate a weaker process of negotiation. Learners make choices about course content or the path they wish to take through materials but do so within fairly well-defined parameters. This is just as well, since the implementation of a strong form of the process syllabus would quite likely run into severe difficulties – a criticism that has also been voiced by Clarke (1991), Kouraogo (1987), and White (1988).

As demonstrated in Example 2, successful innovations must possess certain attributes if they are to be acceptable to users. "Translating" these writers' objections into the language of diffusion research, we can say that potential users of the process syllabus must perceive this innovation to be *feasible* (Kelly 1980). The feasibility of teachers negotiating each course from scratch with learners is the key issue here, but the practical question of whether adequate banks of materials are available is also important. If such banks of materials exist – and often they do not – important decisions must be made about how *original* these materials should be (Mintzberg, Raisinghani, and Théoret 1976; Pelz 1985). Should they be commercially available materials, or should they be produced in-house? Teachers must also see negotiation as a *relatively advantageous* change that is *compatible* with their cultural values, *trialable,* and not too *complex* to understand or use (Rogers 1983). Finally, any innovation must have an *explicit* rationale (Dow, Whitehead, and Wright 1984).

## Some implications for educational change

Arguably, the strong form of the process syllabus exhibits none of the important attributes of innovations described in the preceding section (see Table 2.3). It is thus unlikely to be widely adopted, particularly in teacher-centered educational cultures. Despite the inherent difficulties involved in implementing a strong form of the process syllabus – that

TABLE 2.3. SOME IMPLICATIONS OF THE PROCESS SYLLABUS FOR
EDUCATIONAL CHANGE

| Innovations | Diffusion-related issues | Attributes that promoted (+) or inhibited (−) the adoption of the strong form of innovation |
| --- | --- | --- |
| A truly analytic syllabus Situated within a broadly curricular approach to organizing language instruction Content, materials, methodology, and evaluation procedures not predetermined | Relies on a problem-solving model of change | Its *feasibility* (−) Its *originality* (+/−) Its *relative advantages* (−) Its *compatibility* (−) Its *trialability* (−) Its *complexity* (−) Its *explicitness* (−) |

*task – based* [handwritten annotation]

is, a "designless design," in which nothing is predetermined and everything is up for negotiation – a weak version of this syllabus – a largely
predetermined syllabus, in which teachers use negotiation to *fine-tune*
the implementation of instruction – potentially has considerable relevance for teachers, students, and indeed entire projects in educational
change. Assuming that banks of materials were in place, the originality
of these materials could become a manageable issue. As for fine-tuning
the implementation of a predetermined syllabus through negotiation,
teachers could ask learners to keep journals, in which students record
their impressions of class activities. Through such journals teachers
could solicit questions from learners to make sure they understood what
they were learning or, more ambitiously, solicit feedback on how useful
class activities were. Of course, teachers should explain explicitly what
potential benefits learners might gain from this process. Students would
benefit by being better informed about the course, by having both their
objective needs and subjective wants met more directly, and by feeling
that they had a stake in the success of the course – this latter point
being another manifestation of the issue of ownership already discussed
in Examples 1 and 2. Teachers would benefit by getting feedback about
their own teaching during the course, while they could still act on the
feedback.

A weak version of the process syllabus is also more likely to be implemented than a strong version in terms of compatibility, complexity,
and trialability. The strong form of this syllabus would likely seem in-
timidating to teachers, even if, theoretically, they want to be learner-

centered instructors. For example, returning to the use of journals as an example of a weak form of negotiation, journals allow negotiation that is *compatible* with student-centered instruction. Furthermore, the idea of having students keep journals is less *complex* to understand and use than the abstract idea of a "designless design." Last, journals are *trialable:* teachers can initially request learners to comment on course content and not necessarily on their teaching. As they gain experience with journals, they may then experiment more boldly and ask for feedback about their teaching.

As noted previously, the process syllabus is based on a model of change that is quite different from that which underpins the notional-functional syllabus and, indeed, the ELTO program. In those two examples, we saw that change is an expert-driven, top-down process that emphasizes efficiency and minimizes disruption. In contrast, the process syllabus relies on bottom-up decision-making processes and not only tolerates but encourages the participation of "lay" clients. Furthermore, in Candlin's interpretation of this model, at least, tension is not shunned and functions as a potentially useful catalyst of change. In this view, the interaction between teachers' tactical syllabus design decisions and program directors' strategic curricular guidelines constitutes the engine of curricular innovation.

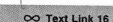

∞ **Text Link 16**
For related discussions of the concept of negotiation, see Text Links 98, 102, and 103; see also Text Links 15, 77, and 155. Finally, see Principle 4 and Text Link 162.

These ideas are difficult to understand in the abstract. To give a brief preview of the practical content of Part II, the model of curricular innovation that informs the CATI project is based partly on a conservative interpretation of Candlin's ideas. This interpretation preserves the distinction between strategic (i.e., curricular) and tactical (i.e., syllabus) levels of planning. However, the syllabus becomes a conventionally predictive document, embodied in task-based materials developed by teachers. For this reason, I add a third level of planning called operational planning (Ellison and Davies 1990), which accounts for actual classroom activities. I also preserve the idea of disequilibrium or conflict as a major driving force of innovation. Just as teachers negotiate learning with students, so must program directors negotiate with teachers how they implement curricular guidelines (see Text Link 16). More specifically, the program director and the teachers negotiate the content and methodology of materials, which yields a syllabus of task-based units. Teachers try these units in class and negotiate unit content and methodology further with students. Used in conjunction with a teacher-generated research program, the trialing process leads to further revision of units. In the long term, all these activities problematize how teachers teach and how they think about their teaching.

# Example 4: The natural approach

## Description

The Natural Approach was first developed as a method of foreign language teaching in the United States to meet the language learning needs of beginning and early-intermediate adult learners (Krashen and Terrell 1983; Terrell 1982; Terrell et al. 1990). Because many of its proposals dovetail so neatly with the theory of second language acquisition (SLA) proposed by Krashen, it is now put forward as an approach that exemplifies the pedagogical application of this particular theory of SLA – namely, monitor theory (Krashen 1981, 1982, 1985). Monitor theory consists of five hypotheses: the acquisition-learning hypothesis, the monitor hypothesis, the input hypothesis, the natural order hypothesis, and the affective filter hypothesis.

The acquisition-learning hypothesis posits that adults can "get" a second or foreign language through the activation of two different systems: (1) *acquisition,* involving subconscious learning processes that allow them to pick up the language "naturally," as in first language acquisition; and (2) *learning,* consisting of the development of formal, conscious knowledge about the grammatical rules of a language. According to this hypothesis, formal instruction does not aid acquisition but is necessary for learning.

The role of conscious learning in adult second language acquisition is explained by the second tenet of monitor theory, which states that conscious learning can be used only to monitor or edit output that has been generated by the acquired system. Even then, monitor use can be effective only if three conditions are met. Performers must (1) have enough time to monitor their output, (2) be focused on form, and (3) know the grammatical rule for the form in question.

The third tenet of monitor theory, the input hypothesis, states that learners acquire syntax and vocabulary by receiving and understanding input that is slightly beyond their current level of competence. By guessing and inferring the meaning of linguistic information embedded in the communicative context, learners are able to comprehend syntax and vocabulary that would otherwise be too difficult for them to understand. This input is known as comprehensible input, or "$i + 1$." Thus, learners gradually acquire (not learn) fluency by being exposed to $i + 1$ in the target language.

The fourth tenet, the natural order hypothesis, proposes that there is a natural and predictable order of development in which adults and children acquire the grammatical structures of the target language. That order of acquisition can occur in adults only when they are focused on language as communication, as when they are "acquiring" rather than "learning" a language. During acquisition, similar errors will occur in learners' interlanguage regardless of their native language.

The fifth tenet, the affective filter hypothesis, states that affective factors, such as self-esteem, anxiety, and social and psychological distance, can impede learners' progress in the target language. Learners who have low affective filters are more likely to seek and obtain more input, to be self-confident in their interactions with native speakers, and to make good acquisitional use of the input they receive.

From a diffusion-of-innovations perspective, the Natural Approach is interesting because it contrasts strikingly with the approaches to language teaching that were current in the United States in the late 1970s and early 1980s – chiefly the Audiolingual Method. Whereas Audiolingualism stressed the importance of habit formation and the prevention of grammatical and phonological errors – both of which are synthetic concerns – the Natural Approach proposes that (1) language classrooms should promote communication in the target language rather than focus on its structure; (2) teachers should allow linguistic competence to emerge over time, rather than try to dictate when and in what order particular linguistic items should be learned; and (3) error correction should focus on meaning, not grammatical form.

∞ **Text Link 17**
See Table 3.2 and Text Links 7, 32, 58, 60–5, and 84. Finally, see Principle 2 and Text Link 160.

These analytic proposals follow from the five constituent hypotheses of monitor theory discussed. The Natural Approach is also interesting for two other reasons. First, although much of the methodology of the Natural Approach (for example, its use of Total Physical Response) predates its subsequent marriage with the theoretical and empirical insights of SLA research, the legitimacy of this approach depends in large part on its association with monitor theory. Rather like the notional-functional syllabus, therefore, the Natural Approach is implicitly based on a research, development, and diffusion model of change – a model that is particularly influential in American work in SLA studies (Crookes 1991, 1992; Larsen-Freeman and Long 1991; Long 1985, 1989a, 1990, 1993). Of course, this model of change can be used to achieve particular ends in particular circumstances, which is why it is important to understand the ideological foundations of different models of change and their strengths and weaknesses. As I argue later, a research, development, and diffusion model of change is best suited to the development and diffusion of complex, technical innovations (see Text Link 17). It is not particularly well-suited to promoting changes in human behavior.

Second, the relative success of the Natural Approach – notably, with Spanish as a second or foreign language teachers who teach in the United States – raises interesting questions about what change is and why it happens. We can analyze the adoption of this innovation in terms of the same attributes discussed in Examples 2 and 3. Despite the *complexity* of the basic research that underpins it, a very *explicit* and *simple* case was made to persuade potential adopters of the value of the Natural Approach. Its pedagogical precepts were *compatible* with what we know about successful bilingualism in naturalistic contexts. Furthermore, Krashen was willing to consider the possibility that the Natural Approach might not be adopted as a complete, internally consistent package – a position that speaks to the issue of *trialability*. Finally, he went to great pains to talk to teachers' groups about the Natural Approach and thus make it as *observable* as possible.

However, the way in which the *compatibility* argument was actually made raises some interesting philosophical issues about what counts as a new idea or practice. Surprisingly, Krashen and Terrell (1983: 16) greatly downplay the innovativeness of the Natural Approach and criticize educators who have been "misled" by grammar-based "innovations and shortcuts" in formal language education. Clearly, the concept of "newness" is an unexpectedly problematic matter.

## Some implications for educational change

Table 2.4 summarizes some of the implications of the Natural Approach for educational change. Krashen and Terrell's argument that the Natural Approach is actually traditional is a variation of the old saw that there is nothing new in education. We might be tempted to dismiss this argument as clever rhetoric designed to bring teachers frightened by the newness of the Natural Approach into the fold of adopters. Evidence that I review later (see Text Link 18) suggests that although potential adopters like

∞ **Text Link 18**
See Table 2.7 and Text Links 13, 55, 56, 89, 90, 96, 111, 117, 124, 139, and Principle 1 and Text Link 159 for discussions of how the attributes of innovations affect their diffusion. Finally, see Principle 8 and Text Link 166.

innovations to be new, they do not like them to be *too* new (Rogers 1983; Stoller 1994).

However, as the discussion of the procedural syllabus in Example 5 also demonstrates, defining what is a new idea or practice is not a simple matter. Fortuitously, Prabhu (the principal developer of the procedural syllabus) independently put forward proposals that were in many ways quite similar to those of the Natural Approach (Prabhu 1987; see Text Link 19). Thus, the *subjective perception* of newness by potential adopters is more important than its

∞ **Text Link 19**
See also Text Links 10, 20, 25, 28, 45, and 46.

*objective* newness. For change agents, this insight means that the management of educational change becomes much more complicated than they might have anticipated.

TABLE 2.4. SOME IMPLICATIONS OF THE NATURAL APPROACH FOR
EDUCATIONAL CHANGE

| Innovations | Diffusion-related issues | Attributes that promoted (+) or inhibited (−) the adoption of this innovation |
|---|---|---|
| A truly analytic syllabus: <br> – focus on communication <br> – linguistic competence emerges over time <br> – focus of error correction on meaning, not grammatical form | Relies on a research, development, and diffusion model of change <br><br> Raises interesting philosophical issues about what counts as new in language education | Its *complexity* (−) or *simplicity* (+) <br> Its *explicitness* (+) <br> Its *compatibility* (+/−) <br> Its *trialability* (+) <br> Its *observability* (+) |

## Example 5: The procedural syllabus

### Description

The procedural, or communicational, syllabus emerged out of the Bangalore Project, an experimental English language teaching project that lasted from 1979 to 1984. The locus of the project was eight classes in primary and secondary schools in southern India, where English is a school subject. Like many other innovations, this project was initiated because of dissatisfaction with the status quo – in this case, a structural syllabus coupled with an Audiolingual methodology (Prabhu 1987) or, according to Tickoo (1996), a form of grammar-translation. Whichever source we follow, the Bangalore Project's developers clearly felt that the current approach was not teaching learners how to use English correctly. To remedy this situation, Prabhu and his associates developed the procedural syllabus (Prabhu 1984, 1985, 1987).

This analytic syllabus type was innovative in at least three respects. First, Prabhu and his colleagues tried to develop a syllabus with a content that was not linguistically based. Instead of organizing instruction in terms of preselected language items, they eventually hit upon the idea of using tasks as the principal carrier of language content. Second, the project team developed a meaning-focused methodology in which students learned language by communicating. Third, Prabhu and his associates tried (at least in principle) to avoid using form-focused activities in the classroom (i.e., explicit grammar teaching or error correction).

From a diffusion-of-innovations perspective, the Bangalore Project is interesting on a number of counts. Arguably, the idea of using games to promote communicative language use predates the beginning of the Bangalore Project by at least two years (Allwright 1977). However, this project objectively constitutes the first conscious attempt to implement analytic pro-

∞ **Text Link 20**
See Text Link 19. See also Text Links 10, 25, 28, 45, and 46 for other discussions of the concept of "newness."

posals for syllabus design through a task-based methodology. As already noted in the discussion of Example 4, these proposals were very similar to those of the Natural Approach (see Text Link 20). Note, however, that Prabhu differs with Krashen and Terrell on the role of comprehensible input in second and foreign language learning. Prabhu argues that $i + 1$ is an inadequate concept for pedagogy because meaning does not reside in syntactic structure; rather, it depends on the uses to which grammar is put for particular communicative purposes – hence the use of tasks in the Bangalore Project. Furthermore, the rationale for the procedural syllabus developed independently of the rationale used to underpin the Natural Approach. This demonstrates that change does not necessarily occur as a result of borrowing; thus, it is theoretically important to distinguish between different types of change (see Text Link 21).

∞ **Text Link 21**
See Text Link 36.

Like the process syllabus – but unlike the Natural Approach, which it otherwise resembles so closely – the procedural syllabus implicitly adheres to a problem-solving model of change, at least in Prabhu's eyes. More specifically, the theoretical principles that underpin this syllabus are said to have evolved over a period of several years through a classroom-based process of trial and error (Prabhu 1987); they were not developed by using a research, development, and diffusion model of change (see Text Link 22). This contrast between the Natural Approach and the Bangalore Project shows that, to quote a vivid Chinese proverb, there is more than one way to skin a cat. Different individuals often reach the same goal by taking different roads. Teachers, unlike researchers,

∞ **Text Link 22**
See Table 3.1. See also Text Link 63.

typically reach the goal of changing their pedagogical behaviors and attitudes on the basis of their own experience (Brindley and Hood 1991). Thus, the Bangalore Project's claimed reliance on a trial-and-error approach potentially allowed teachers to try out the project's task-based methodology in small increments over an extended period of time. To the extent that this actually occurred – and there is evidence that it did, at least in the early stages of the project – this problem-solving model of change probably helped teachers who participated in the project's early stages to develop favorable attitudes toward task-based teaching. As we have already seen, *trialability* is an attribute that can help persuade potential adopters to adopt an innovation.

A problem-solving model of change supposedly promotes high levels of participant ownership. Among the innovative syllabuses discussed in this chapter, only the procedural syllabus has been evaluated formally (Beretta 1989, 1990, 1992a), and one of the most important questions was the extent to which teachers actually implemented and owned the principles of the procedural syllabus. The extent to which an innovation is implemented may be evaluated in terms of so-called levels of use, or implementation, which measure the depth of change that occurs (Gross, Giacquinta, and Bernstein 1971; Loucks, Newlove, and Hall 1975). Based on the work of these educators, Beretta (1990, 1992a) distinguished among three levels of implementation in the Bangalore Project: *orientation* (level 1), *routine* (level 2), and *renewal* (level 3). Level 1 describes teachers who were not well-informed about the Bangalore Project's methodology, did not fully understand how to use it, and did not understand what its effects on learners and teachers might be. Level 2 describes teachers who were well-informed about the methodological implications of the project and whose use of task-based language teaching procedures was relatively stable. Level 3 describes teachers who were confident enough of their mastery of project principles that they were ready to modify its basic precepts.

∞ **Text Link 23**
See also Text Links 40, 72, 136, and 144. Finally, see Principles 5, 7, 8, and 9 and Text Links 163, 165, 166, and 167.

Beretta showed that 47% of Bangalore Project teachers reached a routine level of implementation, and only 13% reached an expert level of implementation. Thus, fully 40% of project teachers were not well-informed about the project's task-based methodology and did not understand how to use it. Nor did they grasp what its effects on learners and teachers might be. Furthermore, few teachers felt that they owned this innovation. The results of this evaluation vividly demonstrate how difficult it is to promote fundamental educational change and reinforce the point made in Chapter 1 that 75% of all innovations fail (see Text Link 23).

Why this unexpected result? Beretta did not analyze the reluctance of teachers to adopt task-based instruction in terms of this innovation's attributes. However, the fact that so many teachers did not understand that using this innovation might affect their own professionalization suggests that issues of *relative advantage* may well have been at play. More specifically, teachers who never got beyond level 1 may not have realized that by participating in this project, they might benefit by enhancing their own professional skills. Yet was this the only factor involved in the low levels of adoption and ownership reported by Beretta?

Let us focus on the change strategies that the project director *actually* used. Were these strategies bottom-up or top-down? What effect did the project director's managerial style have on the ultimate success or failure of the procedural syllabus? The answers to these question are complicated. Teachers who felt that they were part of Prabhu's small inner circle of initiates – "nonregular" teachers who were curriculum specialists and teacher trainers with advanced qualifications in second or foreign language teaching and who were affiliated with the British Council or the Bangalore Regional Institute of English – perceived that the project director relied on a bottom-up strategy of change (Beretta 1990, 1992a).

This bottom-up approach to change is what Prabhu intended to promote in the Bangalore Project (Prabhu 1987). However, it may be argued that Prabhu's intentions largely were not fulfilled (Beretta 1990; Tickoo 1996). Teachers who did not feel part of Prabhu's inner circle (principally, regular teachers allocated to the project by schools that joined after the project had already been running for several years) seem to have perceived the project's communicational methodology as an immutable decision that was imposed on implementers by top management.

A closely related point is just how open and democratic the management style of the project director was. One British observer noted that the evolution of the project's communicational methodology was the subject of ongoing public discussion. Based on these characteristics, Brumfit (1984: 240) claims that the project's organization was "a model of openness and genuine connection with classroom realities." On the other hand, an Indian observer of the Bangalore Project casts considerable doubt on how open the project actually was. Tickoo (1996) argues that hardly any of the early classroom-based comments on the project's strengths and weaknesses influenced the project's subsequent development.

Another fascinating issue raised by the Bangalore Project is just how compatible the procedural syllabus was with instructors' cultural values. Speaking to this issue, Tickoo also castigates the project for its inappropriate methodological radicalism in the "acquisition-poor environment" of English language teaching in Indian primary and secondary schools. This criticism is highly controversial, since the developers and implementers of the innovations that were produced by this project were principally Indians. How, then, could this project be culturally inappropriate? Again, since the project no longer exists, this point is largely moot. For the sake of argument, however, let us assume that this criticism is justified; in so doing, we may get a sense of how ideologically contentious attempts to innovate can be.

The project director was Indian, but he was formally affiliated with the British Council as an English studies officer and also held a Ph.D. from a British university. Many of Prabhu's Indian colleagues also held advanced degrees in language teaching from British or Indian institutions, which have always been strongly influenced by the British tradition of applied linguistics (see, in particular, Palmer 1921). We may therefore advance three reasons why the project's methodology may have been culturally inappropriate for some participants.

First, it is widely accepted that a cultural gap exists between applied linguists and teachers, not just in India but all over the world. As eloquently argued by a high school teacher working in the United States, applied linguists and teachers do not speak the same language: Teachers often view the ideas of applied linguists as irrelevant to the classroom and find their discourse impossibly opaque and difficult to understand (Eykin 1987). Thus, any alleged problems of cultural inappropriateness may have been due in part to the different professional cultures of project participants, some of whom were applied linguists and others, teachers.

∞ Text Link 24
See Text Link 53.

Second, project participants had widely different individual experiences of life. These experiences tend to correlate with the psychological profiles of particular types of adopters (Rogers 1983). Participants who, among other things, travel widely, are highly educated, and have well-developed professional connections tend to be more psychologically open to innovation than individuals who have not had such experiences. Thus, individual teachers' personal openness to change may have influenced their perceptions of the project's cultural appropriateness (see Text Link 24). Third – and this is rather controversial – it is not clear that the development and use of a task-based methodology in the Bangalore Project was a locally developed innovation. It may have been imported from Britain.

There is some anecdotal support for this second interpretation: As Tickoo (1996) notes, at least two project participants felt that the project had imported unacceptably radical foreign ideas into India. This perception raises the question of how *compatible, complex,* and *feasible* the procedural syllabus was. It also suggests that the Bangalore Project may have been based as much on a center-periphery model of development as on a problem-solving model of change.

Project staff had rejected the notional-functional syllabus and Widdowson's (1978) discoursal view of language as inappropriate to the Indian context. Thus, key participants were quite familiar with developments in communicative curricula that were then underway in Britain. For example, Prabhu's (1987: 15) use of information gap tasks parallels the work of Johnson (1982a) and Allwright (1977) in this area. Thus, not only is it unclear that the development of a task-based methodology was a locally developed innovation, but this issue also opens up a Pandora's box of contentious questions that problematize the very possibility of the local development of pedagogical innovation in English language teaching. I discuss these questions in the following section.

## Some implications for educational change

My purpose in giving these contrasting perspectives on the Bangalore Project is not to make any judgments as to which side is "right." We cannot make principled judgments about a project that is no longer functioning, and, in any case, it would be inappropriate for an outsider to make such judgments. Rather, my purpose is to show how complex a "simple" idea – that innovation should be a local initiative – turns out to be. I also want to problematize notions of project success or failure. The Bangalore Project may have failed to change local educational practices in India, but ten years after its discontinuation, it continues to have an impact on theoretical discussions of syllabus design (Long and Crookes 1992, 1993). Furthermore, it is beginning to affect the emerging debate about how to implement and maintain educational innovations (see Table 2.5). Thus, the implementation and maintenance-related issues highlighted by the Bangalore Project go to the heart of any attempt to innovate, in any context of implementation. Even if we believe that the Bangalore Project ultimately failed, its problems can be viewed as what Japanese business managers call "mountains of treasures" (DeCosmo, Parker, and Heverly 1991: 22). That is, we can learn much from the failure or partial success of educational innovations (Fullan 1993).

The previous discussion also shows how difficult it is to manage change (see Text Link 25). This is because change agents deal as much with *subjective perceptions* as with *objective facts*. Thus, a practice – using tasks, perhaps – that one teacher regards as within the mainstream of language pedagogy may strike another as impossibly radical; the amount of effort that a change agent would have to put into persuading these two potential adopters to use the "same" innovation would thus have to be different. Similarly, one person's bottom-up management

∞ **Text Link 25**

For discussion of different models of change, see Table 3.2 and Text Links 60–5. See also Text Links 7, 12, 17, 32, 58, and 84. For discussion of the concept of "newness," see Text Links 10, 19, 20, and 28. Finally, see Principle 2 and Text Link 160.

strategy may be perceived as another's top-down strategy. Finally, teachers' perceptions of a project director's management style is a key

TABLE 2.5. SOME IMPLICATIONS OF THE PROCEDURAL SYLLABUS FOR
EDUCATIONAL CHANGE

| Innovations | Diffusion-related issues | Attributes that promoted (+) or inhibited (−) the adoption of this innovation |
|---|---|---|
| A truly analytic syllabus:<br>− use of task-based instruction as the carrier of syllabus content<br>− focus on communication, with linguistic competence emerging over time<br>− error correction of meaning, not grammatical form | Emerged as the result of dissatisfaction with the prevailing structural syllabus and methodology<br><br>Relies on a problem-solving model of change<br><br>Illustrates the importance of evaluation in determining the degree to which a project in curricular innovation actually achieves its objectives<br><br>Raises interesting philosophical issues about what counts as new in language education<br><br>Suggests that an understanding of how organizations work would be useful to language teaching professionals<br><br>Raises interesting philosophical issues about what counts as a successful project<br><br>Highlights the importance of cultural appropriateness in any process of educational change | Its *trialability* (+)<br>Its *relative advantages* (+,−)<br>Its *complexity* (−)<br>Its *feasibility* (−) |

issue. Whether managers themselves or managed by others, language specialists need to have a basic understanding of what management is, because they are all involved in managing change to a greater or lesser extent (see Text Link 26).

> ∞ **Text Link 26**
> See Figure 4.1 and Text Link 38.

## Example 6: Task-based language teaching

### Description

For the purposes of this book, task-based language teaching is not a distinct type of analytic syllabus, as implied by Long and Crookes (1992, 1993); it is an umbrella term that subsumes the process syllabus, the procedural syllabus, and pedagogical applications of more recent theoretical and empirical work in SLA studies, classroom research, and action research (see, among others, Crookes 1986; Doughty and Pica 1986; Kumaravadivelu 1991, 1993a,b; Long 1985, 1989a,b, 1991; Long and Porter 1985; Loschky and Bley-Vroman 1993; Nunan 1989, 1990, 1991, 1993; Pica, Kanagy, and Falodun 1993; Porter 1986; Samuda and Rounds 1993; Swaffar, Arens, and Morgan 1982). Note, incidentally, that the discussion of task-based language teaching that follows is intended to be no more than a preliminary introduction to this approach to syllabus design. I provide a more detailed review in Chapter 4 (see Text Link 27).

> ∞ **Text Link 27**
> See Text Links 91, 97, 101, and 123.

What are the most important characteristics of task-based language teaching, and what are the most important diffusion-related issues raised by its emergence? What attributes of task-based language teaching might contribute either to its adoption or rejection by teachers? Just as communicative language teaching has no single, monolithic identity, no one version of task-based language teaching has gained widespread acceptance. For example, whereas teacher-led tasks were the norm in the Bangalore Project, small group tasks are common in more SLA-inspired versions of task-based language teaching. Despite such obvious surface differences, however, most tasks display the basic characteristic of posing a problem, the solution of which entails learners communicating in the target language. Figure 2.1 illustrates this idea with a picture that serves as a departure point for a task-based activity.

Let us assume that we are dealing with a class of twenty students. The students must complete the following task within 20 minutes. One student, who does not know what the picture looks like, stands at the board. The rest of the class is divided into five groups of four, who must describe the picture to the student. The student at the board then

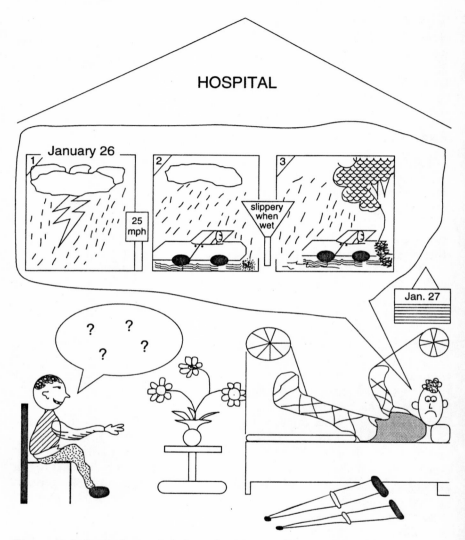

Figure 2.1 Basis for a task-based activity in the classroom.

has to draw the picture within the allotted time to a prespecified level of graphic accuracy – ranging from "getting the gist of the story" to the more demanding criterion of "reproducing the picture with no more than five errors of detail." The student at the board asks for clarifications as needed to understand the groups' drawing instructions.

This task is analytic in that it is specified in *behavioral* rather than in *linguistic* terms. That is, instead of organizing language instruction in terms of preselected grammatical structures or notional-functional categories, the content of learning is specified in problem-solving terms – in this case, problem X is to be solved in Y minutes to a prespecified level of graphic accuracy Z. Of course, this is not to deny that a task-based methodology can be used to implement a covertly synthetic organization of teaching content. As I noted in my earlier discussion of the newness of the notional-functional syllabus, old ways of doing language education can always be dressed in new packaging (see Text Link 28). For example, experience shows that this task typically generates notional descriptions of spatial relationships (e.g., "The crutches are beneath/under/next to the bed") and functional directions (e.g., "Pictures 1–3 are X's story of his accident; put them in a speaking bubble"). This shows that, as Wilkins (1976) foresaw, synthetic and analytic syllabuses are not mutually exclusive: They are actually the poles of a continuum of syllabus design possibilities. In practice, therefore, in weaker forms of task-based language teaching (see Nunan 1989, 1990, 1993, and the implications of Loschky and Bley-Vroman's 1993 work), tasks need not be exclusively analytic constructs. They can also be used to teach preselected categories of language.

> **∞ Text Link 28**
> See Text Link 10, which highlights the covertly structural nature of many materials that were advertised as notional-functional texts. See also Text Links 14, 19, 20, 25, 45, and 46.

This drawing task also combines the characteristics of two types of tasks frequently found in task-based language teaching: (1) the idea that communication occurs when some participants do not have access to information that is available to others, such as the information gap between the student at the board and the rest of the class, and (2) how communication occurs when information is transferred from one medium to another, in this case as students translate graphically represented information into speech and then back into graphic form.

From a diffusion-of-innovations perspective, the key issue facing task-based language teaching is its relative newness on the language teaching scene. Objectively speaking, it has existed in one form or another since 1980. However, to the extent that task-based language teaching is still an emerging technology, the great majority of teachers still do not know much about it (Long and Crookes 1992); therefore, it undoubtedly counts as an innovation. At present, it is still too early to say whether the twenty-first century will judge task-based language teaching to have been a successful innovation or not. However, if tasks like that described here are to achieve widespread acceptance in language teaching, a number of potential objections will have to be met. Let me illustrate this by examining the kinds of problems task-based language teaching will have to resolve with respect to its perceived *feasibility, relative advantageousness,* and *compatibility.*

Perceptions of *feasibility* are potentially a major issue. In the scenario outlined here, for example, I assumed that the size of the class would be no more than twenty students. In many parts of the world, however, normal class sizes run to fifty or sixty students – numbers that, it is often argued, preclude the use of small group work. Yet, the experience of the Bangalore Project – in which teachers had to deal with large class sizes – shows that task-based language teaching is not necessarily tied to using student-centered classroom procedures and that it is possible to develop teacher-centered varieties for such teaching situations. On the other hand, it can be argued that group work is *particularly appropriate* with large classes (Holliday and Cooke 1982). For example, in a teacher-fronted class of sixty learners, a teacher who gave equal time to all students could not allow any one individual to speak for more than 1 minute during a 1-hour class period. Group work, on the other hand, would allow students far more opportunities to use the target language during the same period of time, and the quality of learners' interaction would be far more varied (Long et al. 1976). Both these factors are thought to be beneficial for language learning (Pica 1987).

Of course, these arguments raise other questions, some of which are relatively easy to answer. For example, we could ask: How can teachers develop the kinds of superior classroom management skills that they need in order to implement a small group methodology in large classes? How can teachers develop an entire course along task-based lines? These issues can be addressed by appropriate teacher training. However, the answers to other feasibility-related questions are less obvious, particularly in foreign language teaching contexts. For instance, we might ask how feasible it is for teachers to use task-based language teaching if they cannot communicate themselves in the foreign language for extended periods of time. Furthermore, how feasible is it for teachers to use task-based language teaching if their students' only identifiable need for the target language is to pass a matriculation exam that emphasizes proficiency in translation skills or a passive knowledge of the grammatical structure of the target language?

Teachers who tried to adopt task-based language teaching under such conditions would expose themselves to some quite *disadvantageous* consequences. In theory, of course, it may be advantageous for teachers to upgrade their language skills. In many countries, however, teachers have few, if any, opportunities for advanced language or professional development. Thus, the time, money, and effort that teachers would have to invest in improving their language skills would be prohibitive. Finally, unless the foreign language examinations of many countries change significantly, teachers will probably decide they do not stand to gain much from adopting task-based language teaching.

Another potential problem for task-based language teaching is the extent to which teachers perceive it to be *compatible* with their current beliefs and practices. Some research shows that teachers tend to think about what they do in the classroom in terms of tasks – a warm-up activity, a reading comprehension activity, a dialogue (Swaffar et al. 1982). This might suggest that task-based language teaching has considerable psychological validity for teachers and that it would therefore be compatible with their educational behaviors and values. We must also remember that the analytic characteristics of task-based teaching may seem quite alien to teachers used to using synthetic materials. Such teachers expect to teach discrete structures or notions and functions and may well be disconcerted by the lack of explicitly linguistic content in analytic materials. Thus, task-based language teaching may be met with resistance on these grounds, at least initially. However, this is not to say that such resistance cannot be overcome over time. Finally, all the other attributes of innovations previously discussed in connection with Examples 1–5 – the *form, observability, adaptability, originality, trialability, complexity, feasibility,* and *explicitness* of innovations – can potentially affect the eventual adoption or rejection of task-based language teaching.

## Some implications for educational change

Task-based language teaching represents the cutting edge of syllabus design in the 1990s (see Table 2.6). Since it is still evolving, however, many teachers remain unfamiliar with its basic characteristics. As with the other innovations described in this chapter, its acceptance by language teaching professionals will require time and will be influenced by the same attributes and constraints – both systemic and individual – that determine the ultimate success or failure of all new ideas and practices. Advocates of task-based language teaching should thus anticipate that it will not receive teachers' automatic support. For various reasons, some teachers will always resist such ideas. Thus, if change agents believe that task-based language teaching is a worthwhile innovation, they should not leave its adoption by teachers up to chance – they must manage this process.

# Implications for educational change: A synthesis of examples 1–6

Curricular innovation is a complex, multidimensional phenomenon. As Table 2.7 shows, it is a socially situated activity that is affected by

TABLE 2.6. SOME IMPLICATIONS OF TASK-BASED LANGUAGE TEACHING FOR EDUCATIONAL CHANGE

| *Innovations* | *Diffusion-related issues* | *Attributes that promote (+) or inhibit (−) the adoption of this innovation* |
|---|---|---|
| A truly analytic syllabus, which is organized around the concept of task | Its relative newness on the language teaching scene | Potentially all the attributes discussed with respect to the previous examples: Its *form* Its *observability* Its *adaptability* Its *originality* Its *trialability* Its *complexity* Its *explicitness* The following attributes must receive particular attention: Its feasibility (+/−) Its relative advantages (in foreign language contexts: −) Its compatibility (+/−) |

TABLE 2.7. A SUMMARY OF THE CHARACTERISTICS OF CURRICULAR INNOVATION

| *Curricular innovation defined* | *Factors that affect curricular innovation* | *Innovation attributes that potentially promote (+) or inhibit (−) curricular innovation* |
|---|---|---|
| A complex, multi-dimensional phenomenon | Sociocultural context: − systemic and ethical constraints − the personal characteristics of potential adopters The models and strategies of change that are used to manage the innovation process The perceived newness of an idea or practice | *Relative advantages* (+) *Compatibility* (+) *Complexity* (−) *Observability* (+) *Trialability* (+) *Form* (concrete: +, abstract: −) *Explicitness* (+) *Originality* (+/−) *Adaptability* (+) *Feasibility* (+) |

ethical and systemic constraints, the personal characteristics of potential adopters, the attributes of innovations, and the strategies that are used to manage change in a particular context. The newness of any idea or practice is more a matter of adopters' perceptions than an objectively definable fact. In Chapter 3, I systematize these insights in order to explain the theory of curricular innovation. Part II applies this diffusionist perspective on curriculum development to the design, implementation, and maintenance of the CATI project.

# 3 Issues and definitions

In a society like ours, academic patterns
change more slowly than any others. In
my lifetime, in England, they have crys-
tallised rather than loosened. I used to
think that it would be about as hard to
change, say, the Oxford and Cambridge
scholarship examination as to conduct a
revolution. I now believe that I was over-
optimistic. (C. P. Snow; cited in Miles
1964: 1)

One must learn by doing the thing, for
though you think you know it – you have
no certainty, until you try. (Sophocles,
400 B.C.E., cited in Rogers 1983: 163)

In this chapter, I develop the insights of Chapter 2 into a more formal
discussion of the issues that impact curricular and teacher innovation.
In order to systematize these insights into an appropriate theoretical
framework, I borrow ideas from education, management, medicine, anthropology, sociology, development planning, language planning, and
urban planning. This multidisciplinary framework provides language
teaching professionals with the principles needed to understand the
range of factors that affect the design, implementation, and maintenance
of innovations, regardless of educational context.

## A theoretical framework for understanding innovation: Who adopts what, where, when, why, and how?

A diffusionist perspective on curricular innovation involves (1) explain-
ing differences in the rate of adoption by users in terms of potential
adopters' personal and social characteristics, social system variables,
and the attributes of innovations; (2) analyzing how different channels
of communication (broadcast and print media, electronic mail, face-to-

face communication, etc.) may be used to inform potential adopters about an innovation; (3) identifying the stages potential adopters go through in deciding whether to adopt, maintain, reject, or discontinue an innovation; (4) understanding the personal and social consequences of innovations; and (5) analyzing how change may be designed, implemented, and maintained.

This book is mostly concerned with the last issue. Nevertheless, language teaching professionals must understand how all these issues affect attempts to effect change. In order to clarify these matters, I answer the following composite question, originally posed by Cooper (1982, 1989): Who adopts what, where, when, why, and how? The "Who" section outlines the social roles played by different participants. "Adopts" discusses the decision-making processes potential adopters go through as they decide whether to adopt or reject an innovation. "What" defines curricular innovation. "Where" situates innovation in its sociocultural context. "When" defines diffusion as an interaction between time and the number of users in a social system who adopt an innovation. "Why" lays out the psychological profiles of different adopter types and discusses the attributes that successful innovations possess. "How" classifies different approaches to effecting change.

### *"Who": The social roles played by different participants*

Teachers are key players in all language teaching innovations; however, many other individuals also have a stake in the innovation process (Fullan 1982a). For example, ministry of education officials, various personnel working for donor agencies, school superintendents, principals, deans, heads of department, and other decision makers can all have a say in whether an innovation is implemented or not. In addition, parents and students often participate in determining the fate of any proposal for change. Although the kinds of players who *actually* get involved in deciding whether an innovation is adopted varies from one context to another, all participants assume social roles that define their relationships with other stakeholders. For example, Lambright and Flynn (1980) suggest that stakeholders relate to each other as adopters (or resisters), implementers, clients, suppliers, and entrepreneurs (i.e., change agents) (see Text Link 29). Of course, *adopters* and *resisters* are value-laden terms – by-products of the pervasive pro-innovation bias of the diffusion-of-innovations literature (see Text Link 30). This terminology implies that resisters are irrational or stubborn when they refuse to adopt the ideas of change agents. However, as I

∞ **Text Link 29**
For further discussion of the significance of these roles in the diffusion process, see Text Links 30, 31, 34, 35, 50, 76, 109, and 133.

∞ **Text Link 30**
See in particular Text Link 50.

43

show later in this chapter, there are times when individuals *should* resist innovations that may be harmful to them. This being said, I continue to use these terms in a narrowly technical sense because I do not wish to engage in needless terminological proliferation.

These distinctions can be used to analyze the roles of stakeholders in a British Council materials development project in Tunisia. In this project, ministry of education officials, deans, heads of department, and other administrators were *adopters,* who decided whether the development of these materials was desirable. Curriculum and materials designers were *suppliers* of the new materials. Teachers were *implementers,* who had to make these innovative materials work in the classroom. Students were *clients.* The expatriate curriculum expert was the *change agent* in charge of developing these materials (Kennedy 1988).

∞ **Text Link 31**
See Text Links 29, 30, 34, 35, 50, 76, 109, and 133.

Of course, any of these participants could also have become *resisters,* or people who oppose an innovation. In fact, these different roles are not mutually exclusive (Kennedy 1988). The same person may play several different social roles in practice, either consecutively or concurrently. For example, in the strong form of the process syllabus, the syllabus is a retrospective document that teachers and students construct over time through a process of negotiation. As they construct the syllabus, teachers and learners play other social roles in addition to those of implementers and clients, respectively. When teachers implement curricular guidelines at the level of syllabus design, they also manage change in their own classrooms – that is, *they also act as change agents.* For example, teachers may have to persuade learners that the innovation of negotiating the content and means of instruction is "allowable" in the first place – an idea that learners may initially find quite alien (Budd and Wright 1992). In addition, teachers may have to demonstrate to learners that engaging in a process of negotiation is potentially beneficial to them. Through negotiation, they can obtain instruction that meets their expectations, needs, and wants more efficiently than instruction that does not allow negotiation. As a result of this negotiation process, teachers may also have to act as *suppliers* of materials, either by selecting textbooks from published sources or by developing their own materials. Finally, since teachers should always retain ultimate responsibility for what happens in their classroom, they may either adopt or resist students' requests, thus taking on the roles of *adopters* or *resisters.* Conversely, learners who participate in the construction of a process syllabus are not passive *clients* who consume whatever the teacher hands out to them. As active partners in the construction of the syllabus, they may become *suppliers* by contributing newspaper articles or videos that teachers use as resources for learning. They may also act as *adopters* of, or *resisters* to, learning proposals made by the teacher or other students (see Text Link 31).

Finally, it is worth noting that the change agent's role is particularly complex. How change agents effect change depends on where they operate and whether they are "inside" or "outside" change agents (Havelock 1973). Outside change agents, who come from outside an educational system, typically do not possess any institutional power to force adoption. Thus, potential adopters are likely to view attempts by outside change agents to impose change as illegitimate (Kennedy 1987). Outside change agents function best as consultants who help end users identify obstacles and who facilitate changes users believe are appropriate to their context of implementation.

In contrast, inside change agents are established members of an educational system. Program directors and teachers can both function as inside change agents, provided that the system is open to the initiation of change by individuals at different hierarchical levels. These issues are addressed in more detail in the final section of this chapter. For now,

∞ **Text Link 32**
For other discussions of the notion of contingency, see Text Links 17, 58, 62, 65, and 84. Finally, see Principle 2 and Text Link 160.

suffice it to say that the change strategies inside change agents use can include both mandated and collaborative change. This does not imply that individuals who *can* legitimately use power to mandate change always choose to do so. Indeed, there are important reasons such a strategy may not be the best option. However, the selection of an appropriate, *contingent* style of change agentry is crucial to the success of any attempt to innovate (see Text Link 32).

## "Adopts": The decision-making processes of potential adopters

Adoption is an extended evaluative process that can be divided into at least four phases of decision making (Rogers 1983; Rogers and Shoemaker 1971). These phases involve potential adopters (1) gaining knowledge about an innovation, (2) being persuaded of its value, (3) making a preliminary decision whether to adopt or reject the innovation and implementing this decision, and (4) confirming or disconfirming their previous decisions. This four-stage process is a necessary idealization that allows us to understand the essential characteristics of potential adopters' decision-making behaviors. In practice, the adoption process is more complicated. Although it is always useful to understand that certain logical dependencies define adopters' decisions – we cannot consciously adopt something we do not know anything about – end users do not make such decisions in a strictly linear way. As stage 4 implies, adoption is more typically a circular, iterative process. Furthermore, these four phases are not categorically discrete. Users can gain knowledge about innovations by actually using them. Finally, end users rarely adopt innovations "as is." Given the choice, they typically adapt innovations in order to make them more relevant to their own needs (see Text Link 33). Thus, analysis of some of the innovative syllabuses discussed in Chapter 2, for instance, reveals that the process syllabus employs a model of change that encourages teachers to adapt tasks to meet their students' needs and wants. The procedural syllabus of the Bangalore Project also theoretically allowed teachers to adapt tasks to class needs, although it is not clear whether teachers actually engaged in much adaptation, particularly in the later stages of the project. Finally, the notional-functional syllabus and the Natural Approach both employ models of change that discourage adaptation.

> ∞ **Text Link 33**
> See Text Links 43, 54, 146, and 151. Finally, see Principles 1 and 6 and Text Links 159 and 164.

## "What": A definition of curricular innovation

The following definition of curricular innovation reflects my own perspective as a program director/change agent: *Curricular innovation is a managed process of development whose principal products are teaching (and/or testing) materials, methodological skills, and pedagogical values that are perceived as new by potential adopters.* Innovations are not necessarily always beneficial. This is an important caveat, which must be considered carefully in order to avoid any conscious pro-innovation bias (see Text Link 34). As I have already suggested, some innovations can be harmful. For example, Thalidomide, a drug that was prescribed to pregnant women in the 1960s to treat morning sickness, also caused horrible birth defects (Rogers 1983).

> ∞ **Text Link 34**
> See Text Links 29, 30, 31, 34, 50, and 76. See also Text Links 17 and 35. Finally, see Principle 1 and Text Link 159.

Fortunately, the innovations that language teaching professionals deal in never have such catastrophic consequences for their clients. Nonetheless, although it is difficult to find an example of a bad innovation in language education that is as clear-cut as the Thalidomide example, there are nonetheless many pedagogical innovations that have been attacked as educationally *undesirable.* For example, Brumfit (1981) and Paulston (1981) both argue that the notional syllabus is undesirable because it deprives learners of the opportunity to exploit the generative potential of grammar (i.e., the ability to use syntactic rules to create new sentences) – a resource that both authors claim is indispensable for language learning. Whatever the merits of this criticism (see Wilkins 1981a, b for a refutation of this charge), the larger lesson is clear: We must not adopt innovations just because they are new. We must also recognize that, influenced in part by the roles participants play in a social system, potential adopters will *perceive* some innovations as bad, threatening, or unwarranted (see Text Link 35). Thus, change agents should be careful to avoid treating the nonadoption of their ideas by potential users as either irrational or unfounded.

∞ **Text Link 35**
See Text Links 29, 30, 31, 34, 50, 76, 109, and 133.

Curricular innovation can be analyzed by breaking down the definition into its constituent parts: (1) *curricular innovation* (2) *is a managed* (3) *process of development* (4) *whose principal products are teaching (and/or testing) materials, methodological skills, and pedagogical values* (5) *that are perceived as new by potential adopters.* The following sections discuss, respectively, potential differences between innovation and change, insights from management theory, the links between development and innovations, "primary" and "secondary" innovations, and the subjective nature of newness.

## DIFFERENCES BETWEEN INNOVATION AND CHANGE AND DIFFERENT TYPES OF CHANGE

Some writers treat *innovation* and *change* as different processes, whereas others view them as synonymous. Researchers who distinguish between these terms argue that innovation is a species of the genus change, in which change is an ongoing, almost unconscious process that involves reworking familiar elements into new relationships; innovation, on the other hand, is a willed intervention, which results in the development of ideas, practices, or beliefs that are fundamentally new (Miles 1964; A. Nicholls 1983). I accept that innovation in education should be a conscious intervention. Furthermore, I recognize that in some circumstances – for example, when an institution abandons an "innovative" curriculum and reverts to using a "traditional" curriculum – "change" is probably not coterminous with "innovation."

Nonetheless, for present purposes, I propose to use the words *innovation* and *change* interchangeably. First, it is convenient. Second, other writers do not maintain Miles's distinction (Adams and Chen 1981; Everard and Morris 1990; Fullan 1982a; Kennedy 1988; Rudduck 1991). Third, change agents do not always know a priori whether adopters perceive a change to be fundamentally new or whether they see it as a less radical reworking of familiar elements into new relationships: This may become clear only as adopters implement the innovation. Finally, opinions about how innovative a proposal is often change over time. For example, the notional-functional syllabus – initially hailed as highly innovative – is now judged to be not so new after all (Long and Crookes 1992, 1993).

TABLE 3.1. TYPES OF SOCIAL CHANGE

| Recognition of the need for change | Origin of the new idea | |
|---|---|---|
| | *Internal to the social system* | *External to the social system* |
| *Internal* Recognition is by members of the social system | I. Immanent change | II. Selective contact change |
| *External* Recognition may be by change agents outside the social system | III. Induced immanent change | IV. Directed contact change |

*Source:* Adapted with the permission of The Free Press, a Division of Simon & Schuster Inc. from *Communication of Innovations: A Cross-Cultural Approach* by Everett M. Rogers with F. Floyd Shoemaker. Copyright © 1962, 1971 by The Free Press.

∞ **Text Link 36**
See Text Link 21.

Many examples of social change can be explained in terms of a borrowing process. However, we must not fall into the trap of asserting that this is the *only* way in which change occurs (Kroeber 1923, 1937). This strong position denies the possibility of parallel invention, but such a position is easily refuted. For example, the Natural Approach and the procedural syllabus make almost identical claims about the role of communication in language learning. Yet, these ideas developed independently of each other (see Text Link 36). For this reason, it is now accepted that "social change is caused by both invention (the process by which a new idea is discovered or created) and diffusion, which usually occurs sequentially" (Rogers 1983: 42). Thus, as Table 3.1 shows, modern diffusion theory distinguishes between four types of change, based on who recognizes a need for change and who proposes change.

*Immanent change* (or self-motivated change) occurs when the persons who recognize a need for change and those who propose solutions to a perceived problem are all part of the same social system. It is the most frequently discussed type of change in the education literature – perhaps more as an ideal to be achieved than as widespread, attested practice – because this type of change allows teachers to act as internal change agents and promotes ownership (A. Nicholls 1983; Rudduck 1991; Stenhouse 1975). *Selective contact change* occurs when insiders select an innovation that comes from outside their social system. For example, the practice of ESL composition teachers (at least those who work in North American universities) to use textbooks originally designed for native writers of English with their ESL students is an example of this type of change. *Induced immanent change* occurs when *outsiders* identify problems but *insiders* develop the solutions to these problems. This typically happens when a professional consultant is invited to diagnose the problems of an organization and to help system members devise their own solutions (see Kennedy 1987 for an example of this in language teaching aid work). Finally, *directed contact change* occurs when outside change agents introduce new ideas or practices into a social system in order to fulfill goals that they (rather than the intended users) have determined are important. The kinds of innovations promoted by aid frequently fall into this category of change.

Although directed contact change is the most immediate way for a change agent to promote development, external reasons (however well-motivated these may be in objective terms) for promoting innovation typically result in low levels of ownership and shallow development. Induced immanent change and selective contact change represent more significant, though still intermediary, levels of development, in that end users participate in developing innovations. Finally, immanent change represents the deepest level of development, in that end users take responsibility for identifying and resolving their own problems. This last type of change is what most educational change agents *aspire* to promote. However, it is not an entry-level behavior, particularly for new teachers. Contrary to Henrichsen's (1989: 3) claim that immanent change "is perhaps the simplest type" to promote, I wish to argue that this type of change is *the most difficult to implement well,* particularly when *external* change agents are initially involved in managing the change process. This is because external change agents must not only be *willing* but also *capable* of pulling out from the change process, which is by no means easy to accomplish. In addition, end users must also possess a great deal of sophistication and self-confidence to identify and resolve their own problems successfully. I return to these ideas in the final section of this chapter.

INSIGHTS FROM MANAGEMENT THEORY

The function of management is to make an organization run as smoothly as possible; it involves "the planning of work, organizing the distribution of activities and tasks to other people, direction of subordinate staff and controlling the performance of other peoples' work" (Mullins 1985: 123, cited by White et al. 1991: 24). Borrowing a metaphor from systems theory, we can understand how educational managers effect change by conceptualizing management in terms of five

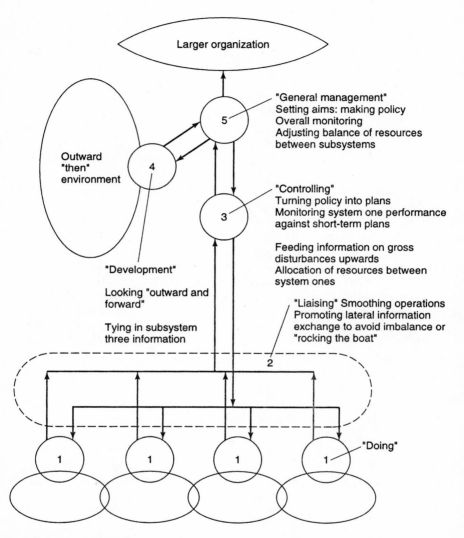

Figure 3.1 A systemic model of organizations. (Reprinted with permission from B. E. Everard and G. Morris, 1990, *Effective School Management*, 2nd ed., copyright © 1990, Paul Chapman Publishing Ltd., London)

interrelated sensing systems (Everard and Morris 1990). As shown in Figure 3.1, these systems include (5) policy making (setting an organization's goals and priorities), (4) development (looking into the outer world and into the future, thus linking the organization to outside developments), (3) controlling (turning policy into plans), (2) liaising (ensuring adequate vertical and horizontal communication between different participants), and (1) doing (implementing policy). In addition, an organization is also linked to larger organizations of which it is part or with which it interacts, as when policy makers communicate with their superiors or with counterparts in other organizations.

Curricular innovation entails a mix of professional, academic, and administrative change (Bowers 1983, 1987; Crocker 1984; Lee and VanPatten 1990; Straker-Cooke 1987; White 1988). Managers must therefore enhance an organization's capacity to innovate through organization development (Everard and Morris 1990; Heller 1982; Schmuck 1982) (see Text Link 37). The final insight to be gained from management theory is that, although teachers typically do not view themselves as managers, the definition given at the beginning of this section covers many of the tasks that teachers actually do in the "mini-organization" of their classes – for example, teachers plan the work that is to be done in class, they organize and distribute tasks to students, and they control and evaluate their performance (White 1988; White et al. 1991). Thus, the management of change is of interest to all participants in language teaching (see Text Link 38).

> ∞ **Text Link 37**
> See Text Links 2, 42, 73, 80, 104, 105, 107, 121, 126, 138, and 157.

> ∞ **Text Link 38**
> See Text Link 26.

THE LINKS BETWEEN DEVELOPMENT AND INNOVATION

> ∞ **Text Link 39**
> See Text Links 49, 67, and 95. Finally, see Principle 6 and Text Link 164.

All productive change is developmental. In order to understand the implications of this statement, we need to unpack its different layers of meaning. As noted earlier in the "Adopts" section, at the simplest level of meaning, innovation involves potential adopters going through a four-step decision-making process. Normatively speaking, individuals first gather necessary information about the innovation; next, they decide whether it is useful or beneficial to them; then they make preliminary decisions to adopt or reject the innovation; finally, they confirm or refute previous decisions. Thus, innovation is developmental in that it involves a *sequence* of decisions that are made *over a period of time*. We can define diffusion in terms of an interaction between two variables: a pool of *potential adopters* and *time* (see Text Link 39). (I return to the time-bound nature of adoption in a later section titled "When.")

At a deeper level of meaning, development and innovation are synonyms: That is, development *is* a self-sustaining process of locally initiated innovation (Jéquier 1976). Defining development in this way is

51

easy, but finding examples of self-sustaining, teacher-initiated innovation is difficult in practice, as the discussion of the Bangalore Project in Chapter 2 shows. Nonetheless, Jéquier's position is theoretically quite interesting (see Text Link 40). He subscribes to a bottom-up approach to development that stresses the importance of *individuals* attempting to control their own destinies, thereby reducing their vulnerability to forces they do not control.

∞ Text Link 40
See Text Links 23, 72, 136, and 144. Finally, see Principles 5 and 7–9, and Text Links 163, 165, 166, and 167.

This notion of vulnerability is a technical construct that "provides a frame for viewing under-development as an initial condition, and development both as a change process and as a terminal state" (Goulet 1971: x).

Goulet's discussion of development focuses on the predicament of underdeveloped societies rather than on the problems of individuals. However, this position can be easily adapted to describe the development problems faced by individuals. This adapted notion of vulnerability not only frames development in individual terms, it also captures another characteristic of innovation: Engaging in change may be necessary, but it is psychologically unsettling. For example, as teachers begin to experiment with new materials or methodologies, they may initially feel that they are *less* effective (Bailey 1992; Kelly 1980). However, with time, they become better at using new ideas and practices. Eventually, they transcend their initial feelings of incompetence and move on to higher levels of professional sophistication and performance. In addition, vulnerability has a psycholinguistic dimension. As language learners acquire "communicative innovations" (Cooper 1989) – target language vocabulary or morphosyntax they perceive to be new – they must be able to tolerate potentially high levels of affective ambiguity whenever their interlanguage is destabilized. Thus, learning to learn and learning to teach are organic, not linear, processes. Finally, defining development in these terms addresses an issue that has been at the heart of language curriculum theory and practice since the mid-1980s: If language education is to be effective, it must attend to both the process *and* the products of teaching and learning (Breen 1984, 1987; Breen and Candlin 1980; Candlin 1984a, 1987).

This discussion holds several implications for graduate level teacher education. If we define development as the reduction of an individual's level of vulnerability, then *how* should teacher education be organized? Furthermore, what should the *content* of teacher education be and how does the *what* of teacher education interact with the *how*? The essential dimensions of a model of in-service teacher education that is consistent with the notion of development outlined earlier should be *field-based, experimental, problem-centered, collaborative, competency-based,* and *open-ended* (based on Tetenbaum and Mulkeen 1986; see Text Link

41). Teacher education programs should ideally dispose of a foreign language teaching program, so that teachers can use their classes as laboratories for curricular innovation. This arrangement would allow teachers to focus on problems that emerge in their teaching. Finally, teacher education should encourage teachers to share ideas, because curriculum development is a collaborative activity. This suggests that appropriate forums for sharing ideas must be set up.

> ∞ **Text Link 41**
> See Text Link 70.

In summary, there should be a link between what teachers do in the classroom and what they discuss in their graduate program classes: If teachers are to become competent language teaching professionals, they must be able to complement experience with theory. Moreover, the process of teacher education does not end with graduation from a teacher certification program or the acquisition of a graduate degree in applied linguistics. It is an open-ended process that involves individual teachers mastering ever more complicated theoretical issues and developing new practical skills on a continuing basis (Larsen-Freeman 1983). Finally, as teachers move from one job to another, not only do they take their knowledge and skills with them to their new jobs, they also adapt these abilities to help them refine their understanding of this new teaching situation.

## DISTINCTIONS BETWEEN PRIMARY AND SECONDARY INNOVATIONS

Changes in teaching (and/or testing) materials, methodological skills, and pedagogical values constitute the core dimensions of teaching and learning (Fullan 1993). They are what I call "primary" innovations. Of course, curricular innovation cannot be reduced solely to the development of these primary innovations. Curricular innovation also depends on organization development, or "secondary" innovations. For example, in order to promote discussion about materials development (a primary innovation), a manager may install an electronic mail system (a secondary innovation) in the school or department (see Text Link 42). The function of secondary innovations is restricted to enabling primary innovations.

> ∞ **Text Link 42**
> For a general discussion of organization development, see Figures 3.1 and 5.1, and Table 5.1. See also Text Links 2, 37, 73, 80, 104, 107, 121, 138, and 157. For related discussions of the institutionalization of e-mail in the CATI project, see Text Links 59, 105, and 113. Finally, see Principles 1 and 3 and Text Links 159 and 161.

The relationship between the three dimensions of primary innovations is complex. As Fullan observes, we might intuitively expect that beliefs change first, and that this leads to new behavior. In practice, however, empirical evidence suggests that beliefs may change as a result

*Defining educational innovation*

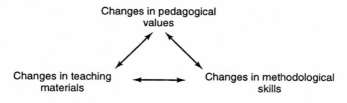

Figure 3.2 The dimensions of curricular innovation.

of experience. Fullan (1982b: 247) concludes that "perhaps it is sufficient for our purposes to recognize that the relationship between beliefs and behaviour is reciprocal – trying new practices sometimes leads to questioning one's underlying beliefs; examining one's beliefs can lead to attempting new behaviour." This reciprocity between beliefs and behaviour is depicted in Figure 3.2 as an "innovation triangle" (Markee 1994b).

The idea that the relationship between beliefs and behavior is reciprocal has obvious implications for teacher and curriculum development. If we accept the idea that teachers should "behave their way into new ideas and skills, not just think their way into them" (Fullan 1993: 15), then this suggests that change agents can use syllabus design and materials development by teachers as a convenient entry point into the larger process of curricular innovation (see Text Link 43). Materials are the most tangible products of innovation. However, innovation must also engage teachers in the more abstract tasks of developing their methodological skills and changing their ideas about what constitutes good teaching. For change agents, the problem is that changes at one point of the innovation triangle need not be accompanied by changes at other points of the triangle (see Text Link 44).

∞ **Text Link 43**
See Text Links 33, 54, 57, 146, and 151. Finally, see Principle 1 and Text Link 159.

∞ **Text Link 44**
See Text Links 57, 146, and 156.

THE SUBJECTIVE NATURE OF NEWNESS

∞ **Text Link 45**
See Text Link 10. In addition, see Text Links 19, 20, 25, 28, and 46.

As shown in Chapter 2, the notional-functional syllabus, the Natural Approach, the procedural syllabus, and weaker varieties of task-based language teaching were perhaps not that new even when they were developed (see Text Link 45). Group work is another example of a "new" procedure that has been described in the language teaching literature and has been implemented by many teachers (at least in Western countries) for many years. Yet, as Long (1989a) points out, individual and whole-class work probably still predominate in many countries of the world, often to the complete exclusion of group work. This suggests that it is individual end users' *subjective perceptions* of newness, rather than any *objective criterion* of newness, that determine whether an approach to organizing language instruction counts as an innovation (Markee 1993a; A. Nicholls 1983; Rogers 1983). In this sense, group work – indeed, any unfamiliar idea or practice – may strike teachers as an innovation. Thus, when Krashen and Terrell (1983) protested that the Natural Approach consists of nothing more than a rediscovery of the underlying principles of traditional direct methods that were popular earlier in the twentieth century, suitably reformulated and updated in light of current SLA research findings, they missed the point that, from a *user's* perspective, some teachers still undoubtedly perceive the Natural Approach as an innovation (see Text Link 46).

∞ **Text Link 46**
See Text Links 10, 19, 20, 25, 28, and 45.

## "Where": The sociocultural context of innovation

Cooper (1989) claims that *where* an innovation is implemented is a sociocultural, not a geographical, issue. However, geographical location *can* affect how well-known an innovation becomes. For example, the Bangalore Project was designed and implemented in India; despite the fact that India is probably the third largest English-using country in the world after the United States and Britain (Kachru 1985), it is nonetheless still relatively isolated from the "mainstream" of applied linguistic work in "center" countries. Consequently, it was not until 1982 at the earliest, when the project had already been running for three years, that some of the first reports of the project's innovations began to filter through to a wider international audience in Britain (Johnson 1982b). Thus, geographical location is not an insignificant factor in the potential diffusion of innovations.

Change agents must recognize the potential impact – positive or negative – of many sociocultural factors (see Text Link 47). Kennedy (1988) suggests that multiple sociocultural systems potentially interact to constrain classroom innovation (see Figure 3.3). In this model, cultural values are the most powerful shapers of participants' behaviors, followed by political conventions, administrative practices, and so on.

∞ **Text Link 47**
See Text Links 4, 48, and 52. In addition, see Text Links 69, 81, 82, and 150. Finally, see Principle 1 and Text Link 159.

Other writers (Munby 1978, 1984; Holliday 1995c; Holliday and Cooke 1982) have addressed the issue of when such factors (for example, political or administrative constraints) should be considered in the course design process.

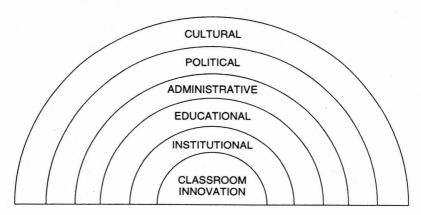

Figure 3.3 The hierarchy of interrelating subsystems in which innovations have to operate. (Reprinted by permission of Oxford University Press from C. Kennedy, 1988, "Evaluation of the management of change in ELT projects," *Applied Linguistics* 9(4), p. 332)

Change agents must certainly bear in mind the factors identified in Figure 3.3 as they manage the implementation of curricular innovation. However, this typology is not a theory that explains how these variables interact, nor is this categorization value-free. For example, a Marxist would dispute the preeminence of cultural factors and argue that economic relationships between different social groups are the driving force of change. Furthermore, such a conceptualization may encourage viewing culture as a monolithic construct (Dendrinos 1992). It then becomes all too easy for language teaching professionals to make stereotypical judgments about groups of learners and to make blanket statements like "All Asian students are passive learners." Such statements are misleading, because they do not take into account individuals' personalities (Willing 1988). Finally, it is probably more accurate to talk about a variety of interrelated cultures – a political culture, an administrative culture, an educational culture – than to posit culture as a separate variable.

Whatever consensus emerges on the relative importance of these factors, it is important to recognize that language teaching professionals are still at the pre-theoretical stage of making checklists of variables that are likely to affect curricular innovation, and these lists are still a long way from being comprehensive. Furthermore, it is probably not useful to argue about which variables are most important, since the relative importance of each factor varies from one context of implementation to another. Finally, different change agents in the same con-

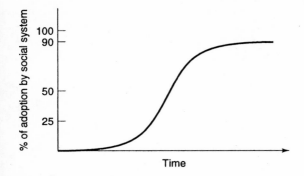

Figure 3.4 An S-shaped diffusion curve (based on Cooper 1982).

text may attach more or less weight to the same set of variables, depending on what their ideological world views are. It is thus more useful to state clearly one's ideological orientations and to analyze *how* different variables cluster together in light of these orientations (see Text Link 48). This provides a relatively objective way of evaluating analyses of sociocultural context.

∞ **Text Link 48**
See Text Links 74 and 82.

### *"When": A quantitative definition of diffusion*

Although some adopters embrace a given innovation relatively quickly, others need more time. Thus, if we know when user A adopts an innovation compared to users B, C, and D, we can specify how fast (or how slowly) an innovation spreads among this

∞ **Text Link 49**
See Text Link 39. See also Text Links 67 and 95. Finally, see Principle 6 and Text Link 164.

particular group of potential adopters. More specifically, we can quantify diffusion as the *percentage* of adopters in a social system (variable 1) who adopt an innovation over a given period of *time* (variable 2) (Rogers 1983). Figure 3.4 shows how these two variables interact to produce the typically S-shaped curve that describes the diffusion of innovations (see Text Link 49). The lazy slope of the toe of the curve shows that adoption occurs slowly at first; depending on the particular kind of innovation that is being adopted, if a critical mass of between 5% and 25% of potential users adopts, the innovation will take off and become self-sustaining (Rogers 1995). At this point, the slope in the midsection of the curve becomes steeper (i.e., the rate of adoption accelerates) as people "jump on the bandwagon." Finally, the curve plateaus as diffusion slows down and eventually tapers off, either because every potential adopter has adopted or else because the innovation stalls. In this latter case, the diffusion process is incomplete.

*Defining educational innovation*

Five different types of adopters can be superimposed on this diffusion curve: *innovators, early adopters, early majority, late majority,* and *laggards* (Huberman 1973; Rogers 1983). As noted earlier, such terms are value-laden (see Text Link 50) and reflect the pro-innovation bias of the diffusion literature; but again, I refrain from coining new terminology just for the sake of renaming terms. Thus, in terms of the diffusion curve in Figure 3.4, innovators and early adopters occupy the first 25% of the curve, early and late majority occupy the steepest portion of the curve, and laggards and resisters occupy the last part of the curve as it forms a plateau.

∞ **Text Link 50**
See in particular Text Link 30; see also Text Links 29, 31, 34, 35, 76, 109, and 133. Finally, see Principle 6 and Text Link 164.

This diffusion curve has practical implications for language teaching professionals. As Figure 3.4 shows, the diffusion process tends to begin slowly; it then suddenly accelerates and finally slackens off. Thus, change agents should be patient and not become discouraged if nothing seems to happen when they initially introduce an innovation into a system. Initial misunderstandings are part of the innovation "turf." Such misunderstandings *must* be clarified, and this takes time. Indeed, not only does innovation take time to implement, *it always take longer to implement than expected.* This characteristic of diffusion should be taken into account during the design and implementation of a project and should also receive proper attention in any summative evaluation of a project (see Text Link 51).

∞ **Text Link 51**
See Text Links 66, 73, and 143. Finally, see Principles 1, 6, and 7 and Text Links 159, 164, and 165.

## *"Why": The psychological profiles of adopters and the attributes of successful innovations*

∞ **Text Link 52**
For discussion of the role of sociocultural factors in diffusion, see Text Links 4, 47, 48, 69, 81, 82, and 150. For discussion of the importance of innovation ownership, see Text Links 9, 23, 40, 72, 129, 136, 137, 144, 147, 154, and 156. See also Principle 1 and Text Link 159.

Why do the adoption behaviors of individuals vary? As we have already seen, the extent to which adopters feel they own the innovations they implement is a key factor in adoption decisions. In addition, sociocultural factors may also constrain innovation (see Text Link 52). In addition, the different psychological profiles of adopters affect implementation (Rogers 1983). For example, early adopters tend to travel widely, are often well-educated, and are upwardly mobile; they tend to seek out and be open to new ideas and tend to have a high degree of exposure to mass media; they often have extensive contacts with other people and tend to be personally or professionally close to change agents; and they are often willing to take acceptable risks and are able to tolerate relatively high levels of uncertainty. Laggards, at the other end, tend to display diametrically opposite characteristics, and types in between exhibit intermediary traits (see Text Link 53).

∞ **Text Link 53**
See Text Link 24. See also Principle 1 and Text Link 159.

Different types of adopters also have different levels of social status and influence within their peer reference groups. Innovators are on the margins of the diffusion curve, as are laggards (see Figure 3.4). That is, they manifest polar opposites of many characteristics. One might expect innovators to play a key role in the adoption process, but research has shown that their social status is low and that they are too different from their colleagues to serve as role models. Indeed, their peers tend to regard innovators as too willing to try out *any* new ideas or practices, however risky and unproven they might be. Thus, although somebody has to be the first to try out an innovation, the influence of innovators on the adoption decisions of other adopters is limited.

The most important category of potential users turns out to be early adopters. Although more conservative than innovators in their adoption behaviors, they are high-status individuals who enjoy the respect of their colleagues. Thus, early adopters' decisions are critical because of their socially influential position as opinion leaders within their

∞ **Text Link 54**
See Text Links 99, 110, 145, and 146. Finally, see Principles 1 and 9 and Text Links 159 and 167.

peer group. Their decisions close an initial "wait-and-see" period following the introduction of an innovation, during which potential users observe the successes and failures of innovators and evaluate whether to adopt the innovation. Thus, when early adopters decide to adopt or reject an innovation, they pave the way for the early and late majorities to follow suit. Thus, change agents should identify early adopters and work through them to encourage later adopters to adopt also (see Text Link 54).

Finally, innovations themselves possess attributes that either promote or inhibit their adoption. Various writers have proposed different lists of attributes (Brickell 1969; Dow et al. 1984; Fullan and Pomfret 1977; Henrichsen 1989; Kelly 1980; Levine 1980; Mintzberg et al. 1976; Pelz 1985; Richards 1984; Rogers 1983; Zaltman and Duncan 1977; see Stoller 1992 for a review). Among these, Rogers' (1983) list, which is based on a cross-disciplinary analysis of 1,500 innovation studies, is the most well-known. These attributes include (1) the *relative advantages* of adopting an innovation, (2) its *compatibility* with previous practice, (3) its *complexity*, (4) its *trialability*, and (5) its *observability*.

∞ **Text Link 55**

See Table 2.7 and Text Links 13, 18, 89, 90, 96, 111, 117, 124, and 139. Finally, see Principle 8 and Text Link 166.

These five attributes are "core" characteristics (see Text Link 55). That is, they influence *all* users' decisions to adopt or reject *any kind* of innovation. Thus, if potential users perceive an innovation to be relatively advantageous to them, they are more likely to adopt it than one they judge to be financially, professionally, or personally disadvantageous to them. The perceived compatibility of innovations is also important. Innovations that lie within a "zone of innovation" (Stoller 1992, 1994) – that is, with a moderate level of innovativeness – are the most likely to be adopted. On the other hand, innovations that are too similar to or too different from potential adopters' current practices and values are unlikely to be adopted. The perceived complexity of an innovation generally has a negative effect on adoption. If potential users believe an innovation is difficult to understand or use, for example, it is unlikely that they will adopt it, particularly if the current alternative is easy to understand and use. The perceived trialability of an innovation is also important, because potential adopters prefer to try out an innovation in incremental stages. Thus, innovations that lend themselves to a piecemeal approach are more likely to win acceptance than innovations that require an all-or-nothing adoption strategy. Finally, the perceived observability of an innovation is also important. Innovations that are easy to observe are more likely to diffuse than those that are not easily observable.

∞ **Text Link 56**

See Table 2.7 and Text Links 13, 18, 55, 89, 90, 96, 111, 117, 124, and 139. Finally, see Principle 8 and Text Link 166.

At least five other attributes have had an impact on the adoption of the examples of educational change discussed in Chapter 2 and have also had an impact on the CATI project described in Part II. These are (1) the *form* an innovation takes, (2) its *explicitness*, (3) its *originality*, (4) its *adaptability*, and (5) its *feasibility* (see Text Link 56). More specifically, innovations that have a tangible form are more likely to diffuse than innovations that are abstract (Richards 1984) – a point also made by Fullan (1982a, 1993), who notes that changes in pedagogical materials are generally easier to introduce than changes in methodological skills and values (see Text Link 57). The explicitness

∞ **Text Link 57**

See Figure 3.2. In addition, see Text Links 43 and 44. Finally, see Principle 1 and Text Link 159.

of the rationale that change agents present to end users also affects adoption (Dow et al. 1984). End users who do not understand what they are supposed to do and why they should do it have good reason to resist changes that may be against their interests. The relative originality of an innovation is also important (Mintzberg et al. 1976; Pelz 1985). For example, change agents need to think through whether specially designed in-house materials meet a program's needs better than either modified textbooks or unadapted commercial materials. The first option requires a high level of originality by teachers, whereas the last requires none. Obviously, each alternative has its own strengths and weaknesses. An in-house solution is more demanding of teachers in the short term but is potentially more rewarding in the long term. Conversely, an off-the-shelf solution is easier on teachers in the short term but may be less rewarding in the long term. Closely related to the issue of originality is the concept of an innovation's inherent adaptability (Dow et al. 1984). As shown in Chapter 2, some innovations are designed to be easily adapted by users. Others, however, are intended to be "teacher-proof." Again, change agents must weigh the relative advantages and disadvantages of the choices they make: In some instances, high levels of adaptability may be required, while in others, low levels of adaptability will prove to be the better option. Finally, end users' perceptions concerning the feasibility of an innovation are a crucial factor in determining an innovation's ultimate success or failure (Kelly 1980). End users are unlikely to adopt innovations unless there is a realistic match between change agents' expectations, the resources that are available to support the introduction of the innovation, and end users' levels of knowledge, commitment, and skills. Change agents must therefore attend to all these factors when they introduce change.

## *"How": Five different approaches to effecting change*

Most of the research on effecting curricular innovation originates in the United States, Canada, Britain, and Australia. These countries have relatively decentralized traditions of educational management, and the models and strategies of change preferred there reflect this general cultural orientation. We must therefore bear in mind throughout the following discussion that other countries may prefer to implement change in a more centralized fashion.

∞ **Text Link 58**
For discussion of models of change, see Text Links 7, 12, 17, 25, 32, 60–5, 84, 125, and 152. Finally, see Principles 2 and 6 and Text Links 160 and 164.

Table 3.2 summarizes five models of change, the strategies of change, and the leadership styles that are typically associated with them (see Text Link 58). For simplicity, the term *approach to change* refers to these three components of change as an integrated concept.

THE SOCIAL INTERACTION MODEL

Most of the empirical work that underpins the social interaction model – for example, the research on adoption phases, diffusion curves, systemic and personal factors, the attributes of innovations – was carried out by rural sociologists in the United States. The aim of these research-

TABLE 3.2. APPROACHES TO CHANGE

| Models of change | Strategies of change | Leadership styles |
| --- | --- | --- |
| Social interaction model | NA | NA |
| Center-periphery model | Power-coercive strategy | Mechanistic |
| Research, development, and diffusion (RD&D) model | Empirical-rational or power-coercive strategies | Open-mechanistic |
| Problem-solving model | Normative-reeducative strategy | Adaptive |
| Linkage model | Normative-reeducative, empirical-rational, or power-coercive strategies | Mechanistic Open-mechanistic Adaptive |

ers was to find out how to persuade farmers to adopt new hybrid varieties of corn most effectively. However, this research has been shown to be relevant to other populations, including educators. For example, educational researchers such as Huberman (1973) have also shown that diffusion curves in education are also S-shaped. This model is different from the other models that I discuss in this chapter because it seeks to explain what motivates clients' actual adoption behaviors, not how to manage change per se. For this reason, the social interaction model has no strategy of change or leadership style associated with it.

What insights does this model offer to language teaching professionals? The most important insight that this model offers change agents is the claim that diffusion is nothing less than a form of communication (Rogers 1983). Speaking to this issue, Cooper (1982, 1989) suggests that languages spread through the establishment of communication networks. This mechanism also accounts for the spread of language teaching-related innovations. A communication network may be conceptualized as in Figure 3.5, in which individuals A, B, C, and D all know each other and interact with every other member of the network, either face to face or via other channels of communication (such as the telephone, electronic mail, or written communication).

As shown in Figure 3.5, an innovation may also spread from network 1 to network 2 because individuals D and E know each other, either through bonds of friendship or because they work with each other or are in the same field. Thus, once E is in possession of whatever information D has about an innovation, E can diffuse this information to F, G, and H in network 2.

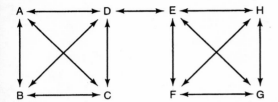

Figure 3.5 The spread of an innovation between two communication networks. (Reprinted by permission of Center for Applied Linguistics from R. L. Cooper, 1982, "A framework for the study of language spread," in R. L. Cooper, ed., *Language Spread: Studies in Diffusion and Social Change*, p. 13., Indiana University Press and Center for Applied Linguistics)

It is in this important sense that diffusion is fundamentally a process of communication. This conclusion implies by extension that change agents cannot leave the formation of communication networks to chance alone (see Text Link 59): They must actively promote their formation and institutionalization.

∞ **Text Link 59**
See Table 5.1 and Text Links 105 and 119. Finally, see Principle 3 and Text Link 161.

## CENTER-PERIPHERY MODEL

International aid agencies have tended to use a center-periphery model of change (see Example 1 in Chapter 2), whereby developed "center" countries transfer institutional models (for example, a university system), resources (teachers, books, the English language), and educational ideologies (the notion of professionalism) to underdeveloped "periphery" countries (see Text Link 60). Note that similar center-periphery relationships exist in the educational systems of developed countries like France and Japan, which are highly centralized. In these countries, the power to promote educational change rests with a small number of senior ministry of education officials who are at the center of the decision-making process. Teachers, who are on the periphery of this decision-making process, merely implement the decisions that are handed down to them.

∞ **Text Link 60**
See Text Links 12, 17, 25, 58, and 61–5. Finally, see Principles 2 and 6 and Text Links 160 and 164.

In its classic manifestation, the leadership style used in conjunction with this model is "mechanistic." Decision makers derive the right to exercise authority based on the hierarchical positions they occupy in a bureaucratically organized institution (Rondinelli et al. 1990). Decision makers typically use a "power-coercive" strategy of change (Chin and Benne 1976) and use rewards or sanctions to ensure that subordinates comply with institutional policies and goals. Rewards and sanctions are two sides of the same coin: Managers reward satisfactory performance with promotions or salary increases, or they punish employees for unsatisfactory job performance.

Although change agents can use this approach to *force* rapid change initially, research in North America, Britain, and Australia suggests it does not promote long-lasting, self-sustaining innovation effectively (Chin and Benne 1976). It is a top-down approach that discourages individual initiative – a quality indispensable to the long-term maintenance of innovations – because it turns teachers into passive recipients of change agents' dictates. In many cases, users do not understand the innovations they are supposed to implement because they have had no hand in their development. This lack of ownership may promote covert resistance, particularly if teachers consider the change agent's use of power illegitimate. Such a result can happen all too easily in international aid work, where external change agents are only temporarily seconded to the institutions they work in (Kennedy 1988).

Of course, in certain contexts of implementation, there is a *cultural predisposition* to rely on such an approach to change (Maley 1984). Might it not therefore be culturally appropriate for external change agents to use a center-periphery model of change in cultures that "do" change in this way? This is the gist of Henrichsen's criticism of the way in which Charles Fries and his associates tried to diffuse the Audiolingual Method in postwar Japan. Henrichsen (1989: 198) argues that "it would have been much better for [Fries and his collaborators] to gain power by establishing linkages with influential people and institutions and then take a vertical, elitist approach, starting at the top of the hierarchy in the Japanese school system and working down to the classroom teachers." This might be a valid change strategy for *internal* (i.e., Japanese) change agents to use, but it is doubtful whether this solution would have been effective in the long term. Even if Henrichsen's solution is technically persuasive, it does not address deeper issues of linguistic imperialism (Phillipson 1992). This is an issue that *external* change agents who seek to promote change in cross-cultural situations always run into. Ultimately, therefore, external change agents should never rely on power to institute change, whether in cross-cultural or other contexts.

## RESEARCH, DEVELOPMENT, AND DIFFUSION MODEL

The RD&D model is the most familiar – and prestigious – model of change among academics. After all, academics produce research. It is therefore natural for academics to assume that developing good innovations depends on their research efforts. The RD&D model originated in macroeconomic management, agriculture, and the space and defense industries, but it has also acquired much prestige in education and the social sciences. This model is rational, systematic, and theory-based (Havelock 1971). It is often used in conjunction with empirical-rational change strategies, which posit that providing high quality products to rational users necessarily ensures adoption (Chin and Benne 1976). Change agents also typically use an "open-mechanistic" leadership style, which "maintains hierarchical authority and central control over decisions but seeks to increase the flow of information about the environment" (Rondinelli et al. 1990: 77). This leadership style is based on the change agent's status as an expert. In centralized educational systems, an RD&D model also may be paired with mechanistic leadership and power-coercive change strategies. This approach depends on long-term planning and involves a division of labor among teams of specialists who work on separate phases of a project to develop a final product. Planning is linear and begins with basic research. This is followed by phases of applied research, development and testing of prototypes, mass production, and packaging and mass dissemination. Proponents of this approach assume that high development costs are offset by long-term benefits of efficiency and by the anticipated high quality of the innovations that are produced (Havelock 1971).

Despite its prestige, this approach to change is open to criticism on the grounds that change agents who subscribe to this approach pay insufficient attention to implementation issues (Milstein 1982). It is instructive that Egon Guba, one of the most important early advocates of the RD&D model in the American educational establishment, has since repudiated his initial adherence to it. Guba came to believe that an RD&D orientation to innovation tends to establish unachievable aspirations, it ignores the idiosyncratic goals of individuals, and, in its attempts to overcome failure provoked by the first two conditions, it promotes frequent policy changes. Aoki (1984) adds that it is excessively centralized. The RD&D model therefore suffers from many of the problems (though not to the same degree) that also afflict the center-periphery model with its power-coercive strategy of change. For example, the RD&D model also relies on top-down change. Consequently, teachers – who are at the bottom of this expert-driven decision-making hierarchy – still do not own the products of this approach and so have little or no stake in their success. The biggest disadvantage of this approach is that it mistakenly assumes rational argument to be sufficient to persuade potential users to accept change. In fact, sociocultural constraints, systemic and personal factors, the attributes of innovations, and so on are frequently much more important than rational argument alone in determining an innovation's success or failure.

∞ **Text Link 61**

See Text Link 12. See also Text Links 17, 25, 58, 60, and 62–5. Finally, see Principles 2 and 6 and Text Links 160 and 164.

The Malaysia Project is an interesting example to illustrate this point. An entire book could be written about this British Council aid project, which sought to diffuse the notional-functional syllabus in Malaysia in the late 1970s (see Text Link 61). However, for present purposes, the current problems encountered by this syllabus are best analyzed as an unintended consequence of the Malay government's language planning policies in the 1970s. When Bahasa Malaysia superseded English as the legal medium of instruction in secondary schools, the standard of English began to decline. However, large numbers of middle-class parents and teachers, many of whom were themselves educated through the medium of English, were unhappy with this decline (Aruchanalam and Menon 1990). They were concerned that children were not achieving the same level of competence in English that they themselves possessed. Such sentiments should not necessarily be interpreted as a neocolonial hankering for English. They are based on the pragmatic assessment that high levels of competence in English are necessary to obtain good jobs. The penalties for children who fail to learn English are potentially high. When parents and teachers observed the declining standards of English, they wrongly blamed the notional-functional syllabus, which they believed does not teach grammar, rather than the language policy decisions that had been made some twenty years ago in the 1970s. In such a situation, rational justifications that this syllabus does cover grammar failed to address the complex ideological roots of the opposition to this syllabus.

∞ **Text Link 62**

See Text Links 12, 17, 25, 32, 58, 60–1, 63–5, and 84. Finally, see Principles 2 and 6 and Text Links 160 and 164.

At the same time, we must recognize that change agents *should* use the RD&D model to produce inherently complex technical innovations, such as language tests. After all, these are the types of innovations that this model of change is best suited to produce. Using an RD&D model on its own, however, does not necessarily lead to a change in pedagogical values and behaviors, because the whole thrust of RD&D efforts – to make innovations "user-proof" – paradoxically results in innovations that are *too* user-proof (see Text Link 62).

PROBLEM-SOLVING MODEL

A problem-solving model coupled with a normative-reeducative strategy of change is theoretically the most popular approach to promoting change in education – at least in English-speaking countries. This approach is qualitatively different from either of the two preceding approaches, in that it is the eventual users of an innovation who identify the need for change. That is, change becomes a bottom-up, not a top-down, phenomenon. Although end users are recognized to be rational and intelligent, this approach assumes that peoples' actions and beliefs are governed by their social values. Consequently, any changes in habitual behaviors and values involve a change in ideology – hence the term *normative-reeducative*. Such deep ideological change results in changes in attitudes, values, skills, and relationships, which go far beyond relatively shallower changes in knowledge, information, or intellectual rationales for action and practice typically promoted by other models of change (Chin and Benne 1976).

In this approach, teachers themselves act as inside change agents (see Text Link 63). Ideally, they use action research to articulate a problem (although see Burns and Hood 1995 for an example of action research used to investigate change imposed at a system level). We may broadly define *action research* as a "small-scale intervention in the functioning of the real world and a close examination of the effects of such intervention" (Cohen and Manion 1985: 174). The action research movement frequently has close links with the critical pedagogy movement (see Candlin 1984a; Dewey 1910; Freire 1976; Pennycook 1989, 1990, 1994; Stenhouse 1975) and encourages teachers to use their own experience to critique what happens in their classrooms. The purpose of such research is to improve on classroom practice and to engage participants in a process of "theorizing from the classroom" (Ramani 1987), which emancipates teachers from the tyranny of unexamined assumptions (Crookes 1993) (see Text Link 64).

> ∞ **Text Link 63**
> See Text Links 12, 17, 25, 58, 60–2, 64–5, and 92. See also Text Link 22. Finally, see Principles 2 and 6 and Text Links 160 and 164.

> ∞ **Text Link 64**
> See Text Links 7, 91, 125, and 152. In addition, see also Text Links 12, 17, 25, 58, 60–3, 65, and 92. Finally, see Principles 2, 6, and 8 and Text Links 160, 164, and 166.

How do teachers articulate the problems they wish to solve? Depending on the problems they face, teachers may act with or without the help of outside change agents. If outside change agents participate in the change process, they act as relatively nondirective resources. To the extent that boss-subordinate relationships exist at all in this approach, leadership is "subordinate-centered," not "boss-centered" (Rondinelli et al. 1990). This means that change agents typically use an "adaptive" leadership style, which is based on experiment, discussion, and persuasion. Having articulated a problem, teachers then diagnose how they want to solve it. Diagnosis is followed by a search and retrieval phase, during which users gather the information they need to formulate and select appropriate solutions. After identifying possible solutions, a process of adaptation, trial, and evaluation follows, during which users assess whether the solutions they have devised really solve their problems. If users judge that the solutions are deficient or unsatisfactory, the process begins again until they find solutions that work (Havelock 1971).

## THE LINKAGE MODEL

Taking their cue from the theoretical literature in education, some applied linguists have begun to advocate using the problem-solving model as an alternative to the better-known RD&D model (Kennedy 1987; Young 1992). Although the problem-solving model should indeed be used as an important mechanism for promoting innovation, it is important to remember that different types of innovations require different approaches to planning and implementing change (Stoller 1992, 1994). For example, new teachers cannot be expected to immediately adopt a problem-solving, action research-oriented approach to change, since this approach is likely to represent a considerable innovation in terms of their currently underdeveloped professional cultures. Thus, as Havelock (1971: 88) remarks, although the social interaction, RD&D, and problem-solving models "represent different and often competing schools of thought, the pragmatic change agent should see them as illustrating different but equally important aspects of a total process."

Havelock calls this synthesis a "linkage" model of change. In this model, a change agent's decision to use a particular change strategy is *contingent* on the problem to be solved (Rondinelli et al. 1990; Stoller 1992, 1994) (see Text Link 65). Thus, in some situations, change agents act as directive problem solvers who simulate solutions for end users, while in others they serve as nondirective facilitators who put adopters in touch with appropriate resources (Havelock 1971). Of course, embracing this multiplicity of roles and approaches is potentially problematic. The linkage model has the advantage of recognizing the complex nature of change processes, but it has the disadvantage that change agents who use this model can expect to be confronted with a very steep learning curve.

> ∞ **Text Link 65**
>
> See Text Links 12, 17, 25, 58, 60–4, and 84. Finally, see Principles 2 and 6 and Text Links 161 and 164.

Answering the question "Who adopts what, where, when, why, and how?" involves defining curricular innovation and examining the social roles of different stakeholders and the phases potential users go through as they evaluate whether to adopt an innovation. Innovation is a time-bound phenomenon, and change is always constrained by sociocultural factors, individuals' psychological profiles, and the attributes that potential adopters perceive a given innovation to possess. The characteristics and the relative strengths and weaknesses of five models of change were discussed. Part II applies this theoretical framework to a curricular and teacher innovation project at an American university.

# II The CATI project: A case study approach

# 4 Issues in project design and implementation

> We are all natives now, and everybody
> else not immediately one of us is an ex-
> otic. What looked once to be a matter of
> finding out whether savages could distin-
> guish fact from fancy now looks to be a
> matter of finding out how others, across
> the world or down the corridor, organize
> their significative world. (Clifford Geertz,
> cited in Swales 1988: 16)

## Some preliminary issues

This section treats the rationale, history, and sociocultural context of the CATI project. It concludes by showing how the insights into change gained from the CATI project can be generalized to other projects.

### Rationale for the CATI project

ESL instruction in North American universities is often provided by part-time teaching assistants (TAs), who are concurrently enrolled as full-time graduate students. Typically, it takes from 1 to 3 years for teaching assistants enrolled in master's programs to graduate. Teaching assistants may have substantial, if not complete, responsibility for teaching a course – a responsibility that, although rarely explicitly acknowledged, informally includes substantial syllabus design and materials development. The CATI project, although closely based on this generic model, differs in one respect: Teaching assistants' de facto syllabus design and materials development responsibilities are explicitly acknowledged and formally included in their job descriptions. The rationale for this is that, in the short term, teaching assistants need to develop their syllabus design and materials development skills, so that they can meet their students' needs in a professional fashion. In the longer term, since many instructors find jobs as curriculum specialists after they graduate, teaching assistants who can show future employers that they have superior curricular skills will be particularly well-prepared to compete in the marketplace.

*The CATI project*

These responsibilities are part of the teaching assistants' job descriptions for four interrelated reasons. First, this arrangement enhances the quality of instruction and provides teaching assistants with experience in curriculum development that is professionally useful to them. Second, it provides a principled way of addressing dissatisfaction expressed by both faculty and teaching assistants at the beginning of the project concerning a perceived lack of coherence in the articulation and content of the ESL courses. Third, it provides a means of building up banks of in-house materials specially tailored to the ESL needs of international students. Finally, it allows project participants to introspect on the process of educational change and on their own professional growth.

## The history of the CATI project

We may distinguish at least three separate phases of the project to date (see Text Link 66). The first, lasting from 1988 to approximately 1990, constitutes the setting-up phase, during which, as a newly appointed faculty member in the department, I learned how to operate in my new surroundings. During this period, I laid the foundations for change by developing a core of teachers who were familiar with task-based teaching. From 1990 to approximately 1992, the second phase of the project, the fruits of the initial setting-up period first began to manifest themselves. These took the form of a sudden burst in the numbers of materials produced *and actually used* by teachers. This is an example of the "bandwagon effect" described by the S-shape of diffusion curves (see Text Link 67). Initially, this materials development activity was confined to instructors teaching parallel sections of one class. It later spread to all the other classes in the ESL courses. This materials development activity continues today at an accelerated pace. The third phase, which began at the beginning of 1993, has involved an expansion of the scope of the project, which now also focuses on promoting change in teachers' methodological skills and attitudes toward teaching (see Text Link 68).

∞ **Text Link 66**

For discussion of the amount of time needed to implement innovations, see Text Links 51, 73, and 143. Finally, see Principle 6 and Text Link 164.

∞ **Text Link 67**

For discussion of this phenomenon, see Figure 3.4 and Text Links 49 and 95. Finally, see Principle 6 and Text Link 164.

∞ **Text Link 68**

See Text Links 125 and 148–152.

## The sociocultural context of the CATI project

In *institutional* terms, the project is located in a research-oriented public university in the United States. *Economically* speaking, although it has suffered budget cuts in the last few years, this university still enjoys

74

many resources, including a large library, well-equipped classrooms, and substantial computer resources. Clearly, faculty and students at this university work in a highly privileged context of implementation.

Turning to *demographic* issues, 36,000 students attend the university. Of these, 26,000 (72%) are undergraduates and 10,000 (28%) are graduate students. International students, who number 3,000 (8%), are almost all graduate students and comprise 30% of the graduate college. The five countries from which the largest groups of students come are the People's Republic of China, the Republic of China, Korea, India, and Japan, accounting for just

∞ **Text Link 69**
For more discussion of the impact of sociocultural factors on curricular innovations, see Text Links 4, 47, 48, 52, 81, 82, and 150. Finally, see Principle 1 and Text Link 159.

over half of all international students. Not surprisingly, students from Asian countries form the majority of learners in the ESL courses. Furthermore, 50% of students admitted to the master's program that hosts the CATI project are from the United States and 50% are international students, most of whom come from the People's Republic of China, the Republic of China, Korea, and Japan. The demographic distribution of students has had an important impact on the CATI project (see Text Link 69).

Whatever their *cultural* and *linguistic* backgrounds, all ESL students are high-intermediate learners who need to develop their academic skills in English. From an administrative point of view, these needs are met by the ESL program that functions as the immediate host of the CATI project. As a faculty member in the master's program, I teach a number of courses in applied linguistics, which graduate students take in order to fulfill the requirements for the master's degree. As director of the ESL program, I supervise the ESL courses, which are divided into two sequences. One sequence is for graduate students, the other for undergraduate students. There are three courses in each sequence. Typically, there are fourteen to seventeen sections of these six courses per semester. The ESL program has an enrollment of 650–700 international students a year, of whom 60% are graduate students.

In summary, the CATI project is based on a *developmental* model of in-service teacher education (see Text Link 70). It is *field-based,* in that there is a very close connection between the ESL program

∞ **Text Link 70**
See Text Link 41.

and the teacher education program that controls the ESL courses. It is *experimental,* in that teaching assistants use the ESL courses they teach to try out and modify the pedagogical ideas and practices to which they are exposed in the teacher education program. It is *problem-centered,* in that teaching assistants focus on resolving issues and problems that occur in their own classes. It is *collaborative,* in that teaching assistants use and modify in-house materials developed by colleagues and predecessors. It is *competency-based,* in that the teacher education program that services the ESL program educates teaching assistants about theoretical issues and problems in task-based teaching. It is also *open-ended,* in that succeeding generations of teaching assistants are inducted into the project on a continuing basis.

## Issues of generalizability versus understanding

∞ **Text Link 71**
See Text Link 77.

The main reason for discussing the CATI project is to develop a grounded understanding of the problems that all change agents must solve if they are to persuade end users to adopt change. How to make this argument is partly a question of methodology (see Text Link 71) and partly a question of making explicit the kinds of questions that should be asked. It is to this latter question that I now turn. Speaking to what could be learned from in-progress reports of ESP materials design projects in the 1980s, Bowers (1980a) notes that case studies are indeed an important part of the professional literature *if* readers can obtain answers to the following questions: (1) How does one project compare with another in terms of approach, content, and the results achieved? (2) What are the design elements of a given project and how can these be reproduced in other environments? (3) What elements of planning and implementation – for example, classroom implementation in a materials design project – are not covered in a project report? (4) How does a project achieve its objectives, and how do these objectives relate to the objectives of other projects? (5) What evaluation measures does the project use and how do they compare to measures used in other projects?[1]

∞ **Text Link 72**
See Text Links 23, 40, and 136. Finally, see Principles 5 and 7–9 and Text Links 163, 165–7.

The first two questions focus on the issue of comparability. I have already addressed this issue in some of the preceding paragraphs; in addition, the six examples of teaching-related innovations discussed in Chapter 2 enable us to make cross-cultural comparisons about the range of factors that influence how innovations diffuse. Recall, for example, that one of the dimensions of Beretta's evaluation of the Bangalore Project involved determining the levels of use and the degree of innovation ownership attained by different teachers who had participated in this project (see Text Link 72). In particular, although Prabhu (1987) does not talk about the implementation of the Bangalore Project in diffusionist terms,

1 Bowers also asks a sixth question about the role of fashion in program design, which I do not take up here.

the evaluations of this project carried out by Beretta (1989, 1990, 1992a) demonstrate how ubiquitous implementation problems are, irrespective of this project's sociocultural context. These are precisely the issues that Tickoo (1996) claims are the most enduring legacy of the Bangalore Project.

As for Bowers' third question, a major focus of this chapter is to develop an empirically based methodology that demonstrates how *intentions* at the strategic level of planning are translated into *actual practice* at the tactical and operational levels of planning. With respect to the evaluation issues Bowers raises in questions four and five, this chapter shows how evaluation is built into the project's design through a planning document called a Project Framework matrix.[2]

> ∞ **Text Link 73**
> For discussion of the amount of time it takes to implement innovations, see Text Links 51, 66, and 143. For discussion of the need to develop an organization's capacity to support innovation, see Table 4.1, Table 5.1, Figure 5.1, and Text Links 2, 37, 42, 80, 104, 105, 107, 121, 138, and 157. Finally, see Principle 6 and Text Link 164.

## The CATI project's negotiated model of curricular innovation

The CATI project's ideology draws on a critical, negotiated approach to pedagogy (Candlin 1984a; Dewey 1910; Freire 1976; Illich 1970; Pennycook 1989, 1990, 1994; Phillipson 1992; Stenhouse 1975; Tollefson 1988, 1989, 1991, 1995) (see Text Link 74). Figure 4.1 shows the project's negotiated model of curricular innovation.

> ∞ **Text Link 74**
> See Text Link 48.

In Part I, we saw that curriculum design involves two levels of planning – strategic (or curriculum) planning and tactical (or syllabus) planning (see Text Link 75). According to Candlin (1984a), syllabuses are retrospective texts that document what teaching actually occurred in a classroom. In the CATI project, however, syllabuses are traditionally predictive documents that are prepared outside the classroom. Consequently, another level of planning is

> ∞ **Text Link 75**
> See Text Links 15 and 16.

---

2 Chapter 5 discusses the resources I have developed to support the process of curricular innovation, including the resources used to monitor and evaluate project success. Chapter 6 provides information on how participatory evaluations – that is, evaluations carried out by *insiders* rather than by *outsiders* – may be used to promote change. This chapter also outlines what *has* been achieved and what has *not* been achieved so far in the CATI project, highlighting some important initial failures in the project and identifying the problems that still await resolution (see Text Link 73).

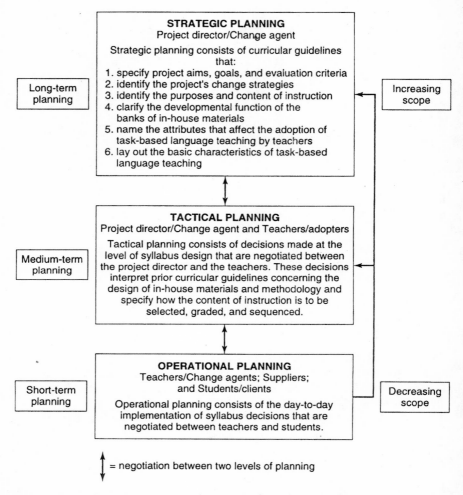

**STRATEGIC PLANNING**
Project director/Change agent

Strategic planning consists of curricular guidelines that:
1. specify project aims, goals, and evaluation criteria
2. identify the project's change strategies
3. identify the purposes and content of instruction
4. clarify the developmental function of the banks of in-house materials
5. name the attributes that affect the adoption of task-based language teaching by teachers
6. lay out the basic characteristics of task-based language teaching

Long-term planning

Increasing scope

**TACTICAL PLANNING**
Project director/Change agent and Teachers/adopters

Tactical planning consists of decisions made at the level of syllabus design that are negotiated between the project director and the teachers. These decisions interpret prior curricular guidelines concerning the design of in-house materials and methodology and specify how the content of instruction is to be selected, graded, and sequenced.

Medium-term planning

**OPERATIONAL PLANNING**
Teachers/Change agents; Suppliers; and Students/clients

Operational planning consists of the day-to-day implementation of syllabus decisions that are negotiated between teachers and students.

Short-term planning

Decreasing scope

↕ = negotiation between two levels of planning

Figure 4.1 The CATI project's negotiated model of curricular innovation.

needed to account for what happens inside the classroom. For this reason, I extend Candlin's basic model by adding a third level of "operational planning" (Ellison and Davies 1990), which accounts for teachers' everyday lesson planning and teaching.

The mechanism that drives innovation forward is the process of communication and negotiation between the principal actors in the teaching–learning relationship (project directors, teachers, and learners), who function as change agents, adopters or resisters, suppliers, and clients of curricular innovations (see Text Link 76). These social roles, which are not mutually exclusive, are formally set out at each level of the model. Strategic curricular planning is the responsibility of the project director or change agent, who supplies knowledge about task-based language teaching to teachers and gives the project its overall direction. The scope of strategic planning encompasses the management of change in an entire project and involves long-term planning.

∞ **Text Link 76**
See Text Links 29, 30, 31, 34, 35, 50, 109, and 133.

Tactical syllabus planning is the shared responsibility of the project director or change agent and teachers. As potential adopters (or indeed resisters) of the innovations specified at the strategic level of planning, teachers interpret curricular guidelines in ways that are personally meaningful and useful to them. It is this process of *critical* interpretation that promotes innovation by teachers, who also function as suppliers of materials and as change agents in their own right. It is in this sense that conflict, which results from this process of critical interpretation and negotiation, functions as a catalyst of change (see Text Link 77). The scope of tactical syllabus planning is narrower than that of strategic curricular planning; it involves managing change in one course (or parallel sections of one course) rather than in an entire program. Thus, tactical syllabus planning is concerned with an increasing level of detail and requires the use of medium-term planning.

∞ **Text Link 77**
See Text Links 15, 16, 98, 102, 103, and 155. Finally, see Principle 4 and Text Link 162.

Operational planning is the responsibility of teachers, which they in turn share with their students. This level of planning also constitutes a potential locus of innovation, in that the implementation of the project's materials involves substantial negotiation between teachers and learners. At this level of planning, teachers function as change agents who "sell" their materials to learners, and students function not only as clients but also as potential adopters or resisters of teachers' innovative materials and methodologies. The scope of operational planning is the narrowest of the three levels of planning described here: It involves managing change with specific individuals in a specific class. Thus, operational planning is concerned with a high level of detail and requires the use of short-term planning, which includes the moment-by-moment decisions teachers make during the course of a lesson. Finally, feedback loops from the operational and tactical levels of planning ensure that curricular guidelines remain in touch with the teachers' and students' sense of reality. As such, they evolve on a continuing basis. Let us next examine empirically how these three levels of planning function (see Text Link 78).

∞ **Text Link 78**
See Text Link 71.

## Strategic planning

The project director's responsibilities include (1) specifying the project's aims, goals, and criteria for evaluation; (2) identifying the change strategies used to implement the project's aims and goals; (3) stating the purposes and the content of the project's ESL instruction; (4) clarifying the developmental function of the project's banks of in-house materials; (5) naming the attributes that affect the implementation of task-based teaching in the project; and (6) laying out the characteristics of task-based language teaching.

### *The project's aims, goals, and criteria for evaluation*

As indicated in Chapter 1, curriculum development and teacher development are indivisible (Stenhouse 1975). Beginning with the 1993–4 academic year, this idea has been succinctly expressed by using the adapted Project Framework matrix shown in Table 4.1 (see Alderson 1992; Boyle 1987; Cracknell and Rednall 1986; and Deyes 1988 for the original version of this matrix).

∞ **Text Link 79**
See Text Links 131, 134, and 142. Finally, see Principles 4 and 7 and Text Links 162 and 165.

By using this framework, which is widely used by American, Australian, European, and United Nations aid agencies (Cracknell and Rednall 1986), we can specify a project's aims and objectives and also outline the criteria used for evaluation in a single, integrated package. Thus, project framework documents can help language teaching professionals to understand the consequences of their decisions and actions (Alderson 1992) (see Text Link 79) – a welcome development, since language program evaluation is still in its infancy (Beretta 1992b).

Table 4.1 consists of two parts. The first part sets out the project's Aims, Objectives, and Outputs as hierarchically organized statements that range from the general to the specific. The second consists of the Inputs required to achieve the project's Aims, Objectives, and Outputs. Thus, in the first column, Project Structure, the first aim is to educate teachers to take on future responsibilities as curriculum specialists. Reading down the column, this aim correlates with the first Project Objective of developing and implementing a program of teacher-implemented syllabus design and materials development activities. Similarly, the second Project Aim of using the ESL courses as a laboratory for curriculum and teacher development relates to the second and third Project Objectives of promoting the critical use of task-based language teaching among teachers and involving students in the project's evolution through continuing negotiation and evaluation of classroom activities. The aims and goals are specified as Outputs, or products that the project seeks to develop. Managers often reserve the Inputs section for specifying the funding that must be committed to a project. This matrix, however, specifies the organizational capacity of the ESL courses to (1) inform teachers about task-based language teaching, (2) help participants communicate with each other about task-based teaching, (3) monitor individual change, and (4) evaluate project success or failure (see Text Link 80). The Indicators of Achievement column sets out the behavioral and attitudinal changes that must occur if the project is to succeed, the Means of Verification column indicates the procedures used to evaluate the project, and the Important Assumptions column specifies assumptions about the potential impact of sociocultural factors on the project.

∞ **Text Link 80**
See Table 5.1 and Figure 5.1. See also Text Links 2, 37, 42, 73, 104, 105, 107, 119, 121, 138, and 157.

This matrix is used in the CATI project in the following way. Reading Table 4.1 horizontally, the first Project Objective – developing and implementing an in-house materials development program – is *achieved* if each individual teacher contributes one required unit to a central bank of materials. The fulfillment of this requirement is *verified* by having teachers develop materials as term projects for a methodology class in the teacher education program. Finally, it is *assumed* that three conditions must exist if Project Objective 1 (and indeed the second objective) is to be achieved: (1) adequate levels of funding for the ESL courses will be maintained by the university; (2) the teacher education degree program will continue to exist as a supporting resource for the ESL courses; and (3) suitable supervisory and teaching staff will continue to be available.

Notice that these three assumptions are motivated by developments in the larger sociocultural environment that circumscribes the CATI project (see Text Link 81). As already noted, the university has experienced financial problems in recent years due to cutbacks in state budget appropriations for

∞ **Text Link 81**
See Text Links 4, 47, 48, 52, 69, 82, and 150. Finally, see Principle 1 and Text Link 159.

higher education. Thus, at the level of Project Aims, it is also assumed that the university will not suffer drastic cuts in the state budget even while it is recognized that the situation is unlikely to get dramatically better. At the level of Project Objectives, this lack of state support for the university has had a noticeable impact on the funding of ESL instruction. Budget cuts by the state have meant that the amount of money committed by the university on a recurring basis to the ESL courses each year has not kept up with demand. Although it has been possible to continue providing ESL instruction in a fairly stable fashion, these factors have still had a negative impact on the ESL courses. ESL administrators must continually ask the university for more funds on

TABLE 4.1. CATI PROJECT FRAMEWORK MATRIX FOR THE 1993-4 ACADEMIC YEAR

| Project structure | Indicators of achievement |
|---|---|
| *Project aims* | |
| 1. To give teachers the knowledge, skills, and abilities they need to fill supervisory positions as ESL curriculum specialists after graduation | 1. By the time teachers graduate, they will be able to solve selected curricular problems in ways that are both practically feasible and theoretically motivated. |
| 2. To use the ESL courses as a laboratory for curriculum and teacher development | 2. Teachers will engage in a process of innovation, the products of which include the development of new materials, methodological skills, and pedagogical values by teachers. |
| *Project objectives* | |
| 1. To develop and implement a program of teacher-generated syllabus design and materials development activities that service the needs of the ESL courses | 1. Each teacher will contribute one *required* unit to a bank of materials. Each teacher will be *encouraged* to continue developing new units after fulfilling the basic requirement. |
| 2. To promote the critical use and understanding of task-based language teaching materials and methodology in the ESL service courses | 2. Each teacher will use in-house task-based materials and will be able to consciously articulate an individual interpretation of task-based methodology. |
| 3. To involve ESL students in the evolution of the project through negotiation and evaluation of the project | 3. Teachers will incorporate student feedback so that students' needs and wants are appropriately reflected in the project's instructional materials. |
| *Outputs* | |
| 1. Professional language teaching specialists who use an evolutionary, innovation-centered approach to teaching | 1. Attested changes in teachers' pedagogical behaviors (development and use of new materials and methodological skills) and values |
| 2. Banks of open-ended task-based materials produced in-house | 2. Ongoing development of new materials; improvement over time in the quality of units produced |
| 3. The ongoing evolution and improvement of the quality of instruction offered by ESL service courses | 3. Data that provide evidence of teacher and student satisfaction or dissatisfaction with the content and methodology of existing ESL courses |
| *Inputs* | |
| Ongoing development of the organizational capacity of the ESL courses to function as a laboratory for teacher and curriculum development, specifically, continuing efforts to improve the project's capacity to: (1) inform teachers about task-based language teaching; (2) enable project participants to communicate with each other about task-based teaching; (3) monitor the processes of change undergone by individuals; and (4) evaluate the extent of project success | The project is able to maintain itself on an ongoing basis as each new generation of teaching assistants is inducted into the ESL courses. |

| *Means of verification* | *Important assumptions* |
| --- | --- |

*Project aims*

1. Satisfactory completion of course requirements for a methodology course in the teacher education program; portfolios that document the professional evolution of teachers

2. Action research contributed to portfolios that document the teachers' own professional evolution; classroom research by the project director; evaluation surveys; TAlist contributions (optional)*

1. No *major* changes in the political/economic situation (both internal and external) that affects the academic unit that hosts the CATI project

2. No major changes in the institutional status of the academic unit that hosts the CATI project

3. No major changes in the educational philosophy of the academic unit that hosts the CATI project

4. No major changes in the demographic profiles of the populations from whom the teaching assistants and ESL students are drawn

*Project objectives*

1. Each required unit will be developed as a term project for a methodology course in the teacher education program.

2a. ESL course supervisors will use a three-step classroom observation process (pre-observation conference, observation, debriefing) to support the teachers' use and understanding of task-based language teaching.

2b. Teachers will keep a portfolio *minimally* consisting of their units and revisions and a journal (a monthly journal of 400–600 words, to be discussed once a month with the director). In addition, they will select a range of self-report data (action research reports, videos of their teaching, etc.) to include in the portfolio.

3. Teachers and supervisors will conduct evaluations of project materials at the end of each year to check the extent to which materials have been revised in light of student feedback.

1. Maintenance of adequate funding of ESL courses

2. Continued existence of the teacher education program

3. Availability of suitable teaching staff and continuity of personnel in supervisory positions

*Outputs*

1. Evaluations of each teaching assistant's materials development projects done in the methodology course; classroom observations; teachers' portfolios

2. Inspection of units contributed to the project's bank of materials

3. Student evaluations and teachers' portfolios

As for *Project Aims* and *Project Objectives*

*Inputs*

There will be yearly anonymous evaluations by teachers of the adequacy of existing organizational resources that support the process of innovation and yearly anonymous evaluations of course supervisors.

Good vertical and horizontal communication networks exist that will help project participants identify what new resources need to be developed.

---

*The TAlist is an electronic list to which all teachers subscribe. For further discussion of how it functions, see Chapter 5.

an ad hoc basis and never know how many ESL sections they can open until the last moment. Frequently, therefore, they cannot hire some teaching assistants until the day before classes begin. As a result, these late hires cannot attend the ESL program orientation before instruction begins. Finally, these cuts have also resulted in an increase in the maximum permitted size of ESL classes. In 1988, the maximum number of students admitted to these classes was eighteen; it is now officially twenty-one – a 16.7% increase in class size in six years.

With respect to the second assumption at the level of Project Aims, the situation is potentially more serious. The university's financial woes has led the administration to seek ways of maximizing efficiency, including downsizing some academic units. This has led to one academic unit being closed and other units, including the one that hosts the CATI project, being targeted for a reduction in faculty numbers. This reduction would affect the capability of the host teacher education program to support curricular innovation in the CATI project. Thus, the continued existence of the teacher education program in its present form is a crucial factor in the ability of the CATI project to meet its developmental objectives. At the time of writing this book, this issue remains unresolved.

Concerning the third and fourth assumptions at the level of Project Aims, it is the unit's philosophy that the teacher education program is not necessarily a "post-experience" degree. Thus, the unit admits some individuals who have never taught ESL (in contrast, master's programs in Britain are all "post-experience" degrees, so that candidates must have a minimum of 3 or 4 years of teaching experience before they can apply to a program). In addition, approximately 50% of students are international students, many of whom come from the People's Republic of China, the Republic of China, Korea, and Japan. The high proportion of international students from these countries can be explained in part by political factors, such as the drive for modernization by the People's Republic of China, and by economic factors, such as the low rate of exchange for the U.S. dollar in recent years, which has made graduate education in the United States attractive for students from Taiwan, Korea, and Japan.

At the level of Project Objectives, this means that staffing the ESL courses can be quite difficult. It is a structural fact of life that all (educational) organizations constantly change because the people who make up the system change (Baldridge and Deal 1983). There is, therefore, a constant need to induct new teachers into the ESL courses and to ensure that experienced teachers pass on their skills and experience to new arrivals before the former graduate. This constant change in personnel, combined with the demographic profiles of master's program students, means that the unit that hosts the CATI project disposes of a limited pool of teachers from which to draw its staff. This is because project teachers must have prior teaching experience and a level of communicative competence in a "native" or "second language" variety of English that enables them to operate effortlessly in the linguistically and intellectually challenging context of teaching ESL at a North American research university.

*Any* student in the teacher education program who possesses these qualities can teach for the ESL program. However, international students who do not come from the English-speaking world are inevitably at a linguistic disadvantage when they compete for jobs against peers who come from countries where English is used for intranational communication. Even though it is common sense that individuals who wish to teach in the ESL program must have an adequate level of communicative competence in English, this situation poses troubling ethical issues with regard to international students who lack access to important opportunities for professionalization that are available to their more communicatively competent peers. This illustrates how the demographic profile of the host teacher education program's student body negatively impacts the CATI project's ability to be inclusive. It also illustrates how sociocultural factors cluster together in unexpected ways. The solutions to these problems remain unclear (see Text Link 82). Finally, the demographic profiles of *ESL students* affects classroom practices. As noted earlier, most ESL students come from Asian cultures, which have different educational traditions from those of North America. Consequently, teachers have to educate many of their students to accept the task-based methodology they use in their classes. It is in this sense that curricular innovation in the CATI project is embedded in a matrix of sociocultural factors that define what is feasible.

> ∞ **Text Link 82**
> See also Text Links 4, 47, 48, 69, 81, and 150.

Turning to the evaluation philosophy that underpins the CATI project, evaluation criteria must produce guidelines that identify (1) the purpose of an evaluation, (2) who will carry out the evaluation, and (3) what kinds of data and research designs will be used (Alderson 1992; Beretta 1992b; Lynch 1996). In the CATI project, the responses to these guidelines are as follows. (1) An evaluation must provide feedback that sustains the process of innovation and contributes to the professional development of teacher-evaluators. (2) The most useful kind of evaluation is that carried out *by* project participants *for* project participants. (3) No single evaluation paradigm can provide a complete picture of project success or failure. We must therefore gather qualitative and quantitative data and use experimental and nonexperimental research designs as appropriate.

Evaluations of language programs and methods are usually done by outside evaluators (Beretta 1992b), whom Alderson and Scott (1992) call "JIJOEs" (Jet In Jet Out Experts). This tongue-in-cheek acronym points up the fact that, although outsiders can provide a fresh perspective on a project's achievements (Alderson and Beretta 1992a), JIJOE evaluations have a number of weaknesses. They are expert-driven, with methods and practices that are often irrelevant to the concerns of teachers. Teachers are therefore unlikely to have any interest in being evaluated and, particularly if the results are unfavorable, are unlikely to accept recommendations for improvement. Thus, the utility of JIJOE evaluations is compromised by the fact that teachers do not own the results of such evaluations. Furthermore, although outsiders may be objective and free of conflicts of interest, they may also simply impose their own agendas on a project without really understanding its aims and objectives. Finally, since outsiders are typically on-site for a limited period of time, they cannot hope to develop a deep appreciation of the values, meanings, and aspirations that teachers project onto the innovations they implement.

In contrast, participants are more likely to own the results of inside evaluations because they have "discovered" them for themselves. Even though inside evaluators must acknowledge potential conflicts of interest, the advantages of such evaluations generally outweigh the disadvantages. Insiders' evaluations are based on the "local knowledge" of teacher-evaluators. Consequently, the interpretation of results reflects the values, meanings, and aspirations of project participants and contributes to the validity of the evaluation for users. The fact that these results are not generalizable is unimportant, since the evaluation serves to sustain a *local* process of change. Inside evaluations also contribute to the professionalization of individual evaluators (Alderson and Scott 1992; Celani et al. 1988). Finally, since no single approach to evaluation should become paradigmatically dominant (Beretta 1992b), projects should be evaluated in a variety of ways. Some evaluations may legitimately analyze specific details of the innovation process, while others may look at the innovation process in more general terms. These different types of evaluations yield different results, which must be pieced together into a composite picture of how innovation works (see Text Link 83).

∞ Text Link 83
See Text Link 136.

## The project's change strategies

The CATI project employs a linkage model of change, which promotes innovation by using top-down and bottom-up strategies of change on a *contingent* basis (see Text Link 84). The model is top-down in that the project director uses authority in two ways: (1) as a faculty member, using the hierarchical position of director within the unit that hosts the CATI project to develop the project's organizational capacity to sustain curriculum and teacher development; and (2) as a curriculum specialist, using academic authority to set out the *general* parameters within which innovation in the

∞ **Text Link 84**
See Text Links 17, 25, 32, 58, 62, and 65. Finally, see Principle 2 and Text Link 160.

CATI project occurs. However, the project director and teachers constantly renegotiate these parameters. In some instances, teachers have rejected the project director's proposals. For example, the project director's first proposals for changing classroom observation procedures involved circulating a standardized form that supervisors would use to observe teachers. The motivation for developing this form, which consisted of a checklist of "desirable" teaching behaviors, was that teachers had complained that observation procedures were arbitrary. Having made the observation form available to teachers, the project director asked for feedback. In response, one teaching assistant forcefully argued that this proposal went against the grain of current research in education, which had moved away from the idea that teaching could be distilled into a checklist of teaching behaviors that were universally "good." The TA further argued that this proposal contradicted the project's avowed aim of promoting teacher development, noting that the observation form was a *quality control* tool, not a

*teacher development* tool. During the course of the debate that ensued, a solid consensus emerged among teaching assistants that the proposed innovation was undesirable. Ultimately, the project di-

∞ **Text Link 85**
See Text Links 114, 127, and 153.

rector withdrew the proposal and subsequently developed the observation procedure described to verify the second objective in the Project Framework matrix in collaboration with the teachers (see Text Link 85).

In sum, curricular innovation in the CATI project is based on the concept of using authority as a tool of empowerment, not as a tool of control. That is, authority is used *with,* not *over,* teachers. As Freire (1976) argues in a different context, authority cannot be exercised by fiat; it is based on praxis. For

∞ **Text Link 86**
See Text Links 64, 92, 125, and 152. Finally, see Principles 4 and 8 and Text Links 162 and 166.

this reason, as the Means of Verification column in Table 4.1 attests, the CATI project primarily employs strategies of change – such as action research – that are bottom-up and nondirective. Thus, when teachers do action research to help them understand what actually happens in their classes, the project director's function is to act as a resource and as a facilitator, who helps teachers bring their action research projects to fruition, and not as a gatekeeper of change (see Text Link 86).

*The CATI project*

## The purposes and content of instruction

International students have a substantial background in grammar and general English when they arrive in the United States. However, they do not necessarily know how to communicate effectively according to the specialized norms of academic discourse. One solution would have been to offer subject-specific English for academic purposes (EAP) instruction – and this has been done in one course. However, due to timetable difficulties and other logistical problems, it was unlikely that a "narrow-angle" EAP solution (McDonough 1986) would be viable. At the same time, this did not mean that a "wide-angle" EAP design was not feasible. In the research-oriented context of implementation in which the CATI project functions, such a solution focuses on teaching the academic skills that all students need in order to carry out research successfully. International students need to be able to process large amounts of challenging information quickly. This information is presented in different forms (books, monographs, articles, etc.) and venues (lectures, seminars, discussion sections) and with different kinds of participants as interlocutors (peers, faculty, and advisors). They therefore need to know how to communicate effectively through different *instrumentalities* (Munby 1978).

∞ Text Link 87
See Text Link 11.

More specifically, students must be able to communicate successfully via both oral and written *media*. They must also be able to handle different *modes* of communication, ranging from "monologues that are spoken to be heard" (i.e., lectures) to "dialogues that are spoken to be heard" (i.e., ordinary conversations). They must be able to communicate through different *channels* of communication, such as face-to-face oral discourse, writing, and electronic mail. Finally, they must learn how to use the university's research facilities, particularly its large computerized library system. In sum, although it is not possible for the *intellectual* content of most ESL courses to be subject-specific, the *procedural* content of these courses (i.e., the kinds of learning activities with which students engage in their ESL classes) can be appropriately derived from the academic tasks that students accomplish in their day-to-day lives. It is this focus on analyzing tasks, rather than analyzing the functional language that realizes tasks, that differentiates analytic from earlier synthetic approaches to needs analysis (see Text Link 87).

## The developmental function of in-house materials

The decision to use an ESP-inspired course design solution naturally suggests that teachers should develop in-house materials, an activity that

has always been important in ESP. However, the
decision to rely mostly on in-house materials is motivated by the more important aim of promoting
teacher development (see also Baumgardner et al.

∞ **Text Link 88**
See Text Link 116.

1986). As we will see later, this means that the materials must be easily
accessible to teachers. Furthermore, adding new units to the banks of
materials and editing existing units should both be easy processes (see
Text Link 88).

## Attributes affecting the adoption of task-based language teaching

Innovations have attributes that either facilitate or inhibit their adoption (see Text Link 89). These can be
used to analyze the factors that potentially affect the
adoption of task-based teaching by teaching assistants. The importance of some of these attributes has
emerged over time. Consequently, they were not all
identified a priori at the start of the project. The im-

∞ **Text Link 89**
See Table 2.7 and Text
Links 13, 18, 55, 56, 90,
96, 111, 117, 124, and
139. Finally, see Princi-
ples 1 and 8 and Text
Links 159 and 166.

portance of the attributes of explicitness, adaptability, and feasibility
emerged during the implementation of the project.

RELATIVE ADVANTAGE

Learning how to develop and implement task-based language teaching
materials is a major undertaking for teaching assistants. It represents a
substantial investment of time and effort and poten-
tially involves learning many new skills. Teaching
assistants should therefore feel that potential benefits will outweigh the costs of producing materials
(Rogers 1983). Thus, teaching assistants develop
their materials in a methodology class in the teacher
education program that hosts the CATI project. In
this way, teachers receive academic credit for their
materials development work. Furthermore, as graduate students who have other obligations and duties, they do not have to invest an unreasonable

∞ **Text Link 90**
To understand how these
various attributes are interrelated, see Text Link
96. For related discus-
sion of the role of inno-
vations' attributes in
diffusion, see Text Links
13, 18, 55, 56, 89, 111,
117, 124, and 139. Fi-
nally, see Principle 8 and
Text Link 166.

amount of time and effort in the CATI project. They also receive considerable guidance and feedback from their peers and the instructor
during the development phase of their materials, which also lessens the
burden of developing these units (see Text Link 90).

COMPATIBILITY

Few teaching assistants come into the service courses using task-based
language teaching as their preferred approach, but many have already

∞ **Text Link 91**
See Figure 2.1. See also
Text Links 27, 91, 97,
101, and 123.

experimented with student-centered techniques (e.g., group work, simulations, language games). Some have already used isolated tasks in their teaching, the most familiar being the kind of information gap task discussed in Example 6 of Chapter 2 (see Text Link 91). Thus, many of the procedures used in task-based language teaching are already somewhat familiar to most instructors. This is important, because innovations that are too different from adopters' current practices are less likely to be adopted (Rogers 1983). In effect, the methodology course in the teacher education program provides many teaching assistants with an intellectual rationale for organizing an entire course along task-based lines and also shows them how to do this. The subjective "newness" of task-based language teaching for most teaching assistants is therefore a matter of degree, which is likely to make it compatible with the current pedagogical practices of most teaching assistants. In turn, this is likely to make task-based teaching an acceptable innovation for most teaching assistants (Stoller 1994).

COMPLEXITY

Task-based language teaching is relatively complex, which makes it potentially difficult to understand and use (Rogers 1983). However, teaching assistants have almost a semester to use task-based materials developed by their colleagues before they produce materials of their own. Since they now enroll in the methodology class in the teacher education program during their first semester of teaching, they also have the opportunity simultaneously to develop their understanding of task-based language teaching theory. Consequently, they are able to draw on both their practical experience of task-based teaching and the theoretical background to which they are exposed in the methodology class to develop their units. Furthermore, teaching assistants receive feedback from the project director and the assistant project director when they are observed teaching their own or their colleagues' materials. Consequently, the level of complexity inherent in task-based language teaching is lessened by these arrangements, so that complexity is not viewed as a major hindrance to its adoption by teaching assistants.

TRIALABILITY

As suggested previously, instructors are not expected to innovate right away. This is important, because innovations that can be tried out in stages tend to be much more acceptable to potential adopters than those that they have to adopt lock, stock, and barrel (Rogers 1983). Since teachers develop their materials as part of a final project for the methodology class, they have approximately 10 to 12 weeks to get familiar with the practical aspects of task-based language teaching before they start producing their own materials. They therefore have the opportunity to understand how such materials work in their classes, and this helps them to understand the materials development problems that they may have to solve in their own units.

## OBSERVABILITY

The more visible an innovation is, the more likely it is that people who observe it will adopt it (Rogers 1983). All teaching assistants should therefore be exposed to the task-based materials produced by their peers and predecessors. To this end, examples of task-based units are included in a teachers' handbook, which new teaching assistants receive before they begin teaching. New teaching assistants also attend a workshop that is part of an orientation to the ESL courses, during which they discuss what task-based language teaching is and produce a mini task-based unit (see Text Link 92).

∞ **Text Link 92**
For discussion of the importance of personal experience in diffusion, see Text Links 64, 86, and 125. In addition, see Text Link 7. Finally, see Principle 8 and Text Link 166.

## FORM

The form an innovation takes is also crucial to its adoption (Richards 1984). Since the notion of teacher education and development is rather abstract and difficult to explain, it is important to engage new teaching assistants in a problem-solving process (i.e., the development of task-based materials) with immediate results that have a tangible, concrete form. This early focus on materials development makes it potentially easier for teaching assistants to understand what they have to accomplish and what their roles are in the project. Note that the attribute of form is related to the characteristics of observability and complexity, in that the tangible nature of the innovation that teaching assistants have to manipulate makes it potentially more visible and also less complex for possible users to understand.

## EXPLICITNESS

The need to make the *aims* and *goals* of the CATI project explicit (Dow et al. 1984) was first identified in Hutchin's (1992) evaluation of the CATI project. This evaluation showed that, although teaching assistants believed that the experiences and practices to which they were exposed in the ESL courses were beneficial, few instructors had consciously made the connection between their materials development activities and the teacher development aspect of the project – a connection that is crucial to the project's success (see Text Link 93). This lacuna has now been corrected by stating this aim in the

∞ **Text Link 93**
See Text Link 1. See also Principle 1 and Text Link 159.

Project Framework document that is prepared each year (see Table 4.1). This document is contained in the teachers' handbook and is extensively discussed during the orientation.

ORIGINALITY

The CATI project relies on the production of in-house materials because this is an effective way of promoting teacher development. This does not mean that commercial materials are not also used in this project – they are, primarily as references and resources for ideas. This acknowledges the fact that commercial materials also promote professional development by providing teachers with practical examples of new ideas – as happened in the case of the notional-functional syllabus (see Text Link 94). Relying on original materials, however, is a potentially complex solution. In the short term, original solutions are demanding of teachers, who have to become suppliers of materials. Another significant cost of adopting such a solution is the time and effort required of the change agent, who has to ensure that revisions to units are kept up to date. In the longer term, however, an original solution is potentially beneficial, in that it engages each teacher in a process of continuing professional development that is based on an experiential, problem-solving approach to teacher education (Tetenbaum and Mulkeen 1986). Furthermore, the management problems involved in keeping revised units up to date can be solved. In the end, change agents decide what trade-offs they are willing to accept. In the CATI project, the high level of originality of project materials is considered a price worth paying to promote a process of change.

> ∞ **Text Link 94**
> See Text Link 13. See also Principle 1 and Text Link 159.

ADAPTABILITY

The philosophy that underpins the CATI project is evolutionary and classroom-based in the sense that teachers constantly revise previously written materials. Consequently, the adaptability of materials is a key issue (Dow et al. 1984). Teaching assistants now perceive the banks of task-based materials as open-ended and routinely adapt them to their own purposes. However, at the beginning of the project, they had many reservations about task-based language teaching because they perceived this approach to syllabus design to be too closed from a methodological point of view. However, once a teaching assistant who was widely respected by her peers began to produce and share her own interpretations of task-based materials with her colleagues, other teaching assistants quickly began to follow in her footsteps (see Text Link 95).

> ∞ **Text Link 95**
> See Text Links 39, 49, and 67. Finally, see Principle 1 and Text Link 159.

## FEASIBILITY

The feasibility (Kelly 1980) of teaching assistants engaging in materials development was initially low. Until the project director persuaded his faculty colleagues that teaching assistants should take the methodology class the first semester that they taught for the ESL courses, teachers were advised to take this class during their last semester in the MATESL program. Consequently, teaching assistants did not receive the necessary theoretical background in task-based language teaching when they most needed it – when they first started to teach in the ESL courses. Furthermore, the opportunity for teaching assistants to develop materials in the methodology class was also greatly delayed. This meant they had few incentives to produce task-based materials *on their own time*. Consequently, teaching assistants initially perceived task-based teaching to be a relatively disadvantageous innovation (see Text Link 96). This situation occurred because there was a mismatch between the project director's expectations and the resources, knowledge, and skills available to teaching assistants.

> ∞ **Text Link 96**
> For other discussions of the impact of this and other attributes on diffusion, see Text Links 13, 18, 55, 56, 89, 90, 111, 117, and 124. Finally, see Principle 8 and Text Link 166.

## *The characteristics of task-based language teaching*

Teachers who participate in the CATI project need to be well-informed about task-based language teaching. More specifically, they need to be able to answer the following three questions: (1) What are tasks? (2) What is task-based language teaching? (3) What criteria may be used to select, grade, and sequence tasks? (see Text Link 97).

> ∞ **Text Link 97**
> See Figure 2.1 and Text Links 27, 91, 101, and 123.

### WHAT ARE TASKS?

A number of definitions of *task* exist in the literature:

A piece of work undertaken for oneself or for others, freely or for some reward. Thus, examples of tasks include painting a fence, dressing a child, filling out a form, buying a pair of shoes, making an airline reservation, borrowing a library book, taking a driving test, typing a letter, weighing a patient, sorting letters, taking a hotel reservation, writing a check, finding a street destination, and helping someone across a road. In other words, by "task" is meant the hundred and one things people do in everyday life, at work, at play, and in between. Tasks are the things people will tell you they do if you ask them and they are not applied linguists. (Long 1985: 89)

A piece of work or an activity, usually with a specified objective, undertaken as part of an educational course, or at work. (Crookes 1986: 1)

An activity which require[s] learners to arrive at an outcome from given information through some process of thought, and which allow[s] teachers to control and regulate that process. (Prabhu 1987: 24)

An activity or action which is carried out as the result of processing or understanding language (i.e., as a response). For example, drawing a map while listening to an instruction and performing a command may be referred to as tasks. Tasks may or may not involve the production of language. A task usually requires the teacher to specify what will be regarded as successful completion of the task. The use of different kinds of tasks in language teaching is said to make language teaching more communicative . . . since it provides a purpose for a classroom activity which goes beyond the practice of language for its own sake. (Richards, Platt, and Webber 1985: 289)

Any classroom work which involves learners in comprehending, manipulating, producing, or interacting in the target language while their attention is principally focused on meaning rather than form. The task should also have a sense of completeness, being able to stand alone as a communicative act in its own right. (Nunan 1993: 59)

Any structural language learning endeavor which has a particular objective, appropriate content, a specified working procedure, and a range of outcomes for those who undertake the task. "Task" is therefore assumed to refer to a range of workplans which have the overall purpose of facilitating language learning – from the simple and brief exercise type, to more complex and lengthy activities such as group problem-solving or simulations and decision-making. (Breen 1987: 23)

One of a set of differentiated, sequenceable, problem-solving activities involving learners and teachers in some joint selection from a range of varied cognitive and communicative procedures applied to existing and new knowledge in the collective exploration and pursuance of foreseen or emergent goals within a social milieu. (Candlin 1987: 10)

These definitions are roughly arranged in terms of a continuum of "real world" to "pedagogical" perspectives on what tasks are. This distinction between the "real" world and the classroom does not imply that the classroom is not a valid social context in its own right (Breen 1985). Nor, indeed, are real world and pedagogical tasks mutually exclusive: There is no reason why tasks cannot have both real world and pedagogical dimensions. However, as implied in the first two definitions provided by Long (1985) and by Crookes (1986), pedagogical tasks should be derived from real world tasks, since analytical syllabuses are based in part on an analysis of learners' behavioral needs (Wilkins 1976).

What are pedagogical tasks? According to Prabhu's (1987: 24) definition, which makes no reference to real world needs, tasks are learning activities that engage learners in logical thinking. Prabhu identifies three kinds of cognitive task types: opinion gap, information transfer, and reasoning gap tasks. An example of a reasoning gap task – the most important task type in Prabhu's scheme – is using railroad timetables or reading maps in order to get from A to B. Prabhu also distinguishes between pre-tasks and tasks, the main difference being that pre-tasks are cognitively less demanding than main tasks. Using railroad timetables as an example, during the pre-task stage, the 12-hour clock is used, only two or three changes of trains are called for, and the teacher takes a leading role in helping students solve the problem. During the main task stage, however, students have to use the 24-hour clock, change trains more often, and solve the problem without the teacher's help. Richards et al. (1985) share Prabhu's concern with how a task is specified and also mention the teacher's role in regulating the teaching and learning process. Similarly, the definitions by Richards et al. and Nunan (1993) emphasize the communicative, meaning-oriented character of tasks. The definitions offered by Breen (1987) and Candlin (1987) emphasize the participatory, negotiable character of pedagogical tasks and stress that they should promote communication-oriented, problem-solving interaction.

The most relevant aspects of these definitions may be summarized as follows. Pedagogical tasks are derived in part from sociolinguistic analyses of real world tasks. In psycholinguistic terms, pedagogical tasks require students to produce chunks of language as learners attempt to communicate by using the linguistic resources they currently possess in the target language. As participants talk, they modify their own and their interlocutors' speech. Learners thereby get and produce negotiated comprehensible input and output that are beyond their current level of communicative competence. This modified interaction sets up the necessary (though not sufficient) preconditions for second language development to occur (Long 1981, 1985, 1989a, 1991; Pica 1987; Pica et al. 1989; Swain 1985, 1995).

## WHAT IS TASK-BASED LANGUAGE TEACHING?

The analytic definitions of task suggest that task-based language teaching focuses as much on the process of learning as on its products and that it is organized in terms of methodologically induced opportunities to use and learn language. Potentially, this "methodological syllabus" engages teachers and learners in two distinct forms of negotiation. They may negotiate the content of instruction and the way in which classes are organized. Or they may negotiate the comprehensibility of the linguistic input and output produced during classroom talk. In theory, either type of negotiation can change traditional classroom power relationships. However, demonstrating that such a change has occurred is an empirical matter, and making such changes actually happen is easier said than done (see Text Link 98). In sum, I define task-based language teaching as an analytic approach to syllabus design and methodology in which chains of information-gathering, problem-solving, and evaluative tasks are used to organize language teaching and learning; these interdependent pedagogical tasks, which combine insights from sociolinguistic and psycholinguistic research, are designed to methodologically simulate the communicative events that learners encounter in specific second language-using environments (Markee 1994b).

∞ **Text Link 98**
See Text Links 15, 16, 75, 102, 103, and 155 for further discussion of these issues. Finally, see Principle 4 and Text Link 162.

## WHAT CRITERIA MAY BE USED TO SELECT, GRADE, AND SEQUENCE TASKS?

As Long and Crookes (1992: 46) note, "little empirical support is yet available for the various proposed parameters of task classification and difficulty, nor has much of an effort been made to define some of them in operational terms." Thus, content selection, grading, and sequencing are undeniably problematic for, but not unique to, task-based language teaching. Long and Crookes further point out that the "identification of valid, user-friendly sequencing criteria remains one of the oldest unsolved problems in language teaching *of all kinds*" (emphasis added; see also Wilkins 1976). Therefore, what principles can be used to select, grade, and sequence tasks?

The definition of task-based language teaching given previously implies that we can select content on the basis of analyses of students' sociolinguistic needs (Long 1985) and psycholinguistic wants (Brindley 1984). We may also select material on the basis of its authenticity (Nunan 1988b) and sequence it according to the logical principle of task dependency (Johnson 1982a). This principle states that task 1 serves as input for task 2, which then serves as input for task 3, and so on.

Other sequencing principles offered by Candlin (1987) are based on notions of (1) cognitive load, (2) communicative stress, (3) particularity and generalizability, (4) code complexity and interpretive density, (5) content continuity, and (6) process continuity. In relation to *cognitive load*, Candlin argues that tasks that can be broken down into clear chronological sequences of activities or that involve the individual actions of individual actors are cognitively simpler than tasks that have no sequential development or that involve multiple actions by multiple actors.

*Communicative stress* includes factors such as learners' familiarity with a topic, the number of interlocutors involved in the interaction, the degree of communicative competence or topic familiarity exhibited by learners' interlocutors, the extent to which a conversation is clearly organized, and the degree to which the talk focuses on the "why" rather than the "how" of task completion. The factors covered by the variable of communicative stress suggest that sequencing decisions can be made by progressively "upping the communicative ante" of tasks.

*Particularity* and *generalizability* refer to how original or how ritualized the interaction is. For example, a task that involves learners telling a story about known past events may be simpler to accomplish than a task that requires students to respond to original questions about hypothetical future events. Thus, the idea of asking students to complete routine tasks before they engage in nonroutine tasks may also serve as a useful principle of sequencing.

*Code complexity* and *interpretive density* refer to the relationship between a text's lexico-syntactic complexity and its interpretive density. Thus, a syntactically simple text is not necessarily easy to interpret. For example, the simplicity of Hemingway's language in his novels and short stories belies the complexity of the interpretive task that readers must accomplish. Candlin therefore advocates that learners' understanding of textually elaborate texts may be promoted by straightforward questions, and that students' understanding of textually simpler texts may be furthered by questions that require learners to engage in in-depth textual analysis.

*Content continuity* takes into account the notion of the authenticity of the pedagogical task in relation to the target task, a notion clearly derived from a prior analysis of students' needs. Given Candlin's emphasis on the process of learning rather than on its products, it is not surprising that he expresses some reservations about the viability of content continuity, since pedagogical tasks that simulate real world tasks may lack verisimilitude. However, Candlin does see a role for such a principle in ESP-type situations.

*Process continuity* involves learners in evaluating what is required to solve a problem in terms of language forms, functions, discoursal strategies, ways of conceptualizing and organizing ideas, and content knowledge. Process continuity is similar to Johnson's notion of task dependency, except that it is learners rather than teachers or materials writers who establish these continuities.

Empirical research also suggests that turn length, the number of elements a text contains, genre, and the referents used to organize discourse all affect the perceived difficulty of aural and written texts (Anderson and Lynch 1988; Brown and Yule 1983; Kiniry and Strenski 1985; Nunan 1985). Such criteria may thus be used to grade and sequence listening, speaking, reading, and writing tasks. Furthermore, some tasks are psycholinguistically more difficult to complete than others. For example, one-way information gaps, in which only one participant holds new or unknown information, promote less obligatory conversational adjustments than two-way tasks, in which all participants hold information that is necessary to solve a problem (Long 1981). This insight into task difficulty has led to the development of a task typology that may be used as a framework for choosing and using tasks (Pica et al. 1993). In addition, as shown by Brock (1986), teachers' use of referential questions affects the syntactic complexity of students' responses more than the use of display questions. (According to Long and Sato 1983, referential questions are genuine requests for new information, whereas display questions are questions to which the teacher already knows the answer; however, this distinction is not black and white. See also Banbrook and Skehan 1990.) This too can inform sequencing decisions. Finally, Prabhu (1987) suggests that the amount and type of information that students must manipulate, the number of steps involved in completing cognitive operations, how accurately students must perform, and the extent to which they must draw on their knowledge of the world to solve problems are all useful criteria for grading and sequencing content in task-based language teaching.

> ∞ **Text Link 99**
> See Text Links 54, 110, and 145 for related discussions of opinion leadership. Finally, see Principle 9 and Text Link 167.

In the following section on the tactical level of planning, I analyze a teaching assistant's task-based materials to show how one teacher interpreted the project director's strategic intentions. I have selected this particular teacher's materials not just because they illustrate task-based language materials, but because the teacher who produced them was an influential opinion leader in the CATI project whose work has served as a model for his peers (see Text Link 99).

## Tactical planning

It is in the model's tactical level of planning that the teaching assistants' task-based language teaching syllabus design and materials development activities are conceptually located. If the project's model of curricular innovation is to work, teaching assistants must understand the theoretical principles upon which task-based language teaching is founded. They must also know how to select texts, grade, and sequence pedagogical tasks. Finally, they must decide how to select appropriate methodological procedures. This section examines how one teaching assistant interpreted task-based language teaching in his materials.

The materials target high-intermediate learners who are graduate students from different disciplinary backgrounds. All four skills are covered by the materials, but the main emphasis is on the development of academic writing skills for research purposes. The thematic content of the unit is archeological discoveries, in particular, the recent discovery in the Italian Alps of a mummified body (dubbed the "Iceman" by the press) dating from 4000 B.C.E. Extract 4.1 gives an overview of the whole unit. Extract 4.2 shows the types of class activities used in the seven sections of the unit; it also shows how nonlinguistic principles are used to select, grade, and sequence content in an analytic approach to syllabus design. Extract 4.3 illustrates how a process-oriented methodology is specified as an integral part of syllabus content. Extract 4.4 illustrates how such a methodology dovetails with a process-based approach to writing. Extract 4.5 shows how learners can negotiate the content of instruction within parameters set by the teacher or materials writer.

As shown by the overview in Extract 4.1, the unit uses the theme of archeological discoveries to carry the unit's content and to take learners through the process of researching and writing an academic essay on cause-and-effect relationships. The unit has the kind of behavioral orientation that characterizes analytic syllabuses in that it engages students in discovering how to carry out research and how to construct knowledge. Focus on the research process is quite relevant to learners' intellectual development as graduate students who use English to conduct research at a U.S. university.

The overview in Extract 4.1 also shows that the range of source materials used as inputs for the unit – primarily written texts from magazines and journals – are all authentic and intellectually challenging. Also included are a videotaped television program and a lecture on the Iceman by a faculty member at the university. As a class activity, students visit a campus cultural museum where they can ask questions on the issues raised in the source materials. The general focus on communication in an academic context and the selection of authentic texts and tasks that address the larger behavioral needs and interests of students are all consistent with the characteristics of task-based language teaching outlined earlier in this chapter.

The summary of activities shown in Extract 4.2 shows in more detail how a large problem (researching and writing an academic essay) is broken down into smaller constituent problems: Introduction (section 1); Information Gathering (sections 2–4); Synthesis (section 5); Output (section 6), and Feedback (section 7). The organization of this unit is thus based on a nonlinguistic metric for *selecting* different types of

# The CATI project

## Purposes

1. To give students practice in recognizing and analyzing cause-and-effect relationships
2. To illustrate a multidisciplinary perspective on problem solving
3. To offer students opportunities to utilize various media as sources
4. To give practice in writing a scientific academic essay in a cause-and-effect rhetorical mode

## Materials

1. *NOVA* video, "The Iceman." Transcripts for "The Iceman" are also available.
2. Fritz, Sandy. (1993, February) Who was the Iceman? *Popular Science.* pp. 46–9.
3. Wernick, Robert. (1988, March) What were Druids like, and was Lindow Man one? (extract). *Smithsonian.* pp. 146–7.
4. Houston, Julie. (1984, February) Sacred slayings. *Science Digest.* pp. 64–7, 102.
5. Green, Timothy. (1972, June) Fifty years later, Tutankhamun's treasures are still a sensation. *Smithsonian.* pp. 14–23.
6. Seidler, H., et al. (1992, October 16) Some anthropological aspects of the prehistoric Tyrolean Ice Man. *Science.* pp. 455–7.
7. Marbach, W. D., and J. Phillips. (1987, November 2) New tools for an ancient dig. *Newsweek.* pp. 80–1.
8. World Heritage Museum (Lincoln Hall) Brochure and Tour.

## Supplemental Materials

9. Warren, K. J. (1988) A philosophical perspective on the ethics and resolution of cultural property issues. *The Ethics of Collecting Cultural Property, Whose Culture? Whose Property?* P. M. Messenger (Ed.). Albuquerque: University of New Mexico Press. pp. 1–25.
10. Sjøvold, Torstein. (1993, April) Frost and found. *Natural History.* pp. 60–3.
11. Bohen, Barbara. (1993) Videotaped lecture about the Iceman.
12. The Hatshepsut affair. (1989, May 13). *The Economist.* p. 49.

Courtesy of David Broersma.

tasks, while *grading* and *sequencing* decisions are made on the basis of increasing conceptual difficulty.

The different sections are graded in a pattern of progressively more demanding work. Thus, section 1 introduces both the rhetorical style and the theme of the unit. Sections 2–4 require students to gather increasing amounts of information from different sources, the relevance of which is dictated by the students' own choices and interests. This focus on gathering information culminates in an out-of-class project in

EXTRACT 4.2 SUMMARY OF ACTIVITIES
___

√Denotes that worksheet(s) go with the activity.

Section 1   √*Introduction:* A brainstorming activity is followed by an analysis of cause-and-effect relationships.

Section 2   √*Information Gathering (Video):* Students watch the [television] video, "The Iceman." When the video is finished, students freewrite and then break into interest sections and discuss cause-and-effect relationships in their group.

Section 3   √*Information Gathering:* Students read articles about the Iceman, the Bog People, and King Tutankhamun with special attention to cause-and-effect information related to their interest sections. Students will solve a problem or discuss a case study related to their interests.

Section 4   *Information Gathering (Tour):* In groups, students develop questions related to their interest sections to ask the tour guide in the World Heritage Museum (WHM). The second half of class is a tour in the WHM in Lincoln Hall.

Section 5   √*Synthesis:* After working through the "abstract" handout, students use their notes from the WHM tour, transcripts of the video, and the articles already read to develop abstracts for their interest sections. After preparing individual abstracts, students present their abstracts to their group members for feedback.

Section 6   *Output:* Based on the abstracts, and utilizing sources, students write a cause-and-effect essay.

Section 7   √*Feedback:* Using the peer editing handout as a guide, students exchange copies of their essays with students from other interest sections, and in groups of three or four have conferences about each paper.
___

Courtesy of David Broersma.

section 4. Section 5 then gives students their first opportunity to organize the material they have gathered and yields an abstract of the paper they will write (see Text Link 100). In section 6, they

∞ **Text Link 100**
See also Text Links 128 and 140.

flesh out the abstract by writing a first draft of the paper. In section 7, they revise these first drafts based on feedback they receive from peer editing and write the final version of the essay. Thus, students begin by gathering information, then synthesize this information, and finally create an original text on the basis of input texts. It is this concern with selecting, grading, and sequencing the conceptual and methodological content of instruction that allows task-based language teaching to be viewed as a bona fide approach to syllabus design (Nunan 1989). Again, these organizing principles are consistent with the characteristics of task-based language teaching outlined earlier in this chapter. The design of this unit is on the analytic, not the synthetic, end of the syllabus design spectrum. The only possibly synthetic element in the design is the goal of getting students to write a cause-and-effect essay; however, most of the tasks in this unit focus primarily on how to organize and develop such essays and only secondarily on the linguistic means used to produce the essay.

As illustrated by section 3 of the materials, reproduced in Extract 4.3, this summary of activities is translated into a methodological syllabus of tasks (Nunan 1988b). Section 3 begins with a specification of the content of instruction. That is, the kinds of authentic source texts that are used as input are identified, as are the purposes these texts serve. At the same time, both the content and purposes of instruction are articulated by giving students detailed methodological instructions that tell how to complete the five tasks that constitute section 3. These tasks range in scope from individual work (activities A and B) through small group work (activities A, C, and D), to a presentation to the whole class (activity E). Notice also how the pedagogical note that follows activity A suggests what kinds of information learners should look for in their articles and how they should organize this information for use in subsequent activities. The articulation of these activities demonstrates how Johnson's (1982a) principle of task dependency works. In activities A–E, there is a progression from small group–mediated information-gathering activities to interpretation tasks carried out in a whole-class context.

Extract 4.4 shows how the task-based methodology of these materials dovetails with a process-based approach to writing. Students write at least two drafts of the same essay. Thus, in activity A of section 6, students write a first draft in class; after they complete activities A (peer editing) and B (conferencing) of section 7, students write a more polished draft as a final homework assignment (activity C).

These methodological directions focus on the learning *process* by encouraging users to identify and repair whatever problems of content, organization, or grammatical and lexical errors occur in first drafts. At the same time, sections 6 and 7 yield identifiable *products* – cause-and-effect essays on the Iceman story. Note that the language work that emerges from activities A and B of section 7 targets the specific problems that individual students manifest in their first attempts to communicate their ideas in written form. Thus, traditional language teaching concerns with formal grammatical accuracy are not ignored but rather are addressed as side products of learners' attempts to produce first drafts.

*Materials*
1. Fritz, Sandy. (1993, February) Who was the Iceman? *Popular Science*. pp. 46–9.
2. Wernick, Robert. (1988, March) What were Druids like, and was Lindow Man one? (extract). *Smithsonian*. pp. 146–7.
3. Houston, Julie. (1984, February) Sacred slayings. *Science Digest*. pp. 64–7, 102.

*Purposes*
1. To gather information for the end-of-unit essay.
2. To reemphasize cause-and-effect relationships.
3. To practice analyzing and evaluating material included in sources.

*Instructions*
Activity A: Reading Source Materials (20 minutes)
The articles for this activity are divided into four groups. Each person within your interest section should read a different group. Therefore, you should have an "expert" in your group on each of the four groups of articles. Quickly decide who within your group will read which group of articles (A, B, C, or D). Then read your article carefully, looking for information that applies to your interest section.
   *Note:* While you are reading your article(s), be sure to underline, circle, or highlight the information that applies to your interest section. Then write notes next to the highlighted information to describe briefly why it is important. Also, keep track of the cause-and-effect relationships you find on your cause-and-effect handout.

Activity B: Comprehension Check (10 minutes)
Answer the questions for your group of articles (see following pages).

Activity C: Reporting (20 Minutes)
Report to the other members of your group about the articles(s) you read. Briefly summarize the content of the article(s), then discuss the information in the article that relates to the interests of your group.

Activity D: Discussing Interest Section Questions (30 minutes)
As a group, discuss the questions (or case studies) designed for your interest section (see "Interest Section Questions" below). Using the information in the articles, develop a position as a group, and then prepare a short, informal presentation to share with the rest of the class. Your presentation should include a brief summary of the question, your group's answer, and the evidence supporting your group's answer.

Activity E: Presentations (20 minutes)
A spokesperson from each group should present the summary prepared in activity D.

Courtesy of David Broersma.

EXTRACT 4.4 OUTPUT AND FEEDBACK

**Section 6: Output**
Activity A: Writing a Rough Draft (100 minutes)
Using your notes and sources from all the previous sections, write a rough draft of a five-page cause-and-effect essay based on the abstract you developed. Some suggestions of paper topics are as follows:

1. What motives underlie the political struggle over the Iceman? What factors do you feel are the most significant, and why?
2. [Students fill in their own suggestion.]

*Remember:* Make sure that the causal relationships you discuss are clearly expressed. For examples of the kinds of language that indicate causality, review the "causality" handout, pages 59–60.
Out-of-class assignment: Before you come to class next period, make three photocopies of your rough draft and bring them with you.

**Section 7: Feedback**
Activity A: Peer Editing (50 minutes)
The teacher will assign you to a group different from your interest section. In your group, exchange the three copies of your rough draft with your group members. Everyone should end up with three different rough drafts. Read the drafts carefully and consider the questions on the "Peer Editing Handout." Write comments on a separate piece of paper for each of the papers you read.

Activity B: Conferences (50 minutes)
For each member of the group, take at least 12 minutes to ask questions and offer suggestions in response to the paper. Try to offer criticism that will help your group members to improve their papers, but don't forget to be gentle (you will have a turn, too!).

Courtesy of David Broersma.

Section 2 consists of the first information-gathering tasks used in the unit. These are shown in Extract 4.5; they exemplify how the negotiation of content by students is built into the unit and how information gap tasks work.

After reviewing cause-and-effect relationships in activity A, viewing the video in activity B, and answering comprehension questions (not reproduced here) in activity C, students evaluate which aspects of the Iceman discovery interest them most. They can now decide what topic they wish to write their papers on. Suggested topics for students to explore include aspects of the scientific, historical/cultural, or political dimensions of the discovery; however, students are not limited to such topics provided they can form large enough groups. The formation of groups is done in activity D; learners use the topics they have chosen as the basis for selecting their partners for the rest of the unit. Thus,

*Materials*
1. Handout with pre- and postvideo questions.
2. [Television] video, "The Iceman."
3. Copies of portions of the transcript for "The Iceman" (optional).

*Purpose*
1. To introduce the topic of the Iceman and other similar archeological finds.
2. To alert students to cause-and-effect relationsips.
3. To allow students to determine which aspects of the topic most interest them.

*Instructions*
Activity A: Reviewing (5 minutes)
As a class, briefly review cause-and-effect relationships and the brainstorming activity from the previous class period.

Activity B: Watching the Video (55 minutes)
Watch "The Iceman." Try to discover cause-and-effect relationships in the video.

Activity C: Answering Questions (10 minutes)
Answer the questions on the handout called "Questions about the Iceman Video" in as much detail as you can. When you finish answering the questions, think about which aspect of the Iceman discovery interests you the most. Which aspect would you most like to write a paper about? Here are some ideas:
*Scientific*
 – the interaction of science with other fields
 – specific scientific applications (for example, carbon-14 dating)
 – factors that can interfere with scientific analysis
 – how the scientific method is applied to archeological finds
*Historical/Cultural*
 – what the Iceman reveals about ancient cultures
 – how the Iceman changes previously held beliefs about ancient peoples
 – the processes historians use to analyze data
 – limitations of the historical method
*Political*
 – how political forces influence scientific research
 – issues involved in the dispute over the Iceman between Austria and Italy (to whom does the Iceman really belong?)

Activity D: Forming Interest Sections (20 minutes)
After determining which aspect of the topic interests you most, try to find three other people who share your interest. Feel free to walk around the classroom to find others interested in the same topic. It is important that the groups consist of at least three people and no more than four. Also, try to find partners with different cultural backgrounds if possible. The teacher will

105

EXTRACT 4.5 (CONT.)

make final decisions regarding the composition of groups if there are too many or not enough people with the same interests, or if there is not enough cross-cultural mixing in the groups. You may choose topics other than the ones listed above if you can find enough other people who are interested in your topic.

After the groups have been formed, in the time remaining, you should discuss within your group the cause-and-effect relationships mentioned in the video that had the most direct connection to the interest of your group. Keep a record of your discussion on your cause-and-effect handout.

Courtesy of David Broersma.

interest groups emerge as a result of negotiations between students who, in finding out which other learners share their interests, have to bridge a complex information gap.

∞ **Text Link 101**
For an example of a task that combines the characteristics of an information gap and information transfer activity, see Figure 2.1.

As we saw earlier in this chapter, information gap tasks consist of a family of tasks, which include information gap, reasoning gap, opinion gap, and information transfer activities (Nunan 1989; Prabhu 1987) (see Text Link 101). The purpose of such tasks is to gather information, solve problems, and to evaluate information. Of course, the use of such tasks predates task-based language teaching and may be found in communicative materials that are not principally task based. However, while the use of such tasks is not unique to task-based language teaching, such teaching is *defined* by its reliance on these tasks. The advantage of relying on information gap tasks is that these activities not only provide psycholinguistically rich opportunities for language learning, but they also give students the chance to negotiate the content of learning and to develop critical thinking skills. An empirical example of negotiated vocabulary learning is given in Excerpts 1 and 2 in the final section of this chapter, "Operational Planning."

Of course, as Clarke (1991) points out, ESL teachers often find that it is difficult to get learners to negotiate the direction of a course, since many students regard this as the teacher's job. However, note that activities C and D avoid this problem neatly by setting up a real communicative need for learners to negotiate the group's composition. First, they must decide what aspect of the Iceman discovery interests them most; second, they must find other people who share their interests; and third, they must collectively identify which of the cause-and-effect relationships in the video may be relevant to their interest group. In short, activities C and D require group members to assume responsibility for their own learning. Since each group member reads different articles, everybody must decide what information they need to highlight for their partners so that the group can develop a broad picture of the Iceman discovery. During the discussion, individual group members must be ready to clarify any information that is unclear. They have to gather information and evaluate it critically in order to accomplish tasks efficiently within the time frame given. These materials thus promote negotiation in both an educational and a psycholinguistic sense (see Text Link 102).

∞ **Text Link 102**
See Text Links 15, 16, 77, 98, and 155 for related discussions of the concept of negotiation. Finally, see Principle 4 and Text Link 162.

## Operational planning

Operational planning is the responsibility of teachers and students and involves the short-term planning and execution of lessons by teachers. This level of planning is also a locus of innovation in that teaching involves negotiation between teachers and learners. Negotiation is built into the ESL courses through student use of academic journals to ask questions about or comment on class content, and to evaluate tasks and provide feedback about how they were implemented. This feedback allows teachers to communicate directly with learners who, for whatever reason, do not ask questions in class. Furthermore, it enables teachers to identify problems as they arise and to negotiate appropriate solutions, whether with individual students or with the class as a whole. Thus, journals allow teachers to fine-tune their teaching in the short term; they are also a valuable resource at the tactical level of syllabus design for revising units in the medium term (see Bailey 1983, 1990; Bailey and Ochsner 1983; McDonough 1994; and Porter et al. 1990 on the use of journals in language research and pedagogy).

Most important, the level of operational planning constitutes the proving ground of methodology as a resource for learning (see Text Link 103). There is empirical evidence that the project's task-based methodology can provide learners with opportunities for receiving and producing comprehensible output (Markee 1994c). As shown in Excerpt 1, three learners (L9, L10, and L11) are discussing a text on the greenhouse effect. L10 has asked her group on four previous occasions what the word *coral* means but has not yet understood her partners' or the teacher's explanations. The excerpt begins with L10's fifth attempt to understand this word (see Appendix 1 for a summary of the transcription conventions used). This excerpt does not come from a class that is using Broersma's unit; however, it is a product of the same kind of information-gathering activities illustrated in Broersma's materials.

∞ **Text Link 103**
See also Text Links 16, 77, 102, and 155. Finally, see Principle 4 and Text Link 162.

*Excerpt 1*
(small group work)

```
 1 L10:  both of them what they say
 2       (1.3)
 3       coral. what is corals
 4       (4)
 5 L9:   <hh> do you know the under the sea, under the sea,
 6 L10:  un-
 7 L9:   there's un:: (+) //how do we call it//
 8 L10:               //have uh some coral//
 9 L9:   ah yeah (+) coral sometimes
10       (+)
11 L10:  eh includ[ə]s (+) uh includes some uh: somethings uh-
12       (++)
13       //the corals,// is means uh: (+) s somethings at bottom of
14 L9:   //((unintelligible))//
15 L10:  //the// sea
16 L9:   //yeah,//
17       at the bottom of the sea,
18 L10:  ok uh:m also is a food for is a food for fish un and uh
19       (+)
20 L9:   food?
21       (+)
22 L10:  foo-
23 L9:   no it is not a food it is like a stone you know?
24 L10:  oh I see I see I see I see I see I know I know (+) I see (+) a
25       whi- (+) a kind of a (+) white stone <h> //very beautiful//
26 L9:                                           //yeah yeah//very
27       big yeah //sometimes very beautiful and// sometimes when
28 L10:          //I see I see I ok//
29 L9:   the ship moves ship tries ((unintelligible)) I think it was the
30       ((unintelligible; the final part of this turn is overlapped by
31       L10's next turn as shown by the slashes))
32 L10:  //oh I see (+) I see the Chinese is uh (+)// [sanku]
33       (++)
34 L11:  uh?
35 L10:  [sanku]
36       (+)
37 L9:   what
38 L10:  c//orals//
39 L11:  //corals//
40 L9:   corals oh okay
41 L10:  yeah
        (Class 1)
```

(Markee 1994c: 104)

From lines 1 to 17, L9 and L10 recycle information from L10's previous four attempts to solve this problem. At line 18, however, L9 and L10 break new ground: L10 guesses that coral is a kind of food for fish. At line 23, L9 incorrectly rejects L10's guess and replies that "it is like a stone." This information triggers a breakthrough in understanding for L10 at lines 24–25; she first vigorously asserts that she has understood this word and then adds the extra information that coral is white and very beautiful. At lines 26–27 and 29–30, L9 corroborates with L10 has said (and also adds some unintelligible information). At line 32, L10 further confirms that she has understood by correctly translating the word *coral* into Chinese, her native language. Since L9 does not understand Chinese, she asks for a clarification at line 34 and again at line 37, when L10 repeats the Chinese word, *sanku,* at line 35. Thus, at line 38, L10 translates the Chinese word back into English; L11, who is also Chinese, almost simultaneously offers the same English translation at line 39, thus corroborating the correctness of the translation.

This evidence shows that L10 has understood what *coral* means, but it does not mean that she has learned this word (Hawkins 1985; Markee, 1994c). Later evidence suggests that L10 has learned this word. The teacher asks L10 during some previous group work to define this word for the rest of the class, which L10 does some 20 minutes later. This is the definition L10 produces:

*Excerpt 2*
(presentation during whole-class discussion)

1 L10  I think the co[l]al is the kind of fossil (+) <h> fossil at the: botto of
        the sea.
2       <hh> the: co[l]al reef you are one of the imp- very important, <hh>
        habitats
3       (+) fo:r fish that support th[ə]:m"

(Markee 1994c: 105–6)

This definition looks "messy," but it displays the classic "An A is a B which does C" structure of formal definitions (Abelson 1967), where A = "coral," B = "fossil at the bottom of the sea," and C = "habitats for fish." Note also that L10 constructs this definition by "cannibalizing" talk from previous excerpts (indicated in boldface type): Thus, one of the sources for the phrase "at the bottom of the sea" in Excerpt 2 is the highlighted talk reproduced in lines 13, 15, and 17 of Excerpt 1. This evidence supports the claim that analytically organized language instruction promotes contextualized opportunities for language learning that reflect students' own learning agendas. It also shows that task-based language teaching provides opportunities for learners to focus on grammar or vocabulary as important resources for language learning. Thus, what differentiates task-based teaching from synthetic approaches to syllabus design is not *whether* to teach grammar and vocabulary; it is what *counts* as grammar and vocabulary instruction, *who* provides the instruction, and *when* formal language work occurs in a lesson.

This chapter has answered at least four of the six questions posed by Bowers (1980a). The CATI project addresses many of the same implementation issues that emerged in the Bangalore Project (Question 1). Thus, both projects can teach us about the problems we must solve as we attempt to promote curricular innovation. The CATI project can also tell us more about such issues, because understanding how curricular innovation works is the explicit focus of this case study. In terms of understanding the key elements of the CATI project, and which of these elements can be reproduced in other contexts of implementation (Question 2), the point of studying the CATI project (indeed, any project) is to gain a grounded understanding of the problems that are involved in managing curricular innovation. One of the most important lessons that we can draw from the CATI project is that change agents must develop contextually appropriate models of curricular innovation and empirically based methodologies for understanding how intentions are translated into actual practice. Thus, this chapter on the design and implementation of the CATI project has developed a model of curricular innovation that involves three levels of planning: strategic (or curricular), tactical (or syllabus), and operational (or day-to-day) planning. For the purposes of this book, the innovation I have used to exemplify the process of curriculum and teacher development is task-based language teaching, but the same kinds of planning decisions would have to be made by project participants whether the innovation being introduced was the notional-functional syllabus or even Audiolingualism. This chapter has also developed an empirically based methodology to illuminate how teachers interpret policy made at the strategic level of curricular planning and how they implement these decisions through a process of adaptation and modification at the tactical level of syllabus planning and at the operational level of planning.

Although the design and implementation of innovative materials have been discussed, issues in project management have not, specifically, the organization development that has been necessary in order to support the materials development activities described here (Question 3). These are examined in Chapter 5.

# 5 Issues in project management: Sustaining change

> One must learn by doing the thing, for
> though you think you know it – you have
> no certainty, until you try. (Sophocles,
> fifth century B.C.E., cited in Rogers
> 1983: 163)

Teachers engaged in developing new materials, methodological skills, and pedagogical values need extensive managerial support if their professional development efforts are to succeed. That is to say, change agents cannot concentrate exclusively on the professional dimensions of educational change. They must also develop their institution's organizational capacity to support teacher professionalization. This chapter sets out in some detail the organization development I have implemented in order to support the CATI project. This illustrates a range of administrative issues and problems that must be resolved in any project in curricular innovation. These issues are highlighted in short summaries at the end of each major section of this chapter.

The CATI project's systemic model of organization development is shown in Figure 5.1, which represents the most mature expression of this model. As I clarify in Chapter 6, the model initially consisted of the central Curriculum Development module, an underdeveloped Knowing module, and a very underdeveloped Evaluation module (see Text Link 104). It has since evolved from this simple (and simplistic) conceptualization of organization development to the more complete model shown in Figure 5.1.

> ∞ **Text Link 104**
> See Table 5.1; see also
> Text Links 2, 37, 42, 73,
> 80, 105, 107, 121, 138,
> and 157.

This model is a language teaching-specific interpretation of the Everard and Morris (1990) model of organization development reviewed in Chapter 3. The central component of the adapted model is the shaded box shown in Figure 5.1, which represents the Curriculum Development module, encompassing the teachers' developmental activities described in the previous chapter. The remaining four components of the model include Communicating, Knowing, Monitoring, and Evaluating modules. The Communicating module subsumes the development of re-

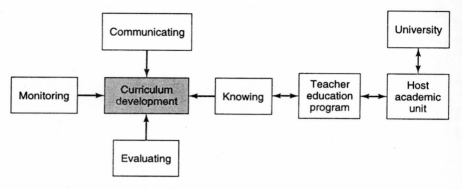

Figure 5.1 A systemic model of organization development.

sources that enable project participants to communicate effectively with each other. These resources include human, administrative, and technological resources. The Knowing component includes the development of classes in the degree-granting teacher education program that inform implementers about task-based language teaching. These classes also connect the CATI project to developments in syllabus design in the outside world. Furthermore, these classes are the organizational bridge that links the ESL program to the host teacher education program and, by extension, to the rest of the university. The Monitoring and Evaluation components include resources ranging from classroom observations to action research projects and evaluations that participants use to monitor and evaluate project implementation.

The four supporting modules of the model subsume ten resources that make it possible to implement curricular innovation. These include human resources (the project director, the assistant project director, and experienced teaching assistants), an orientation for new and continuing teaching assistants, a teachers' handbook, staff meetings, computer technology (an electronic mail list and an electronic database called the ESL Service Courses folder), teachers' journals and portfolios, at least four classes in the teacher education program, a program of classroom observations, and various approaches to doing classroom-based research and project evaluation. Table 5.1 shows that a resource may in some cases have several different functions and therefore appears in more than one of the four modules shown in Figure 5.1 (see Text Link 105).

Most of the curricular resources listed in Table 5.1 are familiar to language program administrators as tools for managing a language program. With the possible exception of the computer resources, none of

TABLE 5.1. CURRICULAR RESOURCES USED TO IMPLEMENT THE CATI PROJECT'S MODEL OF ORGANIZATION DEVELOPMENT

| Communicating: | Knowing: | Monitoring: | Evaluating: |
|---|---|---|---|
| A. *About the CATI Project's aims and goals* | *About task-based language teaching* | *The ongoing implementation of the CATI project* | *The overall success or failure of the CATI project* |
| 1. Human resources<br>  a) Project director<br>  b) Assistant project director<br>  c) Experienced teaching assistants | 1. Teacher education program methodology course used to sustain *development* activities | 1. Classroom observations<br>2. Teachers' portfolios<br>  a) Materials development activities<br>  b) Action research by teaching assistants | 1. Materials development activities<br>2. Research activities<br>  a) Action research<br>  b) Teachers' journals and portfolios |
| 2. TA orientation<br>3. TA handbook<br>4. Staff meetings<br>5. Computer technology<br>  a) TAlist<br>6. Classroom observations | 2. Teacher education program courses used to sustain *research* activities | 3. Action research by the project director<br>4. Surveys |   c) Surveys<br>3. Archive of messages sent to the TAlist |
| B. *About teaching assistants' development and research activities* | | | |
| 1. ESL Service Courses folder<br>2. Staff meetings<br>3. TAlist<br>4. TA journals<br>5. TA portfolios | | | |

∞ **Text Link 106**
See Text Links 3, 5, 8, and 135.

these resources is objectively new. What *is* new in terms of the current literature in language teaching is the way in which I have used these resources to manage change. Change agents must implement organization development of some kind if they wish to introduce and maintain primary innovations. While change agents must determine what parts of their organizations they need to develop in order to support primary innovations, we can probably describe all organization development in terms of the four components shown in Figure 5.1 and Table 5.1 (see Text Link 106).

## Communicating

∞ **Text Link 107**
See Figures 3.5 and 3.6, and Text Links 42, 59, 119, and 121. For more general issues in organization development, see also Text Links 2, 37, 73, 80, 104, 105, 138, and 157. Finally, see Principle 3 and Text Link 161.

Diffusion is a process of communication (Rogers 1983) (see Text Link 107). For this reason, the Communicating module is of major importance in the model. Table 5.1 shows that project participants need to communicate about two things in the CATI project: (1) the project's aims and goals, and (2) the teaching assistants' materials development and research activities. The resources used to communicate about the CATI project's aims and goals include human resources, an orientation, a teachers' handbook, staff meetings, classroom observations, and computer technology, especially an electronic mail list called the TAlist. The resources that are used to communicate about the teaching assistants' materials development and research activities include the TAlist, an electronic data bank for teaching assistants' in-house materials called the ESL Service Courses folder, teachers' journals and portfolios, and staff meetings. These resources enable teaching assistants to document, discuss, and "publish" the development and research activities that they engage in while teaching for the ESL program. The development of such resources also addresses problems that are of wider interest to advocates of action research (see Text Link 108).

∞ **Text Link 108**
See Text Links 116 and 118.

### *Resources used to communicate about the CATI project's aims and goals*

HUMAN RESOURCES

The project director, the assistant project director, and teaching assistants (particularly those with experience) are all important human resources who play specific social roles in the project (see Text Link 109). The project director is the change agent who provides the intellectual direction for the project at the strategic, curricular level of planning and acts as a resource for teaching assistants at the tactical, syllabus level of planning.

∞ **Text Link 109**
See Text Links 29, 30, 31, 34, 35, 50, 76, and 133. Finally, see Principle 3 and Text Link 161.

Many of the project director's responsibilities are discharged in the classes that he teaches as a faculty member in the teacher education program that hosts the CATI project. At the same time, the project director also provides teachers with feedback on their teaching and on their materials by observing classes each semester. Finally, he is responsible for managing the project – that is, he makes decisions that range from determining what new resources need to be developed to supporting the process of curricular innovation to dealing with problems of academic misconduct (e.g., cases of plagiarism by ESL students).

The assistant project director deals with the day-to-day management of the project (e.g., dealing with minor attendance and discipline problems). More important, the assistant project director runs staff meetings, keeps up-to-date minutes of these meetings, shares classroom observation duties with the project director, and generally serves as a resource for teaching assistants whenever they require help. One of the assistant project director's most important functions is to provide feedback on teaching assistants' materials and to interpret curricular guidelines, particularly for new teaching assistants.

The position of assistant project director requires an individual with specific qualities. This person is always a former teaching assistant who has recently graduated from the teacher education program and who is therefore quite familiar with the ESL courses. The person will have taught one or more of the ESL program's courses for a minimum of two years and will have been established as an opinion leader during this time. The assistant project director's status as an established opinion leader is important because this allows leading by example rather than relying on hierarchically derived authority. This status further serves to establish the assistant project director as a change agent.

Teaching assistants are also important human resources in that they all minimally act as implementers of the CATI project. However, teaching assistants are not just passive adopters and implementers of other peoples' ideas. They contribute actively to the ongoing development of the ESL curriculum through their materials development and action research activities. As established teaching assistants gain more experience interpreting the project's aims and goals in personally meaningful ways, they can, like the assistant project director, also act as opinion leaders and change agents vis-à-vis new teaching as-

∞ **Text Link 110**
See Text Links 54, 99, and 145. Finally, see Principles 3 and 9 and Text Links 161 and 167.

sistants (see Text Link 110). For this reason, I use senior teaching assistants who show promise as opinion leaders as peer resources in an orientation for new teaching assistants.

## ORIENTATION

Orientation consists of four days of workshops and some lectures for new teaching assistants and an extra final day of workshops for both new and continuing teaching assistants. New teaching assistants are introduced to the project's aims and goals and its philosophy of negotiated change, with the goal of inducting new teaching assistants into the CATI project as efficiently and as rapidly as possible. This involves giving new teachers the opportunities they need to clarify what is expected of them in terms of materials development responsibilities and to understand how these responsibilities contribute directly to their professional development. Practical workshops run mostly by the assistant project director or continuing teaching assistants give new teachers a peer perspective on a variety of topics and provide them with hands-on experiences that will enable them to interpret and implement curricular guidelines successfully. For example, in one workshop, new teaching assistants are shown some of the practical "tricks of the trade" that experienced peers have used to write their task-based units. In another workshop, new teaching assistants participate in norming activities that ensure comparable standards of grading across sections of the same class. Working with experienced colleagues, new teaching assistants use past ESL students' papers to practice evaluating students' written work. In this way, new teaching assistants not only get an idea of the kind of writing they can expect from students; they also get a sense of how task-based language teaching works in the classroom.

## TEACHERS' HANDBOOK

∞ **Text Link 111**
For other discussions of the potential impact of various attributes on the diffusion of innovations, see Table 2.7; see also Text Links 13, 18, 55, 56, 89, 96, 117, 124, and 139. Finally, see also Principles 1, 3, and 8 and Text Links 159, 161, and 166.

During the orientation, new teaching assistants have to absorb a great deal of information in a short period of time. The teachers' handbook is a reference that summarizes all this information in written form. In addition to the usual rules and regulations that such manuals contain, the teachers' handbook sets out the project's aims and goals and explains in lay terms what these mean. Various appendixes illustrate task-based materials. For example, the teachers' handbook contains the entire Iceman unit discussed in Chapter 4, and it provide guidelines for developing different types of assignments to enable new teaching assistants to organize their own pedagogical activities. Since all the examples of materials in the handbook have been developed by teaching assistants, the handbook provides visible proof for new teaching assistants (who are often initially overwhelmed by their responsibilities) that the CATI project's emphasis on teacher development is not only feasible but beneficial to its participants (see Text Link 111).

STAFF MEETINGS

Teaching assistants who teach parallel sections of the same class meet once a week with the assistant project director. At the beginning of the fall semester, in particular, when new teaching assistants are concentrating on adjusting to a new environment and new responsibilities, participants spend a lot of time discussing how task-based language teaching works in the classroom. The practical advice new teaching assistants receive from peers during these meetings complements the more abstract, theoretically motivated discussions of task-based teaching to which new teaching assistants are exposed in methodology classes in the teacher education program (see Text Link 112). Thus, an important function of staff meetings is to help new teaching assistants bridge the gap between theory and practice in task-based language teaching and to continue the induction process that began with the orientation.

> ∞ **Text Link 112**
> See Text Link 122. See also Principle 3 and Text Link 161.

THE TALIST

As noted previously, the use of computer technology to manage change is probably the only truly new curricular resource discussed in this chapter (see Text Link 113). The TAlist is an electronic mail list to which all CATI project participants subscribe (see also Markee 1994a). A list is the electronic equivalent of an interest group to which people subscribe, much as they would to a magazine. Subscribers send messages to the list via personal computers that are connected to a mainframe by a local area network or modems. The mainframe functions as a "post office" that automatically distributes messages to subscribers. Replies to these messages may be sent either to the list for public consumption or to the private address of the original correspondent.

> ∞ **Text Link 113**
> For other references to the use of computer technology in this project, particularly electronic mail, see Text Links 42 and 105. Finally, see Principle 3 and Text Link 161.

The assistant project director publishes minutes of all discussions that occur in staff meetings on the TAlist. Since the discussions frequently include clarifications of the project's aims and goals by the assistant project director, such comments become publicly accessible to all teaching assistants, not just the people who were present at the meeting. The minutes also allow the project director to provide his own answers to new teaching assistants' questions. Participants also use the TAlist to discuss how to implement the CATI project's aims and goals more efficiently. Thus, the list is used to float ideas about proposed changes, to gather feedback and suggestions for improving these proposals, and to build a consensus around final proposals. For example, the debate summarized in the next section concerning the function of classroom observations in the CATI project was conducted entirely on the TAlist.

CLASSROOM OBSERVATIONS

Classroom observations have traditionally been used as a tool for ensuring quality control in the delivery of instruction. Although it is justifiable to use classroom observations in this way, they can be used more imaginatively as tools of teacher development (Simon 1982). In light of the reactions that were sent to the TAlist by teaching assistants who were critical of the original checklist proposal, an alternative emerged that was more acceptable to teaching assistants and also more appropriate to the CATI project's developmental aims and goals. This revised proposal focused on the role that classroom observations should play in furthering teachers' professional development (see Text Link 114). The solution that emerged was a three-step observation procedure.

> ∞ **Text Link 114**
> See Text Links 85, 127, and 153. Finally, see Principle 3 and Text Link 161.

Teachers who were due to be observed would first contact the observer to contextualize what they were going to be teaching during the observed lesson. In this way, the observer would have a copy of the teacher's lesson plan and would also know what had happened in previous lessons and what would happen in later lessons. Accordingly, the observer would be less likely to make decontextualized criticisms. In addition, teachers would be invited to submit a list of behaviors – for example, giving instructions, asking questions, or managing small group work – about which they wanted to receive feedback. Finally, they would also suggest the kinds of criteria the observer should use to evaluate how successfully they had implemented these behaviors. Once a teacher and the observer had agreed on the focus of the observation and the methodology of the observation, the observer would then observe the class.

During the observation, the observer would take descriptive notes on what occurred in the class. These notes would record the type of activity observed, how long it lasted, and the kinds of visual aids that were used (including information written on the blackboard or on overhead projector slides). In addition, these notes would record the observer's impressions

118

whenever behaviors that had been selected by the teacher in the pre-observation phase were observed. Since the observer's comments were guided by the previously agreed upon evaluation criteria discussed during the pre-observation session, detailed comparisons could be made later between the teacher's intended lesson plan and what happened in the lesson.

During the final stage of the observation process, the teacher and the observer would meet shortly after the observation to debrief each other about what had occurred. The teacher would first be invited to give impressions of how the lesson had gone and to evaluate how effectively he or she had implemented the selected behaviors. Next, the observer would describe to the teacher what he or she had seen and ask whether this description constituted an accurate account of the lesson. Assuming that the teacher agreed with the observer's description, the observer would then give feedback on the teacher's classroom behaviors. When there are differences between the teacher's self-evaluations and those of the observer – often because teachers are more critical of their own performance than observers – the observer and teacher attempt to reconcile such differences so as to achieve a consensual evaluation. Throughout this process, the observer's role is to provide supportive feedback that addresses immediate practical problems that have emerged during the observation process. This feedback also serves to help teachers compare what they currently understand and believe about task-based language teaching with what they actually do in their own classes. Thus, discrepancies between actual behaviors and claimed beliefs are treated not as black marks against teachers but as resources for clarifying teachers' understanding of task-based teaching. Since curriculum development depends on the professional development of individual teachers, this clarification process serves to illuminate the aims and goals of the CATI project in ways that are personally meaningful to the teaching assistants.

## Summary

Six resources help teaching assistants understand the CATI project's aims and goals: human resources, TA orientation, the teachers' handbook, staff meetings, an electronic mail list, and classroom observations. The resources described here serve a function that is crucial to the successful implementation of any project in curricular innovation: *to promote continuous, public, two-way communication between change agents and implementers.* Indeed, probably the single most important lesson to be learned from the CATI project is that projects that do not enable participants to communicate effectively with each other are likely to fail (see Text Link 115).

∞ **Text Link 115**
See Text Link 141 and Principle 3 and Text Link 161.

## Teaching assistants' materials development and research activities

Table 5.1 shows that another important function of the Communicating module is to enable teaching assistants to record and disseminate the results of their materials development activities and action research projects. Three of the five resources (the ESL Service Courses folder, staff meetings, and the TAlist) that have been developed to communicate this kind of information constitute relatively public means of communication about the teaching assistants' interpretations of task-based language teaching. Two (teachers' journals and portfolios) are relatively private forums for discussing teachers' evolving understandings of this approach to syllabus design.

### THE ESL SERVICE COURSES FOLDER

The ESL Service Courses folder is an electronic database located on the ESL program's server (a server is a computer with a large hard disk that is accessible to multiple users). Figure 5.2 shows a print of this folder on a Macintosh computer screen. The folder is represented by the icon to the right of the open document, which shows the folder's contents. This folder contains nine subfolders: (1) a handbook for advisors from other departments; (2) course descriptions for all the ESL courses; (3) technical support information about using computers; (4) the materials used in the orientation for new teaching assistants; (5) examples of research related to the ESL courses; (6) the scales (i.e., the composition evaluation instruments) that teachers use to grade written assignments; (7) an archive of all the electronic messages sent to the TAlist; (8) the teachers' handbook; and (9) the banks of materials that teachers develop as part of their curriculum development responsibilities for whatever class a teaching assistant teaches.

For present purposes, we are concerned only with how the fifth and ninth subfolders are used by the teaching assistants; however, note that the orientation materials and the teachers' handbook, discussed in the previous section of this chapter, are also archived in the ESL Service Courses folder. When teaching assistants wish to access the ESL Service Courses folder, they use the Macintosh's file sharing capabilities. File sharing allows users remote access to materials contained in a folder like the ESL Service Courses folder from another networked Macintosh. In this way, teaching assistants can browse through the contents of this folder on their own computers.

There are several advantages to this arrangement. First, from the project director's perspective, the ESL Service Courses folder is an efficient means of archiving information. For example, when teaching assistants

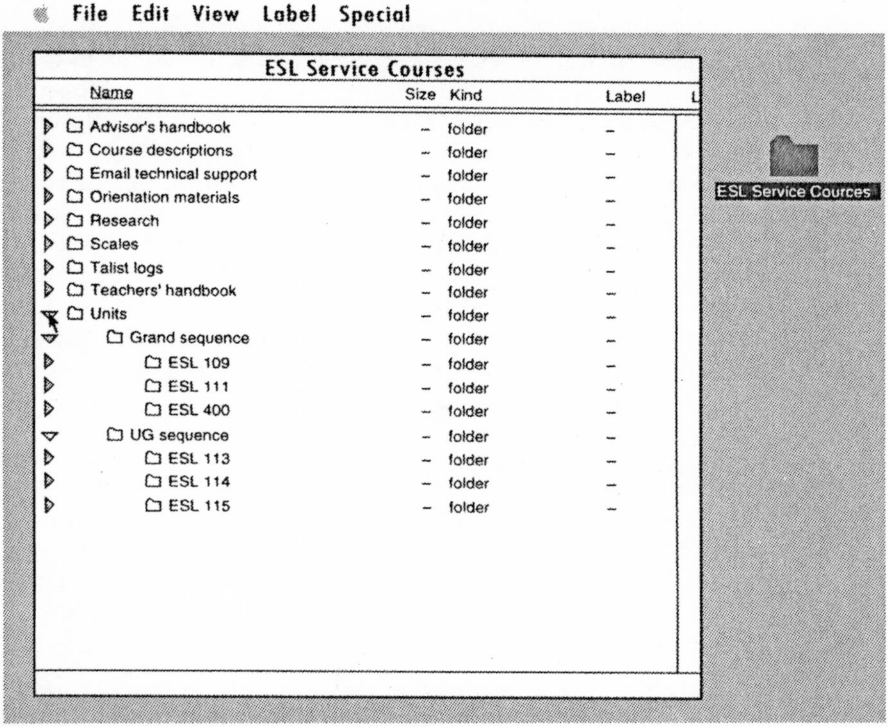

File   Edit   View   Label   Special

## ESL Service Courses

| Name | Size | Kind | Label | |
|------|------|------|-------|---|
| ▷ ▭ Advisor's handbook | – | folder | – | |
| ▷ ▭ Course descriptions | – | folder | – | |
| ▷ ▭ Email technical support | – | folder | – | |
| ▷ ▭ Orientation materials | – | folder | – | |
| ▷ ▭ Research | – | folder | – | |
| ▷ ▭ Scales | – | folder | – | |
| ▷ ▭ Talist logs | – | folder | – | |
| ▷ ▭ Teachers' handbook | – | folder | – | |
| ▽ ▭ Units | – | folder | – | |
|      ▭ Grand sequence | – | folder | – | |
| ▷         ▭ ESL 109 | – | folder | – | |
| ▷         ▭ ESL 111 | – | folder | – | |
| ▷         ▭ ESL 400 | – | folder | – | |
| ▽      ▭ UG sequence | – | folder | – | |
| ▷         ▭ ESL 113 | – | folder | – | |
| ▷         ▭ ESL 114 | – | folder | – | |
| ▷         ▭ ESL 115 | – | folder | – | |

ESL Service Cources

Figure 5.2  The ESL Service Courses folder.

finish writing their materials, they give their units to the project director, who loads them in the appropriate part of the Units subfolder. Similarly, teaching assistants' finished action research reports are placed in the Research subfolder. Second, from a teacher's perspective, on-line materials are easy for teaching assistants to *adapt* and *use*. For example, the course packets they use in the ESL course consist of units like the Iceman unit. Teaching assistants can access the Units subfolder, browse through it, *select* what they want to use, and *edit* and *adapt* the units before distributing them to students. Thus, from a materials development point of view, computers give teachers extraordinary flexibility in accessing, preparing, and revising course materials. From a research point of view, computers enable teaching assistants to "publish" their action research (see Text Link 116).

∞ **Text Link 116**
See Text Links 108 and 118. See also Text Link 88. Finally, see Principle 3 and Text Link 161.

The question of where to publish action research reports represents a continuing problem for advocates of this type of research. Since action research attempts to solve local problems in a teacher's own classroom, solutions to these problems are rarely generalizable. In addition, these reports may be written in a personal style that does not conform to the usual conventions of academic research. For these reasons, professional journals rarely publish action research (Crookes 1993). The Research subfolder provides a nontraditional outlet for teaching assistants' action research reports. While this venue for "publishing" does not carry the prestige of publications in refereed professional journals, the Research subfolder nonetheless plays an important role in the local context of the CATI project. It provides teaching assistants with samples of action research done by colleagues, which they can use to get ideas for doing their own research. In particular, these examples show teaching assistants what kinds of problems action researchers investigate, demonstrates the kinds of insights they can expect to get into their own pedagogical behaviors and values, and provides peer guidance on how to write up their own projects. Thus, the Research subfolder not only gives action research visibility, it helps to demonstrate to teaching assistants its feasibility and advantages. Again, this discussion highlights the contention that an innovation's attributes are powerful determiners of whether it is eventually accepted or rejected (see Text Link 117).

∞ **Text Link 117**
See Table 2.7. See also Text Links 13, 18, 55, 56, 89, 90, 96, 111, 124, and 139. Finally, see Principles 1, 3, and 8 and Text Links 159, 161, and 166.

STAFF MEETINGS

Although the ESL Service Courses folder provides a flexible way of archiving and diffusing teaching assistants' materials research projects, it is not the only nontraditional venue that has been developed to help teachers share their ideas. Teaching assistants often use staff meetings to talk about their materials and research and to receive feedback from colleagues. The discussions that occur in staff meetings typically consist of progress reports on units or action research projects. Through such discussions, teachers become aware of new units that will shortly become available through the ESL Service Courses folder. In addition, new teaching assistants can arrange during these meetings for other teachers to try out their units. In this way, new teaching assistants can revise their materials in light of their own and their colleagues' practical experience. This arrangement not only ensures high levels of ownership of course materials but provides for peer quality control in the materials development process. Ultimately, this arrangement provides diverse opportunities for the continuing professional development of teaching assistants: It enables new and continuing teaching assistants to work as a team and to develop their skills as developers and evaluators of pedagogical materials (see the message in Extract 5.1 for an example of this type of cooperative activity).

The use of staff meetings as a venue for reporting on action research activities also addresses broader issues concerning the status and utility of this kind of research in applied linguistics (see Text Link 118). If action research is to count as research, teaching assistants must be able to articulate their insights into their own teaching behaviors and beliefs and share them with others (Crookes 1993). Thus, the use of staff meetings for this purpose also validates action research as a bona fide research activity. In addition, it ensures that teaching assistants' insights feed back into the continuing development of the ESL curriculum. Finally, the use of staff meetings for these ends creates the formal communication networks that are essential to the diffusion of innovations (see Text Link 119). Indeed, it is the creation of such networks that binds an emerging community of teachers and action researchers together (Crookes 1993). Again, these issues transcend the local nature of the specific solutions that I describe here.

∞ **Text Link 118**
See Text Links 108 and 116. See also Principle 3 and Text Link 161.

∞ **Text Link 119**
See Figures 3.5 and 3.6. See also Text Links 42, 59, 80, 105, and 113. Finally, see Principle 3 and Text Link 161.

## THE TALIST

The last relatively public resource used to disseminate teaching assistants' materials and research results is the TAlist. As Message 1 in Extract 5.1 illustrates, the assistant project director uses the TAlist to publish the minutes of staff meetings. In short, what is important from a diffusionist perspective on curriculum and teacher development is the *public process of communication* that the ESL Service Courses folder, staff meetings, and the TAlist foster. This is because the use of these resources is crucial to the development of formal communication networks upon which planned innovation depends. These formal communication networks do not replace the informal communication networks that teachers construct quite naturally in the staff room. However, as I argue in my discussion of the model's Evaluating module, these formal networks constitute important sources of data for formative and summative evaluations of a project.

## TEACHERS' JOURNALS AND PORTFOLIOS

Teachers' journals and portfolios constitute relatively private channels of communication for teaching assistants. In their journals, for example, teaching assistants systematically document the teaching problems that occur in their classes and reflect critically on their professional development. Since teaching assistants share these insights with the project

## The CATI project

Jen's research unit was highlighted in the Special Features section of the meeting. Jen described the original version of the unit, which consists of seven sections. The first section is composed of introductory activities such as library workshops and learning to use citations. Jen recommended this section be done early in the semester, either with or just after the plagiarism unit. In the second section of the unit, students are given a description of requirements for the writing project. This occurs in the middle of the semester. Section 3 – an analysis of features and conventions of everyday genres – is done in conjunction with section 2. Students then analyze genres in their field of study. Journal articles provide the basis for this activity. After these four sections, students spend time gathering information and composing a first draft. In section 5, the students' drafts are peer-edited. Section 6 involves individual conferences with students. The unit concludes with presentations from students about their research topics.

Tim discussed how he had used Jen's unit. He found the genre analysis very helpful, but skipped the peer-editing section. Tim also remarked that this semester he is using the genre analysis activities as part of his unit on writing a handbook for writing in Economics.

Silva discussed how she had revised the unit. First, she decided to specify an audience for the paper. In her case, she used the [ESL] class as the audience. This required students to meet the expectations of an audience unfamiliar with the topic. Silva also made some changes in the way she proceeded through the unit. Her introductory stage was similar to Jen's except she added a framework for a research report section. Next, Silva's students completed an analysis of genres in their field. Silva held conferences with her students at the pre-draft stage. Students came to the conference with an abstract, outline, and bibliography, and used Silva as a sounding board for their ideas. Students then wrote their first draft and had a peer-editing session. After this, Silva held another set of conferences with her students.

Jen stated that she liked the changes Silva had made.

Courtesy of Patti Watts.

director, these journals function as an important channel of communication between each teacher and the project director. The ensuing dialogue helps teaching assistants clarify issues and resolve problems that occur in their own classrooms. Journals themselves constitute potentially valuable sources of data for doing action research. Although journals are primarily *private* records of individual teaching assistants' insights, they can also – after having been suitably edited – become public sources of data (Bailey 1983). Indeed, as shown in Chapter 6, edited journals can pro-

∞ Text Link 120
See Text Links 141, 149, and 158. Finally, see Principle 3 and Text Link 161.

vide fascinating *public* insights into how teachers' ideas about teaching gradually change – particularly when they are combined with other sources of data like e-mail messages, action research, and survey data to provide an overall picture of change (see Text Link 120).

Teachers' portfolios consist of another relatively private compendium of teaching assistants' professional development activities. Teaching assistants contribute their course materials, journal entries, action research reports, and other documents (such as videotapes) to these portfolios. Portfolios thus provide a multifaceted picture of teaching assistants' evolution as language teaching professionals. As in the case of journals, portfolios can also become public documents if suitably edited. They potentially provide a complete longitudinal record of how teaching assistants develop professionally during the two or three years they teach for the ESL program. Thus, teaching assistants who wish to do action research may use portfolios as a source of data on how their teaching behaviors and beliefs have changed over time. Portfolios constitute another important resource for developing the formal communication networks described earlier in this chapter. As I show later in this chapter, these portfolios are potentially also useful sources of data for formative and summative evaluations of the project, for portfolios will eventually provide evaluators with valuable insights into the process of change over time. They will also provide evaluators with useful information on the extent to which the CATI project has engaged teaching assistants in developing and using new *pedagogical materials, methodological skills,* and *value systems* (see Text Link 121).

∞ **Text Link 121**
For further discussion of organization development-related issues, see Figure 5.1 and Table 5.1 and Text Links 2, 37, 42, 73, 80, 104, 105, 107, 138, and 157. Finally, see Principle 3 and Text Link 161.

## Summary

Five resources – the ESL Service Courses folder, staff meetings, the TA-list, and teaching assistants' journals and portfolios – have been developed to promote communication about the teaching assistants' development and research activities in the CATI project. Although these resources are context-specific, they illustrate wider issues that are fundamental to the successful implementation of curricular innovation in other contexts: specifically, how to ensure that project participants communicate with each other about their professionalization experiences and how to make these individual experiences available to other participants. In addition, this discussion has suggested how to address important issues in action research, such as how to validate this research as an intellectually worthwhile yet practical endeavor.

## Knowing

As Table 5.1 shows, the Knowing component of the model of organization development consists of a number of teacher education program courses. These courses provide teaching assistants with the theoretical background and information about task-based language teaching that they need in order to function as full-fledged participants in the CATI project. One course sustains teaching assistants' materials development activities, and four other courses allow teaching assistants to do action research of various kinds on the ESL courses (see Text Link 122).

> ∞ **Text Link 122**
> See Text Link 112.

### *Teacher education: Sustaining materials development*

A methodology course taught by the project director every semester provides teaching assistants with a broad theoretical background on task-based language teaching (see Text Link 123). In addition to providing teaching assistants with basic information about task-based teaching, this course includes a final project in which participants produce their own materials. By situating teaching assistants' materials development activities in this course, I attempted to circumvent two problems that might derail the in-house development of materials. First, teaching assistants would probably not have the time, nor indeed the inclination, to develop materials on their own time. Second, materials that were developed under unsupervised conditions might be of low quality. From a diffusionist perspective, the first problem demonstrates how a project's implementation can be affected by potential adopters' perceptions of an innovation's attributes – in this case, its perceived feasibility and relative advantageousness to them (see Text Link 124). The second problem shows how important it is for an innovation to improve on what it replaces.

> ∞ **Text Link 123**
> See Figure 2.1. See also Text Links 27, 91, 97, and 101. Finally, see Principle 8 and Text Link 166.

> ∞ **Text Link 124**
> For other discussions of these issues, see Table 2.7. See also Text Links 13, 18, 55, 56, 89, 96, 111, 117, and 139. Finally, see Principle 1 and Text Link 159.

It would have been quite unrealistic to expect teaching assistants to develop materials on their own time. Materials development is complex and time consuming, even when the timetable allows for such development. If time is not available and developers receive no formal recognition for their efforts, however, it is not difficult to predict that teaching assistants would have regarded an extracurricular materials development requirement as an intolerable burden – not least because they have to show the university that they are making good progress toward obtaining their degrees, even when they are teaching. For this reason, I required teaching assistants to produce their materials in the methodology course I teach in the teacher education program. In this way, materials development is not an extracurricular responsibility but is part and parcel of teaching assistants' normal academic workload, for which they receive academic credit. By locating the materials development activities in the methodology class, I am able to monitor the quality of the materials teaching assistants produce.

All students enrolled in the methodology class must present progress reports on their materials development projects to the rest of the class. In the question and answer session that follows their presentations, students receive a critique of their work and suggestions for revisions from both their peers and the instructor. Each individual must then incorporate this feedback into the final version of the project. In addition, teaching assistants who teach for the ESL program have to try out their materials with their classes, in order to make sure that tasks that look good on paper succeed in the classroom. If unanticipated problems arise, teaching assistants must revise the activities before submitting them for inclusion in the Units subfolder of the ESL Service Courses folder. Teaching assistants thus get feedback from various sources throughout their materials development activities. Most of the project director's feedback is given during the methodology class; some suggestions are also given when observing new teaching assistants trying out their materials. In addition, teaching assistants receive advice from their peers in the methodology class and from colleagues during staff meetings.

## Teacher education: Sustaining action research

Four teacher education program courses are available to the teaching assistants as loci for doing action research. As with the methodology course, the availability of these courses* in the teacher education program ensures that teaching assistants receive academic credit for doing action research, thus encouraging them to engage in such research in the first place. In two courses that are taught by a colleague, teaching assistants can do quantitative action research on testing and on composition-related issues, respectively. For example, one teaching assistant completed a project in the testing class on the interrater reliability of teaching assistants' judgments of how students performed on a diagnostic test used to place learners in the ESL program. In two courses taught by the project director (one of which focuses on general curricular issues, the other on action research), teaching assistants can do qualitative action research.

127

In the second of these last two courses, for example, Lai (1995) investigated how her own preconceptions about a female Korean student, Jesun, affected her perceptions of the quantity and quality of Jesun's interactions. Lai had initially judged Jesun to be a shy, low-level learner who did not participate. She based this judgment on the fact that Jesun described herself in her journal as shy. She also claimed to be uninterested in writing. This self-assessment was apparently corroborated not only by Lai's own observations of Jesun's seeming lack of participation during whole-class activities but also by the quality of Jesun's writing. At the beginning of the semester, Jesun's compositions consisted of one-page papers, in which each paragraph consisted of a single sentence.

Lai began her action research by audio- and videotaping two 100-minute classes of her ESL composition class, which was using the Iceman unit at the time of the taping. During one of these classes, Jesun asked a question that captured her fellow students' imagination to such an extent that Lai spontaneously decided to abandon her lesson plan and allow the students to discuss Jesun's question for the remaining 45 minutes of the lesson. This question prompted Lai to ask herself whether Jesun was as passive as Lai had originally thought her to be. Lai therefore transcribed all the talk that occurred during whole-class and small group activities in which Jesun was a potential participant. When Lai read the transcripts of these classes, she found that Jesun behaved in ways that did not conform in the least to her preconceptions.

Lai's quantitative and qualitative analysis of the transcripts shows that, although Jesun had difficulty expressing herself in English, she participated actively during small group work: She took her fair share of turns during group interactions and kept conversation going by using back channels like "yeah, uh-huh, so, ok" at appropriate moments in the interaction. She was able to provide correct explanations of vocabulary items her partners did not understand. Far from being shy, Jesun was quite capable of looking after her own and indeed other students' interests when she needed to. On one occasion, for example, she resisted being talked into doing more than her fair share of reading by another group member. On another, she successfully defended a classmate who had been unjustly accused by another member of the group of not completing some important homework. Furthermore, Jesun helped to keep her partners focused on task and made important contributions to her group's summaries of information that would be presented later to the whole class. She frequently asked questions during small group work, which her partners took up and discussed.

Looking at the textual evidence of Jesun's conversational behavior,

Lai realized that this learner's participation patterns in public were deceptive: Jesun rarely participated much during whole-class activities, but she participated actively in the relative privacy of small group work. In addition, upon rereading Jesun's journals, Lai noticed that Jesun constantly emphasized how important it was to for her to feel interested in the material that she was working with. Lai cross-checked this insight with Jesun's conversational behavior in the transcripts and found that when Jesun was interested in the subject matter, she not only participated actively in the discussion but also persisted in trying to communicate, even when she had difficulty in making herself understood by her classmates. This determination was particularly noticeable when Jesun asked the question that prompted Lai to abandon her lesson plan.

On the basis of these empirically based insights, Lai realized that she had misjudged Jesun. This realization led her to make important changes in her teaching behaviors and also in her definition of good teaching. Lai reports feeling more self-confident as a teacher as a result of her research, which has freed her to experiment with different ways of teaching ESL composition. Most important, she uses classroom materials like the Iceman unit more flexibly. Instead of mechanically completing all of the unit's tasks, she is now more willing to be guided by her students' interests and to exploit the communicative potential of students' questions, even when this means not completing the day's lesson plan. Philosophically, Lai no longer believes that students must participate actively in whole-class activities in order for them to be learning. Although Lai is careful not to claim that changes in her teaching behavior caused any improvements in her students' performance, it is worth noting that, by the end of the same semester, Jesun was producing nine-page papers that were constructed with paragraphs of several sentences instead of one-page papers constructed with one-sentence paragraphs.

In short, this example demonstrates how, by engaging in action research, teaching assistants become active producers of knowledge rather than passive recipients of established authorities' ideas about task-based language teaching. Because this knowledge is built on their own or their colleagues' materials development and teaching activities,

> ∞ **Text Link 125**
> See Text Links 7, 64, 68, 86, 92, 125, and 148–152. Finally, see Principles 2 and 8 and Text Links 160 and 166.

teaching assistants are able to develop their theoretical and practical understanding of task-based teaching (see Text Link 125). As shown in the following section, these projects provide the project director with important sources of data for monitoring and evaluating the extent to which the CATI project is being successfully implemented.

## Summary

Two kinds of courses in the MATESL program have been linked to the CATI project – a methodology course in which teaching assistants develop their materials, and four courses in which instructors can carry out action research projects. This link between the CATI project and the host degree-granting program is probably what differentiates this project from most other projects in curricular innovation. Of course, I am not trying to claim that other graduate-level applied linguistics or ESL programs do not encourage teaching assistants to use their classes as sources of data for research. However, most, if not all, university-level ESL programs that I am familiar with do not have the close relationship between the academic and ESL programs that underpins the CATI project. Of course, developing such links does not guarantee success, but the experience gained through the CATI project suggests that forging such links may well be an important strategy for any change agent concerned about maintaining a program of educational change in the long term (see Text Link 126). This is because teacher education, as opposed to teacher training, is a form of development in which academic input is a key resource for making curricular innovation happen (Lee and VanPatten 1990).

∞ **Text Link 126**
See Text Link 37 and Principle 1 and Text Link 159.

# Monitoring

As Table 5.1 shows, the Monitoring component of the CATI project's model of organization development uses several of the resources already described in the Communicating module to provide formative feedback about the project's ongoing implementation. These include classroom observations, teachers' portfolios (specifically, materials development activities and action research projects done by teaching assistants), action research by the project director, and evaluation surveys.

## Classroom observations

∞ **Text Link 127**
For other discussions of this observation procedure, see Text Links 85, 114, and 153.

As noted earlier, classroom observations have a secondary monitoring function in the model of organization development shown in Figure 5.1 (see Text Link 127): Supervisors' feedback to teachers about their teaching provides teachers with formative evaluations at the end of each semester. If, for example, a teacher has difficulty one semester developing and using a small group methodology, then supervisors and the teacher can work together the following semester on developing this aspect of the teaching assistant's professional competence in task-based language teaching. Furthermore, when teaching assistants graduate from the teacher education program, they have accumulated two or three years' worth of semester evaluations, which provide a record of their development as teachers over time and can be used to provide professional references.

## Teachers' portfolios

From the project director's perspective, two of the most important components in the teachers' portfolios for monitoring purposes are the teaching assistants' materials development activities and action research projects. The development of new materials constitutes one of the most tangible products of the CATI project. As I argue in the following chapter, one of the easiest criteria that we can use to judge the project's relative success or failure in this area is to count how many units teaching assistants have contributed to the ESL Service Courses folder. Although counting the numbers of new units produced each year is an important tool for evaluating the continuing development of the teaching assistants and of the ESL program curriculum, this is not the only – nor indeed the most useful – criterion for evaluating project success. It is also necessary to use qualitative criteria, such as those used to evaluate the Iceman unit (see Chapter 4), and to evaluate the extent to which established units are *revised* by their authors or by other teaching assistants.

Revising materials is less glamorous than producing new units, but it is nonetheless a vital part of the professionalization process and also of the long-term maintenance of the ESL program's curriculum.

∞ **Text Link 128**
See Table 4.1. See also Text Links 8, 100, and 140.

Like any other commodity, materials have a limited lifespan. Their utility and relevance can be lengthened or improved by updating the articles or videos that carry a unit's thematic content. Materials may also be improved by periodically revising the kinds of tasks that students do. For this reason, the Project Framework matrix discussed in Chapter 4 specifies that teaching assistants' revisions should also be taken into account in evaluating the CATI project's relative success or failure (see Text Link 128).

Finally, from the project director's perspective, the teaching assistants' action research allows the director to monitor not only the extent to which individual teachers are using task-based materials, but whether they are developing and using new methodological skills and whether they are reflecting critically on their own beliefs about what constitutes good teaching.

## *Action research by the project director*

The project director, like the teaching assistants, also carries out action research in the CATI project. As I show in the following chapter, this research focuses on assessing the extent to which task-based language teaching is being implemented in the classroom from the perspective of a curriculum specialist. It also problematizes how participants own and understand curricular innovations. This research has focused primarily on trying to document changes in teachers' methodological behaviors and value systems. This type of research presents some particularly difficult problems from a research methodology point of view (see Text Link 129).

∞ **Text Link 129**
See Text Links 9, 52, 137, 147, 154, and 156. Finally, see Principles 7, 8, and 9 and Text Links 165–7.

## *Surveys*

The project director constantly tries to improve the organizational capacity of the Service Courses to support teaching assistants' professional development. The success of this organization development activity is monitored by yearly surveys that evaluate whether the support system is able to meet teaching assistants' professional development needs. Last, but not least, these surveys also provide the project director and the assistant project director with evaluative feedback on their own managerial performance, thus contributing to the professional development of these individuals. Chapter 6 shows how surveys and the other data sources discussed here have been combined to build up a composite picture of the overall success or failure of the CATI project (see Text Link 130).

∞ **Text Link 130**
See Text Link 136. See also Text Link 83.

## *Summary*

Four resources – classroom observations, teachers' portfolios, action research done by the project director, and evaluation surveys – allow the project director to monitor the CATI project. The combination of resources described here is likely to be particular to this project, but the larger point that this discussion makes is how important it is to have a monitoring component built into the design of any project. Although the theoretical need for such a component is widely recognized in the program evaluation literature, it is unfortunately rare in practice for such a component to be included in a project's design. As I show in greater detail in Chapter 6, the CATI project is by no means perfect in this respect. Although formative evaluations were always envisioned as an essential part of the project – and indeed, one was actually carried out in the early stages – they were not scheduled on a regular, yearly basis until the beginning of the 1993–4 academic year, when they were formally mandated by the Project Framework matrix. In retrospect, this was a serious flaw in the CATI project's design, and much wasted time could have been avoided had yearly evaluations

∞ **Text Link 131**

For related discussions of the place of Project Framework documents, see Table 4.1 and Text Links 79, 134, and 142. Finally, see Principles 4 and 7 and Text Links 162 and 165.

been carried out from the beginning. This experience strongly confirms the importance of building a monitoring component into a project's design before it is even implemented. I therefore propose this parameter of project design as a general guiding principle of curricular innovation (see Text Link 131).

## Evaluating

The final component of the model of organization development shown in Figure 5.1 and Table 5.1 is an Evaluating module, in which information is gathered for a summative evaluation of the CATI project. Since the CATI project is a continuing endeavor, no final evaluation has yet been done. However, all the resources that are being used to provide formative feedback about the continuing implementation of the CATI project (see the previous section on Monitoring) will eventually also be used to provide data for a summative evaluation of the project. In addition, all the messages that have ever been sent to the TAlist since it was first set up have been archived as a resource for evaluative research.

### TAlist archives

A technical feature of electronic lists that is potentially useful for evaluative purposes is that all the messages sent to a list are automatically archived by the mainframe computer. The list owner can then download this material every few months to a personal computer. This feature has been used to maintain a complete record of all the activity on the TAlist since it was started. Currently, four years' worth of messages have been archived in this way. Thus, a summative evaluation of the CATI project will be able to analyze messages sent to the list and evaluate whether project participants followed through and implemented changes to which they had agreed in these messages. Since these messages concern documented changes in materials that are contributed to the ESL Service Courses folder – as in Message 1 (see Extract 5.1), for example – evaluators will be able to gain important insights into both the processes and the products of curricular innovation.

133

## Summary

The observations made about the importance of building a monitoring component into a project's design at inception hold just as true for a summative evaluation component. For this reason, I will not repeat the conclusions advanced at the end of the Monitoring section.

In discussing the resources developed in the specific context of the CATI project, this chapter has illustrated how secondary innovations support primary innovations. Curriculum development has to be supported by a systemic model of organization development. This model consists of four interdependent modules. The Communicating module enables project participants to communicate with each other about the aims and goals of a project and about their development and research activities. The Knowing module provides participants with knowledge about the innovations they are implementing and enables a project to sustain teachers' development and research activities. The Monitoring module enables project participants to evaluate a project formatively. The Evaluating module provides a summative evaluation of the overall success or failure of a project. Although every project must develop its own particular mix of secondary innovations to support the primary innovations that occur in the Curriculum Development module, I submit that the model of organization development discussed in this chapter can serve as a basis for organizational change in other contexts of implementation.

# 6 Issues in project evaluation and maintenance: Transformational capacity

> In the real world, innovations are often the result of individual vision, energy and commitment, not rational planning and experimentation. (Alderson and Beretta 1992b: 272)

> The hardest bit is making the familiar classroom strange to yourself. (Peter Medway, cited in Goswami and Stillman 1987: i)

In this final chapter of Part II, I address Bowers's (1980a) last question, on whether a project has achieved its aims and objectives, by evaluating the extent to which participants in the CATI project have changed their behaviors as ESL materials writers and methodologists and whether they have changed their attitudes toward teaching. In addition to evaluating how successfully primary innovations have been implemented to date, I evaluate the extent to which secondary innovations have been successfully institutionalized. First, it is instructive to address some issues that speak to the more general lessons that can be learned from such an evaluation.

## Issues and problems in evaluation

Any evaluation of educational change involves issues and problems that have to be resolved, including (1) deciding whether an evaluation should be carried out by insiders or outsiders, (2) deciding what kinds of data should be gathered to evaluate the project, and (3) understanding how to overcome the practical problems that always affect evaluations.

### Insiders versus outsiders

The evaluation described here is an insider's evaluation of the CATI project. However, as Bowers (1980a) points out, insiders may lack the

135

necessary detachment to interpret project results objectively (see Text
Link 132). This does not mean that insiders' eval-

∞ **Text Link 132**

See Text Links 135 and 143.

uations are fatally flawed. Although it is important
to be aware of the potential conflicts of interest that
exist under such circumstances, *all* evaluations are
value-laden activities. Even evaluations by outsiders
are prone to charges of subjectivity and irrelevance (Alderson and Scott
1992). Furthermore, given the CATI project's philosophy of promoting
educational change by encouraging teacher participation in curricular
innovation, all project participants must be involved in evaluating the
project. As curriculum specialists in training, teaching assistants must
be able to evaluate the behavioral and attitudinal changes they undergo.
As a change agent concerned with promoting local change, I am interested in obtaining feedback that enables me to improve and maintain
the CATI project in the long term.

∞ **Text Link 133**

See Text Links 29, 30, 31, 34, 35, 50, 76, and 109.

In sum, the evaluation activities envisioned here
are participatory and mostly formative. Alderson
and Scott (1992) suggest that three criteria charac-
terize participatory evaluations. First, in participatory evaluations, all participants share duties and
play a variety of social roles in the evaluation process, whereas in non-
participatory evaluations, decision makers do the planning while implementers do all the "donkey work." This idea coincides with the
notion introduced in Chapter 3 that the roles of change agents, adopters, suppliers, and clients are not mutually exclusive (see Text Link
133). The second dimension is a logical extension of the first: Participatory evaluations must involve *all* participants, who should do a fair
share of the planning and "donkey work." Finally, participatory evaluations must provide tangible benefits to all participants.

∞ **Text Link 134**

See Text Links 79, 131, and 142. Finally, see Principles 4 and 7 and Texts Link 162 and 165.

I would like to suggest two further characteristics
of participatory evaluations. First, all project participants should be evaluated, including supervisors.
Thus, in the Inputs part of the Project Framework
matrix (Table 4.1), I specify that the success of organization development efforts must be verified in
part through yearly anonymous evaluations of course supervisors (see
Text Link 134). Such a policy is desirable in terms of ensuring the
smooth running of the project as a whole, and it also helps establish a
climate of trust and cooperation between supervisors and teachers. By
making themselves available for evaluation, supervisors are leading by
example. Thus, through their actions, supervisors can demonstrate to
teachers that evaluation is not one-way and that it is a valuable tool
for improving *all* participants' professional competence in the manage-

ment of change. Second, evaluation reports should document the evolution of a project and discuss the process through which implementation problems were resolved or, in some cases, *not* resolved. Language teaching professionals are only now beginning to become interested in the theory and practice of innovation. We can often learn more about the problems of implementing and maintaining curricular innovations from reports that discuss why a particular innovation *failed* to be adopted than from reports that merely report a project's successes.

Candor about such matters is also important for other reasons. Outsiders who read an evaluation that includes an appraisal of a project's difficulties or failures as well as its successes are more likely to believe its conclusions than one that omits such information. Finally, candid insiders' evaluations are useful to the field of applied linguistics as a whole, not just to a project's participants. Such evaluations illuminate what kinds of implementation and maintenance problems change agents are likely to encounter in all educational change. Again, the solutions that are reported in such documents are project-specific, but what is important is documenting the *process* by which such solutions are reached (see Text Link 135).

> ∞ **Text Link 135**
> See Text Links 132 and 143. For related discussions of the value of case studies as resources for understanding fundamental issues and problems in curricular innovation, see Chapter 1, pp. 4–5, and Text Links 3, 5, 8, and 106. Finally, see Principle 7 and Text Link 165.

## Kinds of data to be gathered

A *range* of data is necessary to document the extent to which a project has achieved its aims and objectives (Beretta 1992b). Thus, using *survey* data, Beretta (1990) established that only 13% of Bangalore Project participants reached a Renewal level of use. In addition, Beretta (1989) made some use of *transcripts* of classroom interaction to evaluate whether the project's focus on meaning was realized in classroom practice. In the CATI project, I use three sources of data to evaluate the project: *action research* by teachers and the project director, teachers' *journals,* and *survey* data from three formative evaluations of the project. Since the CATI project is still evolving, the action research data provide the most illuminating insights into teachers' degree of involvement in developing new materials, methodologies, and values. This innovation triangle represents the CATI project's equivalent of a levels-of-use evaluation methodology (see Text Link 136).

> ∞ **Text Link 136**
> For other references to the evaluation of the Bangalore Project, see Text Links 23, 40, 72, and 144; in addition, see Text Links 83 and 130 regarding the importance of gathering multiple sources of data for evaluation purposes. Finally, see Principles 5, 7, 8, and 9 and Text Links 163, 165, 166, and 167.

## Overcoming practical problems in evaluation

As Beretta (1992a: 250) remarks, most evaluations are "a messy, chaotic series of compromises." The CATI project is no exception to this observation. Unexpected problems in implementing what I thought would be the easiest part of the project (developing new materials) delayed the implementation of subsequent phases. Furthermore, although I have gathered a considerable amount of longitudinal data for evaluation purposes, there are still important gaps in the database, particularly in the early stages of the project. Consequently, only the latter stages of the project can be evaluated in any detail. Finally, some kinds of change are easier to document than others. As I show in the next section on primary innovations, we can sometimes document only the struggle that adopters go through as they attempt to incorporate change into their behaviors and value systems. Demonstrating that certain kinds of change – in particular, attitudinal change – have really occurred is an elusive goal (see Text Link 137). This is because innovation, like evaluation, is also an inherently messy process. Nonetheless, these data are valuable because they highlight the kinds of improvements that must be made to the continuing evaluation of a project, and thus contribute to its evolution and maintenance. This, after all, is the principal objective of insiders' evaluations of local change.

∞ **Text Link 137**

See Text Links 9, 52, 129, 147, 154, and 156 concerning the methodological difficulties involved in demonstrating that change has occurred. Finally, see also Principles 5, 7, 8, and 9 and Text Links 163, 165, 166, and 167 regarding the "messiness" of curricular innovation.

## Primary innovations

∞ **Text Link 138**

These resources are described in Figure 5-1. See also Text Links 2, 37, 42, 73, 80, 104, 105, 107, 121, and 157.

In this section, I evaluate the extent to which teaching assistants have developed new materials, new methodological skills, and new values about what constitutes good teaching. Since the CATI project is still evolving, the evaluation that I offer here is necessarily an interim evaluation, which is based on the resources that have been developed to monitor the project (see Text Link 138).

### Dimension 1: The development of new materials

The Iceman unit discussed in Chapter 4 exemplifies the CATI project's in-house materials. Since these materials are developed in my methodology course, teaching assistants can now choose from a large bank of materials (see Text Link 139). By the end of the 1993–4 academic year, teaching assistants had contributed fifty-five units to the ESL Service Courses folder. Although the distribution of units among the different classes is not equal, all classes now have enough units so that teaching assistants can construct sixty-hour courses from these banks of materials. Teaching assistants who teach parallel sections of the same class meet just before the be-

∞ **Text Link 139**
For an analysis of why these units are developed as part of the methodology course, see Text Link 124; see also Text Links 13, 18, 55, 56, 89, 96, 111, and 117. Finally, see Principle 8 and Text Link 166.

ginning of a semester to download the units they wish to use from the ESL Service Courses folder and construct a course packet. This packet is then printed for subsequent distribution to students. In those courses with enough units to enable teaching assistants to make choices among them, teachers can individualize their packets according to their own preferences. In this case, the thematic content of the units that make up individual teachers' course packets may vary from section to section, but the rhetorical content is the same across sections of the same class.

Materials development work is not confined to the production of new units – which would emphasize the quantity of materials produced rather than their quality. Thus, revising units is also an important activity in the CATI project. As noted earlier, revising materials is less glamorous than producing new units. Nonetheless, this is a vital part of the professionalization process teaching assistants undergo, and it contributes to the CATI project's long-term main-tenance (see Text Link 140). Thus, units like the Iceman unit have been substantially revised over time, both by the original author and by colleagues. These revisions are worth discussing because they

∞ **Text Link 140**
See also Text Links 8, 100, and 127.

illuminate the widely accepted claim that the most valuable classroom materials from a teacher development perspective emerge from an ev-olutionary, classroom-based approach to syllabus design and method-ology (Baumgardner et al. 1986).

Extract 6.1 displays the original version of section 1 of the Iceman unit in column 1. The author's subsequent revisions are displayed in column 2. Although both versions of section 1 begin with a brainstorm-ing activity, the focus of these activities is quite different. In version 1, the subject matter of activity A is directly linked to the thematic content of the unit. However, in version 2, the subject matter of activity A not only leads to a thematically related discussion of the Iceman story but is also based on the students' own lives. This change in version 2 makes the content of the unit – with which students may not be familiar – more accessible than it is in the first version. The subsequent develop-ment of the two versions is also quite different. In version 1, the ma-terials quickly move to a teacher-fronted evaluation task (the reporting

*Version 1*

Activity A: Brainstorming (5 minutes)

Imagine that you discover a very old, dead body while you are out hiking one day. What kinds of things could you discover about the way the dead person lived and died? Make a list on a scrap of paper of as many things as you can think of.

*Remember:* When you are brainstorming, the important thing is to generate as many ideas as possible. Don't stop and think about how "good" an idea is – just write everything down.

Activity B: Reporting (5 minutes)

The teacher makes a list on the chalkboard (or OHP) of ideas which resulted from activity A. Each student reports one idea (in turn) until no one has any more new ideas to offer.

Activity C: Preparing to Watch the Video (5 minutes)

Carefully read the questions on the page entitled "Questions about the Iceman Video." Be watching for the answers to the questions during the video presentation.

*Version 2*

Activity A: Brainstorming (5 minutes)

Imagine that you lose your bookbag today, and it is not discovered for 1,000 years. What kinds of things could be discovered about you? Make a list on a scrap of paper of as many things as you can think of.

*Remember:* When you are brainstorming, the important thing is to generate as many ideas as possible. Don't stop and think about how "good" an idea is – just write everything down.

Activity B: Rethinking (15 minutes)

Now, select three items from your bookbag (they can be anything), and analyze in detail the kinds of information someone could discover about you. For example, if someone found my keychain, they would be able to discover that I drove a car (and which kind I drove), that I probably lived in an apartment (from the number on the keys), that I valued private property and didn't want my things to get stolen, that I had some relationship with Purdue University, etc.

Activity C: Discussing Results (15 minutes)

In groups of three, share the results of the survey of your bookbag. Choose one item from your group which you feel would have the most significance for a discoverer 1,000 years from now, and be prepared to explain to the class why you chose what you did.

Activity D: Reporting (10 minutes)

Each group presents the item it chose and gives a brief rationale for their decision.

Activity E: Cause-and-Effect
Relationships (15 minutes)
Read the "Causal Analysis" handout
from *Readings for Writers*. If you do
not understand any part of the
article, underline it.

Activity F: Discussing (15 minutes)
In your groups, discuss with each
other the parts of the article you did
not understand. If you still have
questions, ask the teacher.

Activity G: Analyzing a Cause-and-
Effect Essay (15 minutes)
Read the article by Bertrand Russell
called "The Unhappy American
Way." Use the article you just read
and the list of cause-and-effect
structures to analyze the causes and
effects mentioned in Russell's article.

Activity H: Discussing (10 minutes)
At this point, the teacher will lead a
class discussion about "The Unhappy
American Way" and cause-and-effect
relationships. Before leaving class the
teacher will introduce the cause-and-
effect handout which students will
use to record cause-and-effect
relationships they discover
throughout the unit.

*Section 2*
Activity A: Reviewing (5 minutes)
As a class, briefly review cause-and-
effect relationships and the
brainstorming activity from the
previous class period.

Activity B: Watching the Video (55
minutes)
Watch the *NOVA* program entitled
"The Iceman." Try to discover
cause-and-effect relationships in the
video.

Courtesy of David Broersma.

task of activity B) followed by an individual prelistening task (preparing to watch the video in activity C by reading some prelistening questions). In contrast, in version 2, the evaluation of the information generated by the brainstorming task in activity A is distributed over three tasks (activities B–D). This evaluation is carried out in more detail and is achieved in a more student-centered fashion (note the reliance on individual or group work during these tasks). Finally, the author developed four new tasks (activities E–H) in version 2 that focus on analyzing cause-and-effect relationships (the rhetorical style that this unit teaches). It is only after students complete these four new tasks in version 2 that they watch the video in activity B of section 2, which was originally activity C of section 1 in version 1.

According to Broersma (personal communication), the author of the Iceman unit, these revisions exploit the pedagogical opportunities of the source texts he was using better and meet the needs of a broader range of students more effectively. He developed the first version of these materials for students who were at a higher level than the students targeted by version 2. Consequently, he had to break down the process of introducing the thematic and rhetorical content of the unit into smaller, more manageable steps for the lower-level learners.

A similar process of breaking tasks down into more explicit subtasks is evident in the revised version of activities B and C of section 5 of the Iceman unit by Tim Noble. Broersma's original version of these activities is shown in Extract 6.2.

Activity B assumes that students know what abstracts are, how they are constructed, and what their function is – an assumption that is not necessarily correct. Extract 6.3 shows how Noble developed subtasks (activities I–III) that train learners in analyzing what an abstract is. In activities IV–V, students practice selecting computer-generated authentic abstracts that may be relevant to writing a particular type of essay and then write their own versions of an abstract. This process of analysis prepares learners for the final discussion of the strengths and weaknesses of the abstracts that each group produces in activity VI.

Broersma's and Noble's revisions develop the scope of activities in the original version of the Iceman unit, but some revisions made by other teaching assistants change the unit's basic focus. Extract 6.4 reproduces Jane Nicholls's revisions to version 1 of the Iceman unit, which changes the unit's original focus on the rhetorical style of cause and effect to comparison and contrast.

Based on such data, it is fair to claim that the materials development aspect of the CATI project is now being successfully implemented. Teaching assistants are developing and using new materials and are also publicly sharing their revisions to established units. Of course, all teachers routinely adapt materials, but this adaptation process is normally a

EXTRACT 6.2. SECTION 5 OF THE ICEMAN UNIT (BROERSMA)

*Activity B: Preparing an Abstract* (65 minutes)
Read the "Abstracts" handout, and then develop an informative abstract for your interest section. The abstract should be about one page long, and it should give a preview of what to expect in a paper about some facet of your interest section.

*Activity C: Discussing Abstracts* (20 minutes)
Exchange your abstract with a partner, and, after reading each other's abstracts, discuss the strengths and weaknesses of each. If there are parts which seem unclear, ask your partner for an explanation. At the end of the class period, give the abstracts to your teacher.

Courtesy of David Broersma.

private matter. It is the public nature of these revisions that contributes to the professional development of all teachers. Since I add all revisions to the ESL Service Courses folder as they become available, these revisions also contribute to the development of the ESL curriculum (see Text Link 141).

> ∞ **Text Link 141**
> See Text Links 115, 119, and 120.

This claim is corroborated by the results of the yearly evaluation of the project prescribed by the 1993–4 Project Framework document (see Text Link 142). In this anonymous evaluation (which uses 4-point Likert scales supplemented by open-ended questions; see Appendix 2), the eleven teach-

> ∞ **Text Link 142**
> See Table 4.1 and Text Links 79, 131, and 134. Finally, see Principle 7 and Text Link 165.

ing assistants who taught during both semesters of the 1993–4 academic year were asked five questions about how well they understood the principles of task-based language teaching and how it could help them solve practical language teaching problems.

Four teaching assistants claimed they understood the principles of task-based language teaching "very well," five claimed they understood these principles "well," one made up a category of "average" understanding, and another claimed to understand the principles "very badly" (question B2). Eight teaching assistants strongly agreed that they had adequate information about the way in which task-based language teaching was used in the ESL courses, two agreed, and one disagreed (question B7). Six teaching assistants claimed they were very well-informed about current developments in syllabus design, four claimed they were well-informed, and one claimed to be badly informed (question C1). The same distribution of answers occurred when teaching assistants were asked how informed they felt about current developments in materials development (Question C2). Since the distinction

EXTRACT 6.3. SECTION 5 OF THE ICEMAN UNIT

---

I. Questions for looking at the abstracts from their fields which they have brought. (In groups according to field of study.) (15 minutes)
   1. What types of articles usually have abstracts?
   2. What is the general purpose of abstracts?
   3. Where can you find abstracts? Anywhere other than at the beginning of articles?
   4. What is the grammar like in an abstract? Are function words (such as articles, prepositions, transition words) left out? What tense is used? Is active or passive voice used?
   5. What sort of information is *not* included in an abstract? What is? Do all abstracts include the same amount of information?

II. Learners read pp. 74 to 75 on abstracts. (Read: 7 minutes. Discuss: 8 min.)
   1. Why have abstracts?
   2. What are the different kinds of abstracts? How are they different?
   3. What should an abstract include?
   4. What should an abstract not include?

III. Look at abstract in the article on Iceman (*Science*) (p. 66) (5 min.) (Esp. for those who read it.)
   1. What kind of abstract is this?
   2. What kinds of information does it include?
   3. Does it effectively summarize the article?
   4. Would you include anything else or delete anything?

IV. (Pairs or groups of three) Abstract choosing activity. (20 to 25 min.)

V. Read the article that is given to you. In pairs, write an abstract for it. Include as much or as little information as you deem necessary. (30 min.)

VI. (Depending on time) Exchange your abstract with another group. After you have had a chance to read it, discuss what you like about it and what might be improved.

---

Courtesy of Tim Noble.

between syllabus design and methodology is blurred in task-based language teaching (Nunan 1988b), it is also appropriate to report that six teaching assistants claimed to be very well-informed about current developments in methodology while five claimed to be well-informed (question C3). Thus, with the possible exception of the single individual who claimed to be badly informed about current developments in syllabus design and materials development, the great majority of teaching

EXTRACT 6.4. THE ICEMAN UNIT: NICHOLLS'S REVISIONS TO VERSION I

**General Comments**

I approached the original Iceman unit differently insofar as I wanted my students to write a comparison/contrast essay. As a result, I encouraged students to get a sense for issues and facts related to each of the three discoveries in question and to archeology as a whole, before defining their specific interest section. Ultimately, they were asked to write a paper which compared and contrasted at least two of the discoveries within a context of a (i) scientific, (ii) historical/cultural, or (iii) political/*ethical* (a category I added to the original) framework.

**Specific Revisions**

1. *Section 2: Information Gathering Activity*
   Activity A: Reading Source Materials and Comprehension Questions
   Rather than breaking students up into interest groups at this point, I had students form three groups, each of which read the article(s) relating to the three archeological discoveries at hand: the Iceman, King Tut, and the Bog People. After students had read and answered the questions in their own groups (i.e., comprehension check), they were redivided into new groups which contained one student from each original group.

   Activity B: Information Gap Activity
   After forming their new groups, information was shared and gathered so that all students could ultimately answer the three sets of questions orally in a "debriefing" whole-group discussion session.

   Activity C: Summarizing
   In groups, students brainstormed similarities and differences they could identify among the three finds. While they were asked to consider facts, the three categories mentioned above were introduced . . . , and students were also asked to consider differences among scientific, historical/cultural, and political/ethical factors. Students worked in their (mixed) groups and used the blackboard for this activity, and a spokesperson for each summarized their conclusions (notably, students were instructed not to repeat overlapping conclusions).

2. *Section 3: Information Gathering Activity (Tour)*
   Students were at this point asked to form groups related to their interest section, and the activity was essentially unchanged except that, rather than discussing one cause-and-effect relationship . . . , students were asked to discuss and make at least one comparison related to something they had learned about on the tour. Students were given this task to do as their journal assignment.

3. *Section 4: Synthesis of Research*
   This section was revised insofar as students worked with the section in Arnaudet and Barrett on "Major Thought Relationships: Contrast and Comparison" (33–43). Also, I did not have students prepare an abstract since I included an additional activity (see below) and did not have time.

4. *Section 5 and Section 6: Output and Feedback*
   No significant revisions other than focusing on comparison and contrast conventions (rather than cause and effect) and I incorporated one additional activity related to Feedback (see below).

## Added Activities

*Information Gathering Activity: Interview and Demonstration*
Students were introduced to the principal conservator for the University of Illinois Krannert Art Museum (who also works on other collections belonging to the U of I), who gave a presentation on a pre-Columbian piece she is currently working on which has created a furor among the art, archeological, and museum communities as it presents particularly interesting ethical questions germane to each of these disciplines.

Students were encouraged to ask questions during the presentation and were then given a kind of "hands on" tour of the art museum, focusing on pieces which were representative of certain political and ethical considerations. Students took notes throughout the tour, and were asked to incorporate information relevant to their topics in the final paper.

*Feedback Activity: Class Discussion*
Three final drafts of the Iceman papers were copied and distributed. Students were asked to read and discuss them in groups, addressing specific concerns while doing so. The class then regrouped and discussed the particular merits and weaknesses of each of the three papers.

Courtesy of Jane Nicholls.

∞ **Text Link 143**
For evaluation issues, see Text Links 132 and 135. For a discussion of the amount of time needed to implement innovations, see Text Links 51, 66, and 73. Finally, see Principles 6 and 7 and Text Links 164 and 165.

assistants claim to be (very) well-informed about task-based teaching. Thus, they seem to feel well-equipped to use the ESL courses as a laboratory for materials development.

However, the successful implementation of the materials development aspect of the CATI project was not achieved overnight (see Text Link 143). An earlier evaluation by Hutchin (1992) demonstrates that the implementation of the materials development aspect of the project took a long time to take off. Hutchin showed that, rather like the teachers in the Bangalore Project (see Text Link 144), the great majority of teaching assistants – specifically, ten out of twelve, or 83.33% of teachers – who participated in the CATI project between 1988 and 1990 reported levels of project ownership that ranged from "moderate" to "quite a lot." Note, however, that whereas Bangalore Project teachers who reported low levels of project ownership joined *later* in the project, the reverse is true in

> ∞ **Text Link 144**
> See Text Link 23; in addition, see Text Links 40, 72, and 136. Finally, see also Principles 5, 7, 8, and 9 and Text Links 163 and 165-7.

the CATI project. That is, teachers who participated in the first four years of the CATI project reported the lowest levels of project ownership.

Teaching assistants during this early period had little personal stake in using the materials that they and their colleagues had developed. Until 1990, when Hutchin began developing materials that she shared with her colleagues – thus providing opinion leadership for her colleagues – teaching assistants relied mostly on commercial materials for classroom instruction (see Text Link 145). Typically,

> ∞ **Text Link 145**
> For related discussions of the role of opinion leaders in the diffusion of innovations, see Text Links 54, 99, and 110. Finally, see Principle 9 and Text Link 167.

they tried out their own materials once, but did not teach them again, much less revise or share them with colleagues. Thus, two years after the start of the project, no banks of materials existed. These disappointing first results – which I discuss in more detail in the section on secondary innovations – are attributable to an initially insufficient amount of organization development. Materials development is supposed to be the easiest dimension of curricular innovation to implement (Fullan 1982a, b), which is why I conceived it as a gateway to further educational change (see Text Link 146). However, the implementation bottleneck that resulted held up the implementation of the other dimensions of curricular innovation until the beginning of the 1993–4 academic year (the 1992–3 year was spent consolidating the implementation of the materials development aspect of the project, which had by then finally started being successful).

> ∞ **Text Link 146**
> For a discussion of the theoretical underpinnings of the claim that materials development is the gateway to further development, see Text Links 33, 43, 44, 54, and 156. Finally, see Principle 9 and Text Link 167.

## Dimension 2: The development of new methodological skills

The number of individuals who have developed new methodological skills as a direct consequence of developing their own materials is lower than the number of individuals who have developed and used new materials. This is particularly true of those participants who taught for the ESL program until the end of the 1991–2 year. However, since then,

∞ **Text Link 147**
See Text Links 9, 52, 129, 137, and 156. Finally, see also Principles 5, 7, 8, and 9 and Text Links 163 and 165–7.

progress has been made in convincing teachers to use their classes as laboratories for developing new methodological skills. Before discussing the evidence that supports this statement, however, I must emphasize that, from a research methodology perspective, documenting how teachers develop new methodological skills is much more difficult than documenting how teachers develop new materials. As Fullan (1982b) explains, the development of new materials represents the most tangible and visible form of change. The development of new methodological skills is not only more difficult to observe empirically, but it is more difficult to describe this dimension of change in a way that allows participants to do something useful with these descriptions (see Text Link 147).

∞ **Text Link 148**
See Text Links 68 and 125.

Action research projects such as Lai's (1995) provide a useful way of describing such changes (see Text Link 148). Instructive though Lai's project is, however, cross-sectional data document only changes that occur at a particular moment in time. We thus need *longitudinal* data to construct a plausible picture of how teaching assistants develop new methodological skills over time. In order to provide such a picture, I cross-reference insights from a journal kept by a teaching assistant during the year that she taught for the ESL program with the results of her action research project (see Text Link 149). In this project, Chinitz (1995) investigated how tasks that she had developed proceeded in her class.

∞ **Text Link 149**
For other discussions on cross-referencing insights from various types of research instruments, see Text Link 120.

Extracts 6.5 and 6.6 (which constitute a single continuous text but have been divided for ease of exposition) come from the journal that Chinitz kept during the fall semester – the first semester that she taught for the ESL courses. Extract 6.5 shows the general criteria that Chinitz used to evaluate how new task-based language teaching seemed to her. Extract 6.6 documents in greater detail some of her attitudes toward using task-based procedures in the CATI project by focusing on the advantages and disadvantages she saw in using information gap tasks. My original comments and questions as project director are included as part of this dialogic text. Extract 6.7 consists of part of Chinitz's final journal entry as a teaching assistant in the ESL program I direct. This entry, which she wrote at the end of the following spring semester, documents her reflections about what she had learned from participating in the CATI project and how she intends to transfer this experience to another ESL program on campus. I then compare these self-report data to the insights that Chinitz

[Text in plain script = comments or responses by Chinitz (LC). Text in bold script = comments or requests for information by the project director (PD). Text in italic script = self-quotations by Chinitz from a previous journal. Text marked with an asterisk = commentary by the project director on a previous journal that is cited by Chinitz. Text in braces = textual gloss by the author.]

*Responses to Your Comments in Last Set of Journals*
PD: **\*General comments: Thanks for a very informative journal. I hope that you will find the feedback as useful! In your next journal, in addition to the info I requested about information gap procedures, could you comment in general terms on how new the 111 materials and methodological procedures seem to you? Also, to what extent is the stuff that we're covering in [the methodology course in the teacher education program] directly transferable to your classroom situation? In other words, are you able to make links between the theory of TBLT in [the methodology course] and the practice in [your ESL class]?**

LC: The materials and methodological procedures used in [my ESL class] are quite new to me. In Slovakia, an EFL situation, there were very few genuine materials to use. The textbooks used were British (situational?) and not bad, but the students' background was a combination of [Audiolingualism] and [grammar-translation] (though I couldn't have expressed that then); they had spent the previous year or two years memorizing verb tenses and other grammar (which they couldn't use to save their lives). I had a hard time getting most of the groups to say anything new, anything that wasn't modelled in their textbook. I couldn't convince them that the sky wouldn't fall if they made a mistake. Also, they were studying English because it was a fad, and because it wasn't Russian, which they had been forced to study for years. They had no clear goals. The best I could get out of them was that they wanted to understand the music they liked to listen to (heavy metal, rap, or top 40). The activities that worked the best with them were cloze activities with popular songs. Of course, that didn't fit into the school's notion: that I should "finish" the textbook. I didn't, of course. In one class, I actually stopped using the Slovak produced text because it was awful. The students were falling asleep. They perked up a bit afterwards, but at the same time, they had no clear plan; I knew what we were going to do, but as there was no text, they didn't. Anyway, had I known about communicative language teaching methodology then, it probably wouldn't have gone over too well.

The following year, teaching Russian speakers in Philadelphia, CLT probably would have worked great, if I had known about it. Whenever we learn something new in [the methodology class], I am always reflecting on how things went then. I remember especially clearly the problems with reading. All of us except the teacher who taught the

---

advanced class worried about finding materials that were not "stupid" but which were not too difficult for the students. I almost always used readings from an ESL textbook, knowing that they were stilted and unrealistic, but not knowing what to do about it. I would be much more willing to use genuine materials now, to get out of it what they can (using pictures and layout and such) and more able to explain to the students that they don't have to understand everything. Of course, collecting genuine materials that highlight what you want to teach can take a long time, but I think it's worth it.

I also picture myself doing exercises from the book or ones which I'd created, which were helpful to the students, but which I could have taken so much further. For example, when we were studying questions, I could have had the students interview people outside the class, to show them what is comprehensible and what isn't, and to get them to negotiate with a NS (who is not as sympathetic a listener as an ESL teacher). I could tell them until I'm blue in the face that asking "When you go home?" will leave the listener waiting for the rest of the sentence. If they could have seen that for themselves, it would have helped a lot.

Specifically regarding the link between the theory in [the methodology class] and practice in [my ESL class]: Am I able to make that link? I guess the answer is sometimes. Some of the theory is quite complicated, and the authors don't always give us examples to help make it clearer. I can't see anything superior to TBLT for preparing the students for their classes in the university. Everything we do must be applicable to their real needs, and they must read authentic texts and perform tasks equivalent to what they do in their other classes. Reading and discussing texts and finally presenting and/or writing a paper based on their research are exactly what they must do outside the walls of [the ESL class]. The feedback that I have gotten from students suggests that they didn't realize that they would get anything out of this class other than writing, but they were pleasantly surprised to see that the class has helped them with their confidence and their ability to discuss things in class and with their classmates in study groups. I think that helps to prove that the tasks are authentic.

---

Courtesy of Lori Chinitz.

gained from her action research project, which she carried out during the spring semester.

Extract 6.5 shows that the use of task-based language teaching is new to Chinitz (as it was for the majority of current teaching assistants when they first arrived on campus; see the answers to question A5 in Appendix 2). Chinitz's initial judgments about task-based materials and procedures are influenced by her previous teaching experience in Slovakia and the United States. As such, Chinitz demonstrates an intuitive awareness of the importance of the sociocultural context in which an innovation is to diffuse (see Text Link 150). Chinitz's response about the extent to which she is able to make connections between the theoretical ideas discussed in the methodology class and her own classroom practice displays a cautious willingness to experiment with task-based language teaching, at least in the context of the CATI project. In short, if we relate Chinitz's responses in Extract 6.5 to the four-stage adoption process outlined in Chapter 3, these data suggest that Chinitz is in the process of gaining relevant knowledge about task-based language teaching and evaluating how useful this innovation is to her and to her current students (see Text Link 151).

> ∞ **Text Link 150**
> See Text Link 47. In addition, see Text Links 4, 48, 52, 69, 81, and 82. Finally, see Principle 1 and Text Link 159.

> ∞ **Text Link 151**
> See Text Links 33, 43, 54, and 146.

Chinitz's evaluation is based primarily on her own experience. As Extract 6.6 shows, she is beginning to experiment with two-way information gap tasks in her class. Extract 6.6 also documents what Chinitz thinks about using such tasks. This extract provides some evidence that Chinitz is using information that comes from the readings in the methodology class – for example, the references to the comprehensibility of students' speech. However, it seems that most of the evidence that Chinitz cites to discuss the advantages or disadvantages of two-way information gap tasks is based on her own experience with using such tasks. For example, in the italicized self-citation from an earlier journal entry, Chinitz reports "feeling good" when she observes that the kind of negotiation for meaning discussed in the methodology class occurred in her own class. I have already noted the role of personal experience as a catalyst of change in the discussion of the problem-solving model of change in Chapter 3 (see Text Link 152).

> ∞ **Text Link 152**
> See Text Links 7 and 64. In addition, see also Text Links 86, 92, and 125. Finally, see Principles 2 and 8 and Text Links 160 and 166.

To the extent that Chinitz feels that the advantages of using two-way information gap tasks outweigh the disadvantages, Extract 6.6 provides evidence that Chinitz has reached the third stage of decision making in the adoption process discussed in Chapter 3. That is, she has made a preliminary decision to adopt such tasks and is beginning to implement this decision. This interpretation of how far Chinitz has progressed in her evaluation of the utility of task-based language teaching is further strengthened by her expression of interest in incorporating such tasks into her future teaching and in using them in teaching environments where they are not currently used. In Extract 6.7, which Chinitz wrote as her final journal before leaving the ESL program that hosts the CATI project, there are indications that she has confirmed her original decisions to incorporate task-based teaching in another ESL program on campus.

# The CATI project

EXTRACT 6.6. CHINITZ'S JOURNAL, FIRST SEMESTER (PART 2)

---

LC: *Today, the students split into four groups with five students each. Each student had to explain her/his group's theme to the other students; they took notes in preparation for answering questions and writing a group summary. I sat in on the groups for a few minutes at a time, and they didn't seem to be inhibited by my presence. I heard some really good communication going on. When we have used terms in [the methodology] class such as "negotiating for meaning," I have been afraid that this is the type of thing that I should be facilitating but that wasn't happening in my class. From the interaction I heard today, I could see that it was happening. The students were motivated to listen to each other by the information gap and the fact that the missing information will be necessary for a future exercise. They asked each other questions to clarify anything that they hadn't understood and shared their ideas about what things meant and what the implications were of certain developments and events about which they'd read. I had a good feeling when the class ended.*

PD: \*Great! In light of my final comment on your last entry {see the first comment by PD in Extract 6.5}, this is exactly the kind of thing which I was hoping to hear from you. For the next set of journals, could you address the issue of how new these information gap activities were for you, what doubts you might have had if you had not used these before, what (dis)advantages you see in their use and any other information which you think might be relevant to your continuing to use such activities?

LC: I have used information gap activities for games and such, but never in two-way communication that was crucial to the outcome of the activity. I never had any doubts in terms of their desirability, only uncertainty about how they work. I think one important thing to keep in mind is that the students must always know that there is some outcome, some reason why they must listen to each other and make sure everything is clear. The <u>advantages</u> are many: students know they must do their homework (if the reading is assigned for homework) or they'll be harming their classmates as well as themselves; they need to listen to each other in order to reach the outcome, so students don't feel that they're talking to a wall; they need to ask questions about anything that is unclear, so students get feedback about the comprehensibility of their speech; everyone has information that is important to the group, so everyone (ideally) gets an equal chance to talk, even the more shy students. The <u>disadvantages</u> are that some students will not care if their not doing their homework harms anyone, including themselves (fortunately I don't have anyone with that bad an attitude now), and student-centered, group work activities can really be ruined by non-cooperation; some students are less articulate than others, and some

EXTRACT 6.6 (*CONT.*)

more advanced students may get frustrated or otherwise cause the less advanced students to feel constrained (of course, some students will feel constrained even with the most helpful partners); the teacher can't always tell if the necessary information really is getting transferred unless s/he checks at each step, and that's intrusive. I think that the advantages outweigh the disadvantages, and I have no problem in continuing to use information-gap activities. They are something that I would like to incorporate into my future teaching, and I look forward to using them as an innovation in some teaching environment where they are not used.

Courtesy of Lori Chinitz.

In this extract, Chinitz specifically mentions developing materials and possibly using action research and journals as some of the skills and habits that she would like to maintain, but she does not specifically mention learning anything new in terms of classroom methodology. In order to get more detailed insights into what new methodological skills Chinitz has developed, we must turn to her action research project, which she carried out at approximately the same time that she wrote this entry. In her project, Chinitz (1995) returns to a theme that relates closely to the issues she discusses in Extract 6.6: the relative merits of opinion sharing tasks versus information gap tasks. In order to carry out her project, Chinitz first audiotaped the interaction that occurred during activities A and B in her unit on advertising (see Extract 6.8) and then transcribed and analyzed the data that she obtained.

Drawing on previous research by Long and Porter (1985) and Pica (1987), Chinitz's research focused on the extent to which opinion sharing tasks that are mediated through small group work enable learners to do talk that is normally the preserve of teachers in teacher-fronted classrooms, such as making suggestions, inferences, and qualifications; asking for clarifications; nominating topics; allocating turns; and providing feedback. As Chinitz notes, her results are in line with previous findings: Tasks that do not force learners to engage in two-way exchanges of information do not necessarily cause meaning to be negotiated by all group members. In particular, she found that a lack of negotiation is inevitable in groups in which one or more members is dominant and concluded that careful control of both task type and group makeup may sometimes be necessary.

More specifically, Chinitz investigated the extent to which Hwaling, a Korean female, was able to participate during activity A, when she was a member of an all-Korean group of learners. Chinitz then con-

## The CATI project

LC: This is my last journal as a [teaching assistant in the program that functions as a laboratory for the CATI project]. I have very mixed feelings, because I've learned a lot and had some great experiences. But I think the [other ESL program on campus] will provide me with some really great experiences, too. I am looking forward to applying what I've learned in [the methodology and action research courses] and in my [teaching in the CATI project] to a different kind of teaching situation, with lower level students. I look forward to creating materials for my classes (whatever they turn out to be; I don't know yet) and to continuing research (on a more informal basis, most likely).

I didn't really think the journals were the greatest idea at first; I just thought they'd be more work. But I can see that they've really helped me to think some issues through and to provide a record I could look back to at any time. I am not the most introspective person in the world, so I probably could have done some more along those lines, but I think I've been able to do more than I expected. I'd like to continue with a journal, although I don't know how well that will work if I know that no one's collecting them.

---

trasted Hwaling's participation patterns during activity A with her participation patterns during activity B, when Hwaling was part of a group of learners who came from different cultural and language backgrounds. Chinitz is able to show that the inclusive leadership and conversational style of Dong-wan, a male student who self-selected as group leader in the all-Korean group, allowed Hwaling to participate relatively actively in the conversational work of activity A. During activity B, however, the more aggressive leadership and conversational style of the self-selected group leader, Lupita, a Mexican female, negatively affected Hwaling's ability to participate in group work.

What new methodological skills did Chinitz develop as a result of doing this action research project? Most important, Chinitz obtained some firsthand insights into how different groups' interpersonal dynamics affected the implementation of the tasks she had designed. As a result, she realized how the composition of small groups can affect a task's success. This led her to reevaluate her preference for not controlling the composition of group members. In addition, she began to critique the methodological principles that she had used to design her tasks:

I believe that the insights gained have affected me both as a researcher and as a teacher. If my materials are well-planned, then my job as a teacher should be much easier. But if I am worrying about design while I am teaching, then I cannot be as effective in the classroom as I would like. It is fortunate that the taping was done when the class was working on materials that I had cre-

EXTRACT 6.8. CHINITZ'S ACTION RESEARCH PROJECT

---

**ADVERTISING: Should It Be Regulated?**

*Section 1: Introductory Activities*
Activity A: Brainstorming/Focusing (20 minutes)
1. What is your definition of advertising? What is its purpose? Where does it appear? Who benefits from it?
2. List the ways in which it benefits/harms consumers and give reasons why.
3. How does advertising in the U.S. differ from that in your home country?
4. Is advertising regulated in your home country? How?
5. As far as you can tell from your experience, is advertising regulated in the U.S.? How?
6. Should advertising be regulated? Why or why not? Are there special categories of advertising which should or shouldn't be regulated? Why or why not?

Activity B: Sharing Ideas/Preparing for Presentations (40 minutes)
Review your answers to the questions with classmates from your home country. Did you agree? Why or why not? If you disagreed, on what issues did you disagree? Were there any issues of which you hadn't been aware?

Guidelines for Presentation Preparation
– Prepare on an overhead an outline for a 5-minute presentation to the whole class, discussing the issues above. The presentation should not be a list of questions and answers. Rather, focus on the points most relevant or interesting to your group, including whether or not advertising is regulated in your country.
– Each presenter will be responsible for acknowledging and building on the information presented in all previous presentations, as one would when discussing an issue in a class or seminar.
– As you are listening to the presentations, note any points made with which you strongly agree or disagree. These may help you when formulating an argument for the debate.
– In groups, you will be writing a list of the main points of all the presentations, and you will also be writing an individual summary. In order to do that most efficiently and effectively, you should take notes during the presentations and ask questions about anything that is unclear to you.

---

Courtesy of Lori Chinitz.

ated, thus allowing me to be more critical and to think about why I had designed something a particular way and how I could make it more effective. (Chinitz 1994)

Are the changes Chinitz went through representative of changes experienced by teaching assistants as a group? As I noted earlier in this section, action research is a recent development in the evolution of the CATI project. Consequently, I cannot document empirically the extent to which all teaching assistants have developed new methodological skills as a direct result of participating in this project. Nonetheless, the limited data that exist to date suggest that a promising start has been made in promoting such change, at least among current teaching assistants. In an anonymous evaluation of the action research course I first taught during spring semester 1994, I asked teaching assistants to evaluate how useful their final projects had been as a professional learning experience and how (if at all) this project had affected the way they thought about and actually did teaching.

In general, the response was very positive. It is worth noting, however, that only five of the eleven teachers who took this course were participants in the CATI project, while the remaining six were teachers in other language teaching programs on and off campus. Nonetheless, even though it is impossible to separate the responses of CATI project participants from those of nonparticipants, the picture that emerges suggests that almost all participants thought that the course promoted important changes in both their methodological behaviors and philosophies of teaching. Ten out of eleven students who completed the course filled out the evaluation. The most negative response given to the question about the extent to which the teaching assistants' final projects had changed their way of thinking about and actually doing teaching was the following:

It was a useful experience for me more as a student than as a teacher. It created, I guess, a greater awareness of student opinions in my class, but no tremendous effect on my teaching, I'm afraid.

However, this comment was atypical of the responses given as a whole. The most positive of these responses was the following:

This project has affected my thinking about teaching and my teaching even before it was completed. This research caused me to ask questions of myself, determine what my objectives are for everything I do in the classroom, and better interpret my students' work and behavior.

Of the remaining eight responses, seven rated the project as "very useful" and one rated it a "useful learning experience." The writer of this last evaluation continues:

[The project] will definitely affect my teaching in the fall semester. I have built up my own philosophy of organizing group work more efficiently in order to promote independent learning in class. I have become aware of a number of variables that have an impact on group work procedures and how the teacher can handle them beneficially. The project exposed my shortcomings and incited self-repair strategies that would improve my teaching methodology to a good extent.

Thus, both the quantitative and qualitative feedback suggest that all but one of the participants enrolled in this class have indeed begun to reflect critically on their teaching and to develop new methodological behaviors. Of course, the intention to implement an innovation cannot be interpreted as proof of actual implementation (Kelly 1980). For this reason, it is worth noting that all of the members of this class who were participants in the CATI project subsequently signed up for other action research projects in later semesters.

The question remains as to whether the current teaching assistants who have not had the opportunity to do action research engaged in similar processes of methodological change. The evidence that speaks to this question is based entirely on survey data rather than on a mix of survey data and empirically observed classroom talk. However, *all teaching assistants make similar claims of methodological change*. In the anonymous end-of-year evaluation for 1993–4, I asked teachers to evaluate how strongly they agreed or disagreed with the statement that postobservation discussions helped them to identify strategies that would enhance future lessons or materials (see Text Link 153 and question D23 in Appendix 2). In response, eight teaching assistants strongly agreed, two invented an intermediate category of "strongly agree/agree," and one agreed. Several of the responses teaching assistants gave to open-ended questions like D13, which solicited feedback on weekly staff meetings, suggest that peer discussions of action research and materials development projects were valuable sources of ideas about teaching. As three teaching assistants note:

∞ **Text Link 153**
See Text Links 85, 114, and 127.

I think the range of different things we did in the [staff] meetings was terrific. I think in the future, the TAs should continue to discuss issues and articles of interest to them. I think discussing TA projects was also very worthwhile. I would want that to continue.

Presentations, talks with specialists, discussions on literature related to our teaching goals and concerns have been really very effective.

I thought the presentations provided us with a lot of fodder for discussion and caused a lot of new ideas to arise.

In sum, obtaining data that speak to the question of whether teaching assistants are developing new methodological skills is a difficult task. Nonetheless, we can claim to know what range of data should ideally be gathered to document methodological change. We can also claim that, although it has taken a long time for the CATI project to promote changes in methodology, five out of eleven teaching assistants who

157

taught in the 1993–4 academic year implemented methodological change as a result of doing action research projects. Although survey data are less convincing than analyses of empirically observed teachers' behaviors, the remaining six teachers probably implemented methodological changes as a result of being exposed to their colleagues' action research projects and also as a result of participating in the classroom observation process (see Text Link 154). The tentative nature of this latter conclusion points to the need to strengthen the action research component of the CATI project, so that future generations of project participants are engaged in this dimension of curricular innovation as soon as possible during their tenure as ESL program instructors.

∞ **Text Link 154**

See Text Links 9, 52, 129, and 147. Finally, see Principles 5, 7, 8, and 9 and Text Links 163 and 165–7.

## Dimension 3: The development of new pedagogical beliefs and value systems

The previous section presented some examples of teaching assistants developing their philosophies of teaching. This section illustrates some important aspects of individuals' decision-making processes as they evaluate and change their values about teaching, in particular, what constitutes "good teaching" (see Text Link 154). Also included are some survey results that speak to how successful the CATI project has been in promoting change in this most abstract dimension of curricular innovation.

How can we document changes in teachers' pedagogical beliefs? Let me answer this question by giving an example of what was arguably a *lack* of methodological and attitudinal change by an individual teacher and then show how teaching assistants as a group reacted to the analysis that I presented to them. The data come from an investigation I carried out into whether teaching assistants' discoursal behaviors during small group work resulted in classroom talk that was qualitatively different from the kind of talk normally found in teacher-fronted classrooms (Markee 1995).

In teacher-fronted instruction, participants organize talk by implementing a three-turn sequential structure. As Excerpt 1 shows, this conversational structure consists of an opening question (Q) turn by the teacher, an answering (A) turn by a learner, and a commenting (C) turn by the teacher, which closes the sequence. This C-turn provides learners with feedback on the adequacy of their A-turn.

*Excerpt 1*

1 T [Q]  what does X mean
2 L [A]  X means Y
3 T [C]  yes good that's right

In this turn-taking system, teachers do all Q-turns and C-turns. Thus, teacher-fronted discourse is constructed in such a way that the teacher controls how the discourse develops during a lesson. The teacher thereby controls the teaching agenda for that lesson (Cazden 1988; Kasper 1985; McHoul 1978; J. Nicholls 1993; Pica 1987; van Lier 1988). This iterative Q-A-C turn-taking system exemplifies a discourse of unequal power. As we saw in Chapters 2 and 4, advocates of the process syllabus are concerned with equalizing the power relationships that exist between teachers and learners through negotiation. Although it would be naive to suggest that classroom talk should resemble natural conversation at all times, task-based language teaching practitioners should arguably aim to diminish the level of teacher control during at least some of the talk that occurs in the classroom (see Text Link 155). A possible advantage of such a development might be that students would take greater responsibility for their own learning, a goal that many communicative methodologists regard as

> ∞ **Text Link 155**
> See Text Links 15, 16, 98, 102, and 103. Finally, see Principle 4 and Text Link 162.

desirable. One way to achieve this goal would be to change the practices of classroom interaction at certain times so that these more closely resembled the open-ended rules of talk found in ordinary conversation. This would not only redistribute power in the classroom, it would also be valuable from an SLA point of view, since the ability to perform a broad range of communicative acts in the target language may promote target language development (Pica 1987).

Tasks that involve student-student talk in small groups simulate many of the practices of ordinary conversation: Turns are not pre-allocated and all participants have equal rights to contribute to the conversation. As the discussion of the Iceman unit in Chapter 4 shows, small group work is common in CATI project materials. What happens, however, when students ask teachers questions during small group work? Does the teacher answer the question – as normally happens in equal power discourse – or does the teacher do something else that reestablishes a discourse of unequal power? Markee (1995) shows that, at such decision points, teachers hardly ever answer a student's question directly. Indeed, only one teacher out of the five whose classes have been transcribed ever answered a student's question directly. Instead, teaching assistants tended to answer student questions with "counterquestion" (CQ) turns of their own (Markee 1995; J. Nicholls 1993). This CQ strategy is exemplified twice in Excerpt 2 (see lines 3 and 6–7):

*Excerpt 2 (condensed)*

1  L13: [Q]   . . . what's that mean (1) coastal vulnerability
2          . . .

```
 3  T:    [CQ]  what d'you think it means
 4               (1.3)
 5  L14:         uh?
 6  T:    [CQ]  what what d'you think a- where are areas of coastal vulnerability
 7               (++) <h> if you think about uh:m
 8  L14: [A]    it's not safe[t] (+) areas which are not safe[t] (1) right?
 9  L13: [A]    it's very easy to be:: (+) damage
10  T:    [C]    yea:h (+) especially by (+) water, (+) by flooding,
                 (Class 1, group 4)
```

By doing these CQ turns, the teacher puts L13 and L14 in the sequential position of having to do A-turns in lines 8 and 9 and is herself in position at line 10 to do a C-turn that closes this sequence (see Appendix 1 for transcription conventions). Whatever the teacher's intentions may have been, her CQ turns thus have the technical effect of reinstating a discourse of unequal power at this decision point in the interaction. That is, the teacher (probably quite unconsciously) takes back from the students the right to control the trajectory and content of these sequences. Ironically, therefore, the "small group" talk illustrated in Excerpt 2 is almost indistinguishable from the talk that occurs in "traditional" teacher-fronted classrooms.

When I asked the teacher who had taught this class to comment retrospectively on her answering strategies at this decision point in the interaction, she articulated some interesting beliefs about what she considered to be good teaching. Note that this teacher was the only instructor who had ever answered a student's question directly. However, when I questioned her about this, she replied that she was surprised that she had ever used an A strategy at all. According to her, the CQ strategy exemplified in Excerpt 2 was "better teaching" because it helped reduce teacher talking time (TTT). She also believed that this strategy gave knowledgeable students an opportunity to practice giving definitions of unknown words and that it was a student-centered way of managing the small group interaction – that is, it emphasized the value of cooperative rather than competitive learning. She thought that students were more likely to remember definitions they produced than definitions produced by a teacher who used an A strategy. She justified her opinions by noting that her previous teacher training had taught her to redirect questions to other students rather than answer them herself – illustrating how powerful previous experience can be in shaping teachers' behaviors and beliefs. However, she recognized that her teacher trainers had assumed that teacher-fronted instruction was the target norm for teacher trainees.

The teaching assistant I questioned thought that these beliefs about teaching were consistent with task-based language teaching. Notice, however, that reducing TTT is a "tenet of good teaching" that Audi-olingual teachers would have had no trouble in accepting. Arguably, this ideological leftover from previous theories of language teaching has nothing to do with task-based teaching. Indeed, I maintain that, at decision points such as those analyzed here, teachers who wish to distribute power more equally in their classrooms should provide direct answers to students' questions, even if this momentarily results in small increases in TTT. The use of small group tasks in which teachers are infrequent participants reduces the overall amount of TTT so that the "problem" of too much TTT evaporates. Furthermore, since learners typically ask teachers to help them only after they fail to get answers from peers, teachers who use a CQ strategy at such a decision point are using class time inefficiently.

When I discussed this teacher's beliefs about what constituted good teaching with current teaching assistants, there was considerable disagreement as to whether my analysis or the teaching assistant's was more convincing. One teaching assistant reacted by saying that using a CQ strategy did promote collaborative learning and that she therefore wanted to learn how to do CQ turns more effectively. An intermediary group of seven teaching assistants took note of the conversation analysis but were not convinced that the use of a CQ strategy at such a decision point was unjustified. They argued that teachers have to juggle with multiple contingencies in classroom talk. For them, a conversation analytic perspective fails to take into account teachers' practical concerns, which include getting through the material on time, making sure that all learners get a chance to participate, and the like. Finally, the remaining three teaching assistants agreed with the conversation analysis in principle but wondered how to apply this information in the classroom. Some teaching assistants were troubled by the larger philosophical implications of this analysis concerning the utility of concepts such as "teacher-centered" and "learner-centered" instruction (see Extract 6.9):

EXTRACT 6.9. A TEACHING ASSISTANT'S VIEW ON TEACHER- VS. LEARNER-CENTERED INSTRUCTION

The goal of student-centeredness is to give students more control over their educational experiences. But there always seems to be a point at which the teacher is making the classroom do what he or she (as the teacher) perceives to be best. In other words, the teacher makes the decisions about what is best for the students. Now, I think there is definitely room for teaching professionals to be able to claim that they know what is best for their students, but I wonder about calling a classroom student-centered when the teacher is still making all the decisions that count. For example, in my classroom, my students are involved in a lot of group work, which I mandate, and which, on the whole, they have been pretty willing to do. In [their responses to questions about their learning style preferences], however, although my students said they would not like lecture all the time, they indicated that they wished that I would talk to them more, and more often.

I'm afraid I am not making sense. It seems as though a distinction needs to be clearly made in how we are defining the expression *student-centered*. It can either mean making the student do the work of the classroom or letting student desires and goals dictate what happens in the classroom. It seems like the CQ strategy issue deals with this distinction: Do we as teachers just give the students what they want (a direct answer) or do we make them work for an answer by first drawing on their own resources? I know your research shows that they have already drawn on their own resources before they ask the questions, which is a key point; nevertheless, I think there is a sense where CQing is a relatively minor manifestation of a larger conflict. Do we really want student-centeredness that gives students the power to ask us to lecture? Also, my experience as student and teacher makes me believe that people get very uncomfortable when their expectations about relationships are violated. Perhaps students, if given what they really want, will say, "You be in charge. Tell me what to do and I will do it."

Courtesy of David Broersma.

This extract illustrates how difficult it is to bring about changes in our own or others' pedagogical values, *even when we are ready to change our beliefs*. All innovation ultimately depends on participants engaging in a meaningful process of values clarification (Henrichsen 1989; White 1988). Thus, the teaching assistants' resistance to the conversation analysis of the function of CQ turns in pedagogical discourse was caused by the fact that this analysis leads to initially counterintuitive methodological conclusions. As Extract 6.9 makes clear, commonly used terms like *student-centered teaching* suddenly become controversial and difficult to define. Of course, this is all part of the process of values clarification, but this process raises interesting problems that go to the heart of any attempt to innovate. For example, if we cannot agree on the meaning of common terms like "student-centered teaching," it becomes extremely difficult for us to change our ideas. Furthermore, we can see that suggestions for apparently small changes (like teachers using an A strategy instead of a CQ strategy to answer students' questions) can open up a Pandora's box of unexpected problems, to which there may be no obvious solutions. Frustrating though this may be, we must nonetheless confront such issues because it is only by clarifying our beliefs that we can develop new pedagogical value systems.

The analysis of CQ turns illustrates the insights we can gain into curricular innovation processes when we treat our classrooms as unfamiliar places. This discussion also shows the complex interrelationships between the three dimensions of primary innovations and why changing teachers' values is so difficult to implement (see Text Link 156). Let us move on to the obvious question: Has the CATI project promoted change in all teaching assistants' pedagogical beliefs and value systems?

∞ **Text Link 156**
See Text Links 6, 9, and 44. Finally, see Principles 5 and 7–9, and Text Links 163 and 165–7.

In the yearly evaluation for the 1993–4 academic year, I asked teachers to evaluate how strongly they agreed or disagreed with the statements that postobservation discussions helped them to: identify their strengths as teachers (Appendix 2, question D21); identify their weaknesses as teachers (question D22); identify ways of improving their subsequent teaching (question D23); and reflect on their teaching methodology and materials (question D24). In response to question D21, ten teaching assistants strongly agreed and one agreed that this procedure had helped them to identify their strengths as teachers. In response to question D22, seven strongly agreed, one agreed, another agreed but added the rider of "not entirely," and two disagreed that this procedure had helped them to identify their weaknesses as teachers. In response to question D23, eight teaching assistants strongly agreed, two invented an intermediate category of "strongly agree/agree," and one agreed that this procedure had helped them improve their subsequent teaching. In response to question D24, seven strongly agreed, one invented the intermediate category of "strongly agree/agree," and three agreed that this procedure had encouraged them to reflect on their teaching methodology and materials.

These results indicate that all teaching assistants believe they have engaged in a process of attitudinal change. However, the different patterns that are observable in the answers to questions D21 and D22 suggest that not all teachers experienced the same type or degree of change. The five teaching assistants who took the action research course probably underwent the greatest amount of attitudinal change, because they received more varied opportunities to reflect intensively on their teaching than did their colleagues who did not take the course. Of course, this does not mean that individuals who did not take this course failed to undergo significant attitudinal change. For example, Broersma, the writer of the journal entry reproduced in Extract 6.9, had not taken this course, yet his comments about the difficulties involved in changing his attitudes toward teaching are particularly insightful. As a whole, however, it seems that keeping a journal is *by itself* a less effective tool for promoting attitudinal change than observationally based action research on classroom discourse that is optionally complemented by journals. For this reason, most teaching assistants who have not taken this course have probably been less engaged in a process of attitudinal change than those who have.

In sum, the materials development aspect of the project initially got off to a bad start. Indeed, this aspect of the project was almost completely unsuccessful for the first two years of the project, and it took another two years to consolidate the implementation of this gateway to curricular innovation. However, these initial problems have been corrected and the development, revision, and use of new materials by teachers has now been successfully institutionalized. The picture concerning teachers' development of new methodological skills and pedagogical attitudes is more complex. Because it took four years to work out the problems with the implementation of the materials development aspect of the project, project participants have only recently been able to pay attention to these less tangible dimensions of curricular innovation. Thus, the implementation of methodological and attitudinal changes has been uneven and has not progressed as far as the implementation of changes in materials. Nonetheless, important progress has been made recently toward institutionalizing a more balanced implementation of all the CATI project's aims and goals. Finally, this evaluation has highlighted the methodological difficulties that are involved in demonstrating that curricular innovation has occurred, especially at the more abstract levels of methodological and attitudinal change. Despite these difficulties, the data gathered to date have all proved useful in fine-tuning the CATI project's implementation and maintenance.

## Secondary innovations

As noted earlier, Hutchin's (1992) evaluation uncovered serious problems with the implementation of the CATI project's in-house materials development program. This led to substantial delays in the implementation of the rest of the project. Why did these problems occur and what solutions were subsequently devised to resolve them? From my perspective, I thought I had clearly explained that materials development was a catalyst for other behavioral and attitudinal changes. Yet, it became painfully clear that most teaching assistants surveyed by Hutchin had not understood that the principal function of having teachers develop materials was to contribute to their professional development: Eight teaching assistants understood that the CATI project was supposed to promote curriculum development, but they did not understand how this contributed to their own development. Ten out of twelve (83.33%) teachers reported levels of project ownership that ranged from "moderate" to "quite a lot."

Thus, Hutchin demonstrated that there was a serious lack of communication between me and teaching assistants regarding the CATI project's fundamental goals. I therefore had to correct this problem if the CATI project was to be anything more substantial than a figment of my own imagination. In the short term, I took two preliminary steps to improve the level of communication between the teaching assistants and me. First, Hutchin posted a summary of the evaluation's results on the TAlist at my behest so that all teaching assistants could become familiar with the project's implementation problems. Second, after all list subscribers had had a chance to digest the evaluation's findings, I then invited all teaching assistants to discuss Hutchin's results with me on an individual basis. During these consultations, I went over the project's aims and goals with each teaching assistant and also solicited each teacher's advice concerning how to make the CATI project more of a reality. This consultation process served to clarify for all teachers what the CATI project's aims and goals were. The teaching assistants' feedback to me suggested that, in the longer term, the ESL courses were currently too underdeveloped from an organizational point of view to sustain a project in curricular innovation. In other words, I could not use the methodology course as the only forum for discussing the project's aims and goals: I had to diversify the number and range of systemic resources used to support the CATI project.

A range of solutions that took into account the systemic complexity of educational change was required to correct the problems identified by Hutchin over the long term. Hutchin suggested that one possible reason for the low level of project ownership reported by teaching assistants was that they did not take the required methodology course early enough in their teacher education careers. For historical reasons, faculty advisors had advised teaching assistants to take the methodology course during their last semester in the teacher education program. However, Hutchin's evaluation showed that this had a negative effect on the project. From the teaching assistants' perspective, taking this course at this time meant that while they could *develop* materials, they had few opportunities to *use* them. Thus, there was no incentive for them to do anything more than fulfill the materials development requirements for the methodology course, since they would have no further opportunity to experiment with their materials in subsequent semesters. As a result, teachers did not contribute to the banks of materials, they did not use each others' materials, and they did not revise materials that theoretically already existed but that in practice disappeared after their authors graduated from the teacher education program. In short, while anonymous evaluations of the methodology course carried out by the university's evaluation service consistently identified the materials development project as one of the most enjoyable and valuable parts of the methodology course, the materials that teachers developed in this class did not contribute to the long-term development of the ESL program's curriculum. For this reason, I persuaded my faculty colleagues that teaching assistants should enroll in the methodology course during the first semester they taught in the ESL program – when it would be most useful to both the teaching assistants and the project.

∞ **Text Link 157**

For discussion of organization development-related issues, see Text Links 2, 37, 42, 73, 80, 104, 105, 107, 138, and 146.

In short, Hutchin's evaluation showed that an expanded program of organization development was necessary (see Text Link 157). The CATI project's initial model of organization development had focused excessively on developing the knowledge that teaching assistants had to have in order to implement task-based language teaching. Consequently, organization development had been limited to the development of a single methodology course. I recognized that this narrow focus on Knowing was inadequate for servicing the needs of project participants. For this reason, the model of organization development I presently use includes Communicating, Monitoring, and Evaluation modules. This more mature model of organization development has evolved gradually over the two years that have elapsed since Hutchin's evaluation and provides me with the multiple tools I need to support the CATI project's aims and goals.

This program of organization development seems to have been successful in correcting the problems identified by Hutchin. I have expanded the Knowing module to include three courses I teach. Subsequently, nine out of eleven teaching assistants whom I surveyed in the 1993–4 end-of-year evaluation rated the overall usefulness of the methodology course to their professional development as very high, and two rated it as high (see Appendix 2, question C4). Two teaching assistants rated the utility of the curriculum design course as very high, six responded that the question was not applicable because they had not taken the course (which, unlike the methodology course, is an elective), and two did not answer (see question C5). Finally, four rated the usefulness of the action research course as very high, and two rated it as high. The question was not applicable for four respondents, and one did not answer (see question C6).

From an organization development point of view, the Communicating module has proved to be as, if not more, important than the Knowing module as a resource for diffusing the project's innovations (see Text Link 158). Thus, it was important to find out how effective my assistant and I were in communicating the project's aims and

∞ **Text Link 158**

See Text Link 120.

goals to participants. I asked respondents to the 1993–4 evaluation to answer seven questions (see questions D1–D7) that address these issues. Five teaching assistants believed that communication between them and the project director was very effective, and six rated it as effective (question D1). Four respondents replied that the project director was very accessible, and seven thought he was accessible (question D3). Nine respondents believed the project director to be administratively very effective, and two effective (question D5). Thus, progress in the area of communication has been made.

In addition, I asked teaching assistants to evaluate the other resources used to communicate the project's aims and goals. These resources include the orientation for new teaching assistants, weekly staff meetings, teachers' portfolios and journals, the TAlist, the ESL Service Courses folder, and the classroom observation process. Almost all respondents either strongly agreed or agreed that these observations had been useful (see questions D21–24 in Appendix 2). In most cases, the remaining resources received similarly high ratings.

More specifically, four teaching assistants thought the *orientation* for new teachers was very helpful and another four thought it was helpful. Two responded that the question was not applicable, and one did not respond (see question C7). Seven respondents rated the overall usefulness of weekly *meetings* as very high and three as high; one did not respond (see question D8). More specific questions about the utility of teachers' *presentations* and *reports* at these meetings yielded the following information. Six respondents expressed very high levels of satisfaction with presentations, and five expressed high levels of satisfaction (see question D9). Seven respondents expressed very high levels of satisfaction with teaching assistants' presentations on their materials development and action research projects, three expressed high levels of satisfaction, and one claimed the question was not applicable (see question D11). Six respondents expressed very high levels of satisfaction with the usefulness of outside guest speakers' contributions to their meetings, three expressed high levels of satisfaction, and two did not answer (see question D10). Seven respondents strongly agreed that portfolios were useful as a resource for documenting teachers' professional evolution, three agreed, and one disagreed (see question D15). A similar pattern emerged concerning the utility of journals: Four strongly agreed that journals were useful, six agreed, and one disagreed (see question D16). In addition, six respondents strongly agreed that the TAlist was a useful tool of communication among project participants, four agreed, and one disagreed (see question D17). Finally, nine respondents strongly agreed that the ESL Service Courses folder was a valuable professional resource for disseminating and archiving teaching assistants' in-house materials, and two agreed (see question D18).

Given these favorable evaluations of the individual resources developed to sustain the implementation of primary innovations in the CATI project, it should not be surprising that the teaching assistants judged that the project was either very helpful or helpful to both their current and future professional development. Ten out of eleven teaching assistants rated the experience of teaching in the ESL courses as very helpful to their ongoing professional development; one rated it as helpful (see question B4). Moreover, seven TAs rated the experience of teaching in the ESL courses as very helpful preparation for their long-term career goals, and four TAs rated this experience as helpful (see question B5). In contrast with Hutchin's largely negative results, eight teaching assistants claimed very high levels of project ownership, while three claimed high levels of project ownership (see question B1). This result was corroborated by the answers given to question B3: Ten teaching assistants felt very free to initiate innovations and one felt free to do so. These answers are logical, because people are most likely to own innovations that they have initiated themselves. Thus, all teaching assistants surveyed at the end of the 1993–4 academic year perceived the ESL courses to be a valuable resource for their professionalization in both the short and the long terms – a result that translates into much more satisfactory levels of project ownership than Hutchin had found in her earlier evaluation of the CATI project.

In conclusion, the current success of the CATI project has been built on a careful analysis of its initial failures. The setbacks at the beginning of the project were translated over time into a more highly integrated design for the implementation and maintenance of the project. Implementing the CATI project has involved a mix of professional, academic, and managerial change. Thus, the teaching assistants' achievements in developing the primary innovations of new materials, methodological skills, and pedagogical values would not have been possible without the development and implementation of the secondary innovations described in this chapter. In short, the CATI project is now a mature project that possesses the organizational capacity to transform the behaviors and attitudes of its participants. Despite the fact that teaching assistants stay with the CATI project's host teacher education program for only two or three years before graduating, the project has proved itself capable of maintaining curricular innovation. At the level of materials development, for example, units like the Iceman continue to be used and adapted despite the fact that its author has now graduated. New teaching assistants continue to carry out action research on their own and their colleagues' teaching, thus further developing their methodological behaviors and values about teaching.

# III Educational innovation revisited

# 7 The lessons of the CATI project

> Be not the first by whom the new are tried,
> Nor the last to lay the old aside.
> (Alexander Pope, 1711, *An Essay of
> Criticism,* Part II, cited in Rogers 1983:
> 241)

In Chapter 1, I asked why some new ideas or practices spread while others do not. In Chapter 2, I discussed six defining examples of language teaching-related innovations that have been implemented in different kinds of institutions in various parts of the world. These examples allowed me to present in an inductive fashion the specific issues and problems that are raised by investigating diffusion. Having identified these issues, I then formalized the insights derived from Chapter 2 into a deductively presented theoretical framework in Chapter 3, which was developed by answering the question "Who adopts what, where, when, why, and how?" Chapters 4, 5, and 6 showed how this theoretical framework has been used to design, implement, and maintain a project in curriculum and teacher innovation at a research university in the United States.

What, then, are the most important lessons that inform our understanding of educational change, as illustrated by the CATI project? Although effecting change will always be an inexact science – or perhaps it is better called an art – I believe that at least nine general principles about the management of curricular innovation may be abstracted from the CATI project. These principles reflect my own experience as a change agent, but they also echo the collective insights of other applied linguists (Bowers 1987; Brindley and Hood 1991; Henrichsen 1989; Stoller 1995a; White 1988) and also those of writers in education (Fullan 1982a, b, 1993; Fullan and Pomfret 1977; A. Nicholls 1983; Rudduck 1991; Stenhouse 1975), sociology (Rogers 1983; Rogers and Shoemaker 1971), and development planning (Jéquier 1976; Rondinelli 1983, 1987; Rondinelli et al. 1990). We may therefore be reasonably confident that these principles are not particular to the experience gained in the course of implementing the CATI project.

# Some general principles of curricular innovation

PRINCIPLE 1: Curricular innovation is a complex phenomenon (see Text Link 159).

∞ **Text Link 159**
For discussion of the issues that are relevant to formulating Principle 1, see Figure 2.7. Figures 3.1–3.6, and Tables 3.1 and 3.2. In addition, see Text Links 1, 4, 13, 33, 34, 42, 43, 47, 51, 53, 54, 57, 69, 81, 89, 93, 94, 111, 117, 124, 126, and 150.

The definition of curricular innovation proposed in this book – a managed process of development whose principal products are teaching (and/or testing) materials, methodological skills, and pedagogical values that are perceived as new by potential adopters – underlines the complexity of this phenomenon. First, it explicitly emphasizes the fact that the primary goals of any project in curriculum and teacher innovation must be to promote deep, ongoing professional change, which specifically involves engaging teachers in developing new materials, methodological skills, and values. However, the implementation of these primary innovations depends on the institutionalization of secondary administrative and academic innovations, which are products of ongoing organization development by the change agent. Examples of administrative innovations include orientations, staff meetings, and computer technology, and examples of academic innovations include graduate level courses in applied linguistics. In short, we can see that curricular innovation requires an appropriate mix of professional, academic, and administrative change. Teachers are most concerned with implementing primary innovations and often do not appreciate the important role played by secondary innovations in successful educational change. However, change agents in supervisory positions must not only promote the development of primary innovations, they must also develop secondary innovations to enhance the transformational capacity of the host organization to support primary innovations.

Second, this definition implicitly suggests that curricular innovation always takes place within a matrix of cultural, political, economic, institutional, and administrative variables that directly influence the ability of project participants to innovate in meaningful ways. Third, it also implies that the extent to which innovations are accepted or rejected by adopters is influenced by the personalities and previous experiences of participants and by a number of attributes (relative advantage, complexity, form, explicitness, etc.) that all innovations possess to a greater or lesser extent. All of these different variables interact in often unpredictable ways and affect the eventual success or failure of both primary and secondary innovations.

PRINCIPLE 2: The principal job of change agents is to effect desired changes (see Text Link 160).

Effecting change is dependent not only on change agents knowing how change works in theory, but also on their understanding of what change strategies are appropriate to use in solving a particular problem. The choice of a particular change strategy is contingent on the status of the change agent and on the nature of the problem that is to be solved.

> ∞ **Text Link 160**
> For discussion of the issues that are relevant to formulating Principle 2, see Text Links 7, 12, 17, 25, 32, 58, 60–5, 84, 125, and 152.

External change agents should never attempt to use power-coercive strategies, because these individuals do not have the hierarchical authority to do so. Thus, any attempt by external change agents to impose a solution will be seen by potential adopters as illegitimate. Internal change agents may use such a strategy to solve routine administrative problems if little or no innovation is involved. When the problem involves the implementation of primary or secondary innovations, however, a great deal of flexibility is required.

The change agent must always provide strong leadership. This involves providing potential adopters with a clear rationale for curricular innovation at all times and articulating an explicit framework that will give adopters a sense of purpose and direction. Thus, as will be argued in Principle 3, good communication is vital to the success of any project in curricular innovation. When the process of innovation is highly technical and is easily evaluated through statistical procedures – like the development of a test, for example – a research, development, and diffusion strategy may be employed. Change in this instance will be primarily top-down and directed by the change agent. However, when the process of innovation is both complex in human development terms and is not easily evaluated through statistical procedures – like the development of new pedagogical values, for example – a problem-solving, action research approach is both more appropriate and also more effective as a means of promoting fundamental change. Under these conditions, change is largely a bottom-up or horizontal process, in which the change agent's principal role is that of a consultant rather than a manager. In order to promote such a process of professional change, change agents must understand the complex interrelationships that exist between primary and secondary innovations. As already noted, without appropriate organization development in the area of secondary innovations, primary innovations will either not be implemented at all, or they will eventually disappear for lack of long-term institutional support. Change agents must therefore develop appropriate negotiating skills so that they can persuade their administrative superiors to put the resources and prestige of the host institution behind the implementation of secondary innovations. They must also energetically explain the relevance of these innovations to teachers, who may otherwise see these innovations as intrusive busy work that takes away time and energy that they could otherwise be devoting to their teaching.

In order to foster the development of an innovative professional culture among teachers, it is important that change agents encourage teachers to view curriculum work as an ongoing opportunity to experiment with new ideas and practices in their own classrooms. This means that there must be a high tolerance for error, since teachers must be able to learn from their own experiences. Consequently, curricular innovation must be viewed as an iterative process that leads to the gradual improvement over time of both teachers and the curriculum. At the same time, change agents must be careful to provide enough support and guidance so that teachers do not get lost in a directionless process of experimentation for experimentation's sake.

PRINCIPLE 3: Good communication among project participants is a key to successful curricular innovation (see Text Link 161).

> ∞ **Text Link 161**
> For discussion of the issues relevant to formulating Principle 3, see Figures 3.5, 3.6, and 5.1 and Table 5.1. In addition, see Text Links 42, 59, 107, and 109–121.

Of the five systemic components that make up any model of educational organization development (Curriculum Development, Communicating, Knowing, Monitoring, and Evaluating), the Communicating component is arguably the most important factor for the successful implementation of both primary and secondary innovations. Change agents must develop formal communication networks among participants: Indeed they *cannot* afford to leave the development of such communication networks to chance. Furthermore, they should not rely on one channel of communication to the exclusion of all others in their efforts to communicate their ideas to implementers. Change agents should use different resources to communicate with adopters, so that adopters may receive the same basic message from different sources and may discuss this message in different forums and at different times. Thus, for example, the implications of the idea that curriculum development and teacher development are two sides of the same coin should be discussed in teachers' handbooks, during orientations for new and continuing teachers, during staff meetings and, where applicable, in the teacher education program's various classes on methodology, testing, action research, and so on. Electronic mail lists can also be used to discuss the implications of the idea that curriculum development and teacher development are indivisible. The bottom line is that change agents should never assume that they have successfully communicated their message by discussing it once or twice. Teachers must be given multiple opportunities in different forums throughout their association with a project to discuss how their professional development activities not only benefit themselves but also feed into the development of a program's curriculum.

PRINCIPLE 4: The successful implementation of educational innovations is based on a strategic approach to managing change (see Text Link 162).

As we saw in Principle 2, change agents can select from a number of approaches to change that are theoretically available to them. Having selected an appropriate approach – and this is largely a contingent decision – change agents must develop an appropriate strategy for planning change. In this respect, probably one of the most difficult issues that must be addressed is the extent to which a project director relies on long-term planning versus medium- and short-term planning to resolve potential problems.

∞ **Text Link 162**
For discussion of the issues that are relevant to formulating Principle 4, see Table 4.1 and Figure 4.1. In addition, see Text Links 15, 16, 77, 79, 86, 98, 102, 103, 131, 134, and 155.

Successful change efforts rely on all three types of planning. At a strategic or curricular level of planning, the long-term aims, goals, and evaluation criteria used to assess project success are most efficiently articulated via a Project Framework matrix. The use of this planning tool ensures that the design, implementation, and evaluation of a project are conceptualized as a single, integrated package. There must also be room for flexibility, so that participants can interpret curricular guidelines in ways that are personally meaningful to them. Thus, there will always be a certain amount of tension between the long-term, strategic perspective of curriculum planning and the medium-term, tactical perspective of syllabus design. In turn, a similar tension will exist between the medium-term, tactical perspective of syllabus design and the short-term, pragmatic perspective of operational planning. It is this tension between different levels of planning that drives the process of curricular innovation forward.

Clearly, the extent to which these tensions will be explicitly negotiated by the various participants in a curriculum and teacher innovation project will vary considerably from project to project. Thus, in some projects, there will be much more negotiation built into the project's model of curricular innovation, while in others there will be considerably less. Regardless, it is essential that change agents have a clear idea of how the model that they are using is actually going to promote a consciously willed and consciously articulated program of change.

On the basis of research carried out primarily in countries with relatively decentralized traditions of educational management – such as the United States, Canada, Britain, and Australia – it seems that managing the process of curricular innovation ideally involves change agents

(1) identifying a problem; (2) consulting with potential adopters to identify potential solutions, clarify misunderstandings, and solicit suggestions for improvement; (3) modifying the proposed solutions in light of feedback received from potential adopters; (4) arranging for the development of whatever supporting resources are necessary (e.g., teacher training); (5) implementing the solutions on a trial basis; and (6) evaluating the solutions when enough experience has been gained and redesigning the solutions if necessary.

It is important to note, however, that such a model of curricular innovation is very much an artifact of the sociocultural context that gave birth to this view of how to manage change. It is therefore quite likely that other models and strategies of change may be culturally more appropriate in contexts of implementation that have more centralized traditions of how to manage change. This aspect of the educational change literature is very much underdeveloped, and further research is needed.

The decentralized, iterative approach to managing change described previously represents an idealization of how the process of change actually happens in practice. Even when such a methodology is consciously used by educational change agents – and often it is not – it is important to note that there is no guarantee that unforeseen events will not change the direction of a project. The same is true of managing change in relatively centralized contexts of implementation. For this reason, I propose Principle 5, which balances the rational view of change expressed in Principle 4 with a more pragmatically informed view of innovation.

PRINCIPLE 5: Innovation is an inherently messy, unpredictable business (see Text Link 163).

∞ **Text Link 163**
For discussion of the issues that are relevant to formulating Principle 5, see Text Links 9, 23, 40, 72, 136, 137, 144, 147, 154, and 156.

Even if change agents consciously use the six steps described earlier to manage curricular innovation, effecting change always turns out to be far messier and more unpredictable than Principle 4 implies. In the context of projects that have the principle aim of promoting human rather than technical development, in particular, participants will always be faced with very high levels of uncertainty and vulnerability. Changes that change agents may perceive to be rational, necessary, and easy to implement may be opposed by potential adopters because, from the perspective of these individuals, these innovations seem entirely irrational, unnecessary, and impossible to implement – thus resulting in low levels of ownership. Alternatively, change agents and adopters may seem to agree that change is necessary, but may have entirely different views as to what change should be implemented and how it should be done. Again, this will lead to low levels of innovation ownership. For

176

these reasons, successful projects in curricular innovation are typically characterized by constant clarifications of participants' understandings and intentions, by backtrackings, and by any number of false starts and changes of direction. This conclusion leads us naturally to Principles 6 and 7.

PRINCIPLE 6: It always takes longer to effect change than originally anticipated (see Text Link 164).

However well-designed a program of change may appear on paper, implementing change will always take longer than anticipated because change agents do not control how potential adopters react to innovations. Adopters need to go through their own decision-making processes in evaluating a proposed innovation, and the time it takes for individuals to reach a decision inevitably varies considerably from

∞ **Text Link 164**
For discussion of the issues that are relevant to formulating Principle 6, see Figure 3.4. In addition, see Text Links 5, 7, 33, 39, 49–51, 58, 60–7, 73, 95, and 143.

person to person. Thus, the realistic change agent outlines time frames within which, on the basis of experience, it may be expected that different phases of a project will be implemented. However, the change agent must also treat these time frames as guidelines that, in practice, are more likely to be honored in the breach than in the observance. On the other hand, although it is important to recognize that change agents cannot control the adoption of innovations by potential end users, it is equally important to recognize that skillful change agents can certainly influence the decision-making processes of adopters.

Obviously, the key question is how potential adopters' decision-making processes are most effectively influenced. As we saw during the discussion of the issues pertaining to Principle 2, change agents can select from a number of quite different change strategies. Although the effective change agent knows how to mix and match different strategies to different problems, the use of persuasion over power to promote change will generally be favored. Although the use of power – even legitimate power – may seem more efficient in the short term as a strategy for making end users behave in a certain fashion, their "innovative" behaviors tend to be very mechanistic and superficial. As a result, when coercive pressure is removed, implementers will heave a sigh of relief and revert to their previous ways without any regrets. In order to promote fundamental change, potential adopters must be given choices and opportunities to work out their own interpretations of what a particular innovation means to them. Not surprisingly, if individuals do not feel coerced into behaving and thinking in a certain way, they will be much more likely to consider adopting an innovation. It is for this reason that participatory, problem-solving approaches to change tend to be much more effective in the long term than coercive approaches. It is also the reason why fundamental change mediated through problem-solving approaches to change takes so long to put into place.

PRINCIPLE 7: There is a high likelihood that change agents' proposals will be misunderstood (see Text Link 165).

**∞ Text Link 165**
For discussion of the issues that are relevant to formulating Principle 7, see Table 4.1. In addition, see Text Links 5, 9, 23, 40, 51, 72, 79, 129, 131, 134-7, 142-4, 147, 154, and 156.

Even when change agents appreciate the importance of communicating their aims and objectives to implementers as explicitly as possible, it is still quite likely that they will be at least partly misunderstood by potential adopters. Change agents must accept the fact that misunderstandings are inherent in promoting change. Rather than regarding such miscommunications as tiresome distractions, wise change agents will exploit such naturally occurring breakdowns as welcome opportunities to engage potential adopters in an ongoing dialogue about the aims and goals of a project and to clarify whatever concerns they may have. However, change agents should not wait for such opportunities to occur spontaneously: *They should make them happen on a regular basis as a means of promoting participants' sense of owning a project's innovations.* For this reason, evaluations must be built into any project in curricular and teacher innovation, preferably through an instrument such as a Project Framework matrix. By laying out *what* changes are desired, by identifying *how* these changes are to be evaluated, and by specifying *when* evaluations are to occur, a formal mechanism is built into projects that allows participants to check on a regular basis whether they are all operating under the same basic assumptions. If it transpires that this is not the case, then adequate steps must be taken to develop an appropriate consensus.

PRINCIPLE 8: It is important for implementers to have a stake in the innovations they are expected to implement (see Text Link 166).

**∞ Text Link 166**
For discussion of the issues that are relevant to formulating Principle 8, see Table 2.7. In addition, see Text Links 9, 13, 18, 23, 40, 55, 56, 64, 72, 86, 89, 90, 92, 96, 111, 117, 123, 125, 129, 136, 137, 139, 144, 147, 152, 154, and 156.

Innovations possess a range of attributes that either promote or inhibit their diffusion. Clearly, these attributes are not all equal. Experience suggests that teachers are much more likely to commit themselves to using an innovation if they (1) have a clear idea of what it is, (2) believe it to be feasible, (3) believe that it addresses a real need, and (4) believe that the costs of innovating in terms of time, energy, and commitment to learning new skills will be outweighed by the advantages that will accrue to them as a result of adopting the innovation. These advantages need not be financial; they may include a sense of greater professionalism, increased recognition and job satisfaction, and the like. All things being equal (and, of course, they never are), the best way of meeting these concerns is to ensure that teachers feel they *own* the innovations they implement. In order for this to happen, teachers must have the opportunity to actually use – and, in the process, also adapt and modify – an innovation. In this way, they can assess its relative advantages and disadvantages on the basis of their own experience.

PRINCIPLE 9: It is important for change agents to work through opinion leaders, who can influence their peers (see Text Link 167).

As already noted in Principle 6, change agents cannot control adopters' reactions to innovations, but they can influence the way in which teachers react to their proposals in important ways. Tactically, for example, it is important for change agents to work through early adopters. As respected opinion leaders within a peer group, early adopters encourage later adopters to adopt new pedagogical ideas and practices by modeling particular adoption behaviors. There are two distinct types of opinion leaders. They can be individuals who hold formal positions in the administrative hierarchy of an organization, an obvious one being a teacher who has "risen through the ranks" to a supervisory position. Opinion leaders of this type have some institutionally derived authority to wield power, but their real power base is the respect of their peers. Consequently, they must be seen to be independent from project directors and change agents so that they are not perceived as puppets whom the change agent is manipulating for personal purposes. If this delicate balancing act can be achieved, formal opinion leaders can contribute very effectively to the diffusion of innovations and to adopters' sense that they own the innovations that they are adopting. However, often as not, opinion leaders are individuals who hold no formally recognized position of authority within the hierarchy. The source of informal opinion leaders' influence among their peers is based exclusively on their experience and perceived excellence as language teaching professionals.

> ∞ **Text Link 167**
> For discussion of the issues that are relevant to formulating Principle 9, see Text Links 9, 23, 40, 54, 72, 99, 110, 129, 136, 137, 144–7, 154, and 156.

It is particularly important that change agents identify opinion leaders as early as possible and that they communicate with them clearly and frequently, since opinion leaders play a key role in the horizontal diffusion of new pedagogical behaviors and attitudes among their colleagues and peers. At critical points in the decision-making process – for example, if there is widespread opposition to a proposal for change – change agents may elect to take a back seat in the discussion and not argue the case for change themselves. Instead, they may rely on opinion leaders who support their position to persuade fellow potential adopters of the necessity and desirability of an innovation. In this way, the proposed innovation will ultimately be perceived to be the teachers' own – particularly if it has been modified in the process of negotiation – and will therefore be much more likely to be adopted. Perhaps the best compliment that can be paid a change agent in such circumstances is for the viability of a proposed change to be attributed to the skill of opinion leaders' powers of persuasion, even if, objectively speaking, the change agent was the originator of the proposal for change.

## Conclusion

Because innovation is always a highly context-specific phenomenon, it is most unlikely that the specific solutions devised to resolve problems in one particular project will be directly transferable to other contexts of implementation. However, as I have argued throughout this book, we can learn a great deal from case studies like the CATI project about the kinds of issues and problems that all change agents are likely to encounter in managing change, whatever kinds of changes they are trying to implement and whatever context of implementation they work in.

Given the fledgling nature of the change literature in applied linguistics, there is a continuing need for further research that documents how innovations of different kinds have been designed, implemented, and maintained in a variety of contexts of implementation. Case studies will enable language teaching professionals to further develop their knowledge and understanding of what is involved in effecting educational change. At the same time, there is also a need for experimental research, which can provide a complementary perspective on the management of educational change. It is also important that the insights that such a research program can provide be fed into the mainstream of applied linguistics, and thereby into the content of graduate teacher education programs. I hope that this book has contributed in a small way to the adoption of what is still an innovation in second and foreign language teaching – namely, a diffusion-of-innovations perspective on curriculum and teacher innovation.

# Appendix 1    Transcription conventions

| | |
|---|---|
| T | teacher |
| L1, L2, etc. | identified learner (learner 1, learner 2, etc.) |
| L | unidentified learner |
| L3? | probably learner 3 (L3) |
| LL | several or all learners simultaneously |
| /yes/ /yah/ /ok/ / | overlapping or simultaneous listening |
| / / /huh?/ / /oh/ / / | responses, brief comments, etc., by two, three, or an unspecified number of learners |
| = | (a) turn continues below, at the next identical symbol<br>(b) if inserted at the end of one speaker's turn and the beginning of the next speaker's adjacent turn, indicates no gap between the two turns |
| (+) (++) (1) | pauses; (+) = a pause of between .1 and .5 of a second; (++) = a pause of between .6 and .9 of a second; and (1) (2) (3) = pauses of one, two, or three seconds, respectively |
| ? | rising intonation, not necessarily a question |
| ! | strong emphasis with falling intonation |
| ok. now. well. | period: falling (final) intonation |
| so, the next thing: | comma: low-rising intonation suggesting continuation |
| e:r, the::: | one or more colons: lengthening of the preceding sound |
| *emphasis* | italic type: marked stress |
| SYLVIA | capitals: increased volume |
| °the next thing | degree sign: decreased volume |
| (radio) | single parentheses: unclear or probable item |

(Adapted with permission of Longman Group UK Ltd. from L. van Lier, 1988, *The Classroom and the Language Learner*, pp. 243–4.)

*Appendix 1*

| | |
|---|---|
| ((coughs)) | double parentheses: comments about the transcript, including nonverbal actions |
| ((unintelligible)) | a stretch of talk that is unintelligible to the analyst |
| no- | hyphen: abrupt cut-off, with level pitch |
| Peter | capitals: used only for proper names, not to indicate beginnings of sentences |
| [si:m] | brackets: phonetic transcription |
| hhh | in-drawn breath |
| hhh | exhaled breath |
| (hhh) | laughter tokens |

# Appendix 2 ESL Service Courses TA Evaluation, 1993–4

Please respond *anonymously* to the questions below by entering your answers directly into the electronic document you are now reading. When you have finished responding to the questions, please date your evaluation in the space provided below and print a paper copy. Please hand in the paper copy and the electronic version of this evaluation to [the administrative secretary] by Friday May 5 at 12 noon. The purpose of this evaluation is to meet any concerns that emerge from this survey and to improve the management of the ESL Service Courses.

Date:

A: Background Information (TAs)

Please highlight your answer to each question in **bold script**. Please select *one alternative only* for each question:

1. You teach in the graduate/undergraduate sequence of courses.

Graduate: 7
Undergraduate: 4
$N = 11$

2. You have taught in the ESL Service Courses for:

1/2/3/4/5/6/7/8/9/10 semesters

Range: 2–7 semesters
Average: 3 semesters

3. Before joining the ESL Service Courses, you had taught ESL for up to:

1/2/3/4/5/6/7/8/9/10 years

Range: 1–18 years
Average: 3.82 years

4. What are your career aspirations? Please briefly describe in the space provided below what kind of job you would like to have after you graduate, where you would like to work, and whether you would ultimately like to get a Ph.D. in applied linguistics or a related field.

---

Career aspirations:

---

5. Please rate your level of familiarity with task-based language teaching (TBLT) before you joined the ESL Service Courses:

| | |
|---|---|
| Very familiar | 1 |
| Familiar | 2 |
| Unfamiliar | 4 |
| Very unfamiliar | 3 |
| [Other] | 1 |

(I utilized tasks extensively in my teaching prior to coming here, but I was unfamiliar with the formal theories behind the use of tasks. I simply felt that students would learn best by being given opportunities to use the language.)

6. Please feel free to provide any further information which you feel should be included in this section of the evaluation:

---

Extra information:

---

B:  General Information (TAs)

1. Please rate your level of ownership of the ESL Service Courses:

| | |
|---|---|
| Very high | 8 |
| High | 3 |
| Low | 0 |
| Very low | 0 |

2. Please rate how well you feel you understand the principles of TBLT:

| | |
|---|---|
| Very well | 4 |
| Well | 5 |
| [Average] | 1 |
| Badly | 1 |
| Very badly | 0 |

3. Please rate how free you feel to initiate innovations in the ESL Service Courses:

| | |
|---|---|
| Very free | 10 |
| Free | 1 |

Constrained        0
Very constrained   0

4. Please rate how helpful the experience of teaching in the ESL Service Courses has been to your ongoing professional development as a language teaching professional:

Very helpful     10
Helpful          1
Unhelpful        0
Very unhelpful   0

5. Please rate how helpful the experience of teaching in the ESL Service Courses has been to help you prepare for your long-term career goals:

Very helpful     7
Helpful          4
Unhelpful        0
Very unhelpful   0

6. Please indicate whether you agree or disagree with the following statements:

TAs are encouraged to interact with teachers who teach other courses and levels:

Strongly agree      5
Agree               6
Disagree            0
Strongly disagree   0

7. TAs have adequate information about how TBLT operates in the ESL Service Courses:

Strongly agree      8
Agree               2
Disagree            1
Strongly disagree   0

8. TAs have sufficient information regarding the way in which individual courses interface with others in the ESL Service Courses.

Strongly agree      7
Agree               3
Disagree            1   (I am assuming that "individual courses"
                         refers to student's field-specific courses.)
Strongly disagree   0

9. Please state where you do the bulk of your "ideas sharing." Please select only one option.

| | |
|---|---|
| All in your office | 4 |
| At weekly level meetings | 6 |
| On the TAlist | 0 |
| Other (please specify) | 1 — in classes, such as 367 & 312 |

10. Do you think there is a need to find new ways to foster this kind of "ideas sharing" within the ESL Service Courses? If so, how do you think this need might be met?

_____

Please elaborate:

_____

11. Please feel free to provide any further information which you feel should be included in this section of the evaluation:

_____

Extra information:

_____

C: Professional Support

1. Please rate how well-informed you feel about current issues in syllabus design insofar as these issues have a direct impact on your practical responsibilities as a TA:

| | |
|---|---|
| Very well-informed | 6 |
| Well-informed | 4 |
| Badly informed | 1 |
| Very badly informed | 0 |

2. Please rate how well-informed you feel about current issues in materials development insofar as these issues have a direct impact on your practical responsibilities as a TA:

| | |
|---|---|
| Very well-informed | 6 |
| Well-informed | 4 |
| Badly informed | 1 |
| Very badly informed | 0 |

3. Please rate how well-informed you feel about current issues in methodology insofar as these issues have a direct impact on your practical responsibilities as a TA:

| | |
|---|---|
| Very well-informed | 6 |
| Well-informed | 5 |
| Badly informed | 0 |
| Very badly informed | 0 |

4. Please rate the overall usefulness of EIL 367 (Introduction to Communicative Approaches to Second and Foreign Language Teaching) to TAs' professional development:

| | |
|---|---|
| Very high | 9 |
| High | 2 |
| Low | 0 |
| Very low | 0 |

5. If you took EIL 487 (Action Research), please rate the overall usefulness of this course to TAs' professional development:

| | |
|---|---|
| Very high | 2 |
| High | 0 |
| Low | 0 |
| Very low | 0 |
| Not applicable | 6 |
| [No answer] | 3 |

6. If you took EIL 312 (special section for experienced TAs taught by the Academic Coordinator), please rate the overall usefulness of this course to TAs' professional development:

| | |
|---|---|
| Very high | 4 |
| High | 2 |
| Low | 0 |
| Very low | 0 |
| Not applicable | 4 |
| [No answer] | 1 |

7. If you have ever participated in a week-long orientation for *new* TAs, please give your retrospective assessment of how helpful this orientation was in preparing you for your duties as a TA:

| | |
|---|---|
| Very helpful | 4 |
| Helpful | 4 |
| Unhelpful | 0 |
| Very unhelpful | 0 |
| Not applicable | 2 |
| [No answer] | 1 |

Please elaborate:

8. If you have never participated in a week-long orientation for *new* TAs, but were given an "abbreviated" orientation instead, please give your retrospective assessment of how helpful this "abbreviated" orientation was in preparing you for your duties as a TA:

   | | |
   |---|---|
   | Very helpful | 1 |
   | Helpful | 2 |
   | Unhelpful | 0 |
   | Very unhelpful | 0 |
   | Not applicable | 6 |
   | [No answer] | 2 |

Please elaborate:

9. If you have ever participated in an orientation for *continuing* TAs, please give your retrospective assessment of how helpful this orientation was in preparing you for your duties as a TA:

   | | |
   |---|---|
   | Very helpful | 0 |
   | Helpful | 2 |
   | Unhelpful | 0 |
   | Very unhelpful | 0 |
   | Not applicable | 6 |
   | [No answer] | 3 |

Please elaborate:

10. Think about the first week of your first semester. How could this time have been made easier for you?

Please elaborate:

11. What were some of the highlights of your experience in the ESL Service Courses? What were some of the low points? What recommendations would you make for improvement based on your own experience of teaching in the ESL Service Courses?

Please elaborate:

12. Please feel free to provide any further information which you feel should be included in this section of the evaluation:

Extra information:

D: Administration of the ESL Service Courses

1. Please rate the effectiveness of communication between TAs and the Academic Coordinator:

| | |
|---|---|
| Very effective | 5 |
| Effective | 6 |
| Ineffective | 0 |
| Very ineffective | 0 |

2. Please rate the effectiveness of communication between TAs and the Visiting Teaching Associate:

| | |
|---|---|
| Very effective | 11 |
| Effective | 0 |
| Ineffective | 0 |
| Very ineffective | 0 |

3. Please rate the accessibility of the Academic Coordinator:

| | |
|---|---|
| Very accessible | 4 |
| Accessible | 7 |
| Inaccessible | 0 |
| Very inaccessible | 0 |

4. Please rate the accessibility of the Visiting Teaching Associate:

| | |
|---|---|
| Very accessible | 8 |
| Accessible | 3 |
| Inaccessible | 0 |
| Very inaccessible | 0 |

5. Please rate the overall administrative effectiveness of the Academic Coordinator:

| | |
|---|---|
| Very effective | 9 |
| Effective | 2 |
| Ineffective | 0 |
| Very ineffective | 0 |

6. Please rate the overall administrative effectiveness of the Visiting Teaching Associate:

| | |
|---|---|
| Very effective | 9 |
| Effective | 1 |
| Ineffective | 0 |
| Very ineffective | 0 |
| [No answer] | 1 |

7. Please rate your level of satisfaction with the way in which attendance problems, student complaints, and student proficiencies were handled:

| | |
|---|---|
| Very high | 9 |
| High | 1 |
| Low | 1 |
| Very low | 0 |

8. Please rate your level of satisfaction concerning the usefulness of weekly level meetings:

| | |
|---|---|
| Very high | 7 |
| High | 3 |
| Low | 0 |
| Very low | 0 |
| [No answer] | 1 |

9. Please rate your level of satisfaction concerning the usefulness of presentations at weekly level meetings:

| | |
|---|---|
| Very high | 6 |
| High | 5 |
| Low | 0 |
| Very low | 0 |

10. Please rate your level of satisfaction concerning the usefulness of guest speakers at weekly level meetings:

| | |
|---|---|
| Very high | 6 |
| High | 3 |
| Low | 0 |

Very low          0
[No answer]       2

11. Please rate your level of satisfaction concerning the usefulness of EIL 367- and EIL 312-related project discussions at weekly level meetings:

Very high         7
High              3
Low               0
Very low          0
[Not Applicable]  1

12. Please rate your level of satisfaction concerning the amount of time devoted to "sharing ideas" with colleagues at weekly level meetings:

Very high         7
High              3
Low               1
Very low          0

13. Please comment on the weekly level meetings: What did you like about them? What didn't you like about them? What suggestions would you make for next year's meeting format?

Please elaborate:

14. Please indicate whether you agree or disagree with the statements in 14–18:

End-of-semester TA evaluations accurately and fairly represented your work.

Strongly agree         7
Agree                  2
(Agree – but I haven't
seen this semester's yet.)  1
Disagree               1
Strongly disagree      0

15. The teachers' portfolios are a useful resource for documenting TAs' professional evolution.

Strongly agree         7

Agree             3
Disagree          1
Strongly disagree 0

16. The teachers' journals are a useful resource for documenting TAs' professional evolution.

Strongly agree    4
Agree             6
Disagree          1
Strongly disagree 0

17. The TAlist is a valuable tool of communication in the ESL Service Courses.

Strongly agree    6
Agree             4
Disagree          1
Strongly disagree 0

18. The ESL Service Courses folder is a valuable professional resource for disseminating and archiving the in-house materials produced by TAs.

Strongly agree    9
Agree             2
Disagree          0
Strongly disagree 0

19. Did you find the classroom observations process (i.e., preobservation, observation, and postobservation) generally useful? If so, how did this process contribute to your ongoing professionalization and development as a teacher? If not, what could be done to enhance this process?

_____

Please elaborate:


_____

20. Postobservation discussions effectively helped to address your criteria for evaluation.

Strongly agree    8
Agree             3
Disagree          0
Strongly disagree 0

21. Postobservation discussions effectively helped to identify your strengths as a teacher.

| | |
|---|---|
| Strongly agree | 10 |
| Agree | 1 |
| Disagree | 0 |
| Strongly disagree | 0 |

22. Postobservation discussions effectively helped to identify your weaknesses as a teacher.

| | |
|---|---|
| Strongly agree | 7 |
| Agree | 1 |
| [Agree, but not entirely] | 1 |
| Disagree | 2 |
| Strongly disagree | 0 |

23. Postobservation discussions effectively helped to identify strategies to enhance future lessons and/or materials.

| | |
|---|---|
| Strongly agree | 8 |
| [Strongly agree/Agree] | 2 |
| Agree | 1 |
| Disagree | 0 |
| Strongly disagree | 0 |

24. Postobservation discussions effectively helped to encourage you to reflect on your teaching methodology and materials.

| | |
|---|---|
| Strongly agree | 7 |
| [Strongly agree/Agree] | 1 |
| Agree | 3 |
| Disagree | 0 |
| Strongly disagree | 0 |

Please elaborate:

Thank you for completing this evaluation. We appreciate the time and effort you have put into providing this feedback and will make every effort to incorporate your suggestions for improvement.

# References

Abbs, B., A. Ayton, and I. Freebairn (1975). *Strategies*. London: Longman.

Abelson, R. (1967). Definition. In P. Edwards (Ed.), *The encyclopedia of philosophy*, vol. 2, 314–24. London and New York: Macmillan and Free Press.

Abu Samah, A. (1984). The English language (communicational) curriculum for upper secondary schools in Malaysia: Rationale, design and implementation. In J. A. S. Read (Ed.), *Trends in language syllabus design*, 193–215. Singapore: SEAMEO-RELC.

Adams, R. S., and D. Chen (1981). *The process of educational innovation: An international perspective*. London: Kogan Page/UNESCO Press.

Alderson, C. (1992). Guidelines for the evaluation of language education. In C. Alderson and A. Beretta (Eds.), *Evaluating second language education*, 274–304. Cambridge: Cambridge University Press.

Alderson, C., and A. Beretta (1992a). Editors' postcript to Alderson and Scott paper. In C. Alderson and A. Beretta (Eds.), *Evaluating second language education*, 58–60. Cambridge: Cambridge University Press.

———. (1992b). Editors' postcript to Beretta paper. In C. Alderson and A. Beretta (Eds.), *Evaluating second language education*, 271–3. Cambridge: Cambridge University Press.

Alderson, C., and M. Scott (1992). Insiders, outsiders and participatory evaluation. In C. Alderson and A. Beretta (Eds.), *Evaluating second language education*, 25–58. Cambridge: Cambridge University Press.

Alderson, J. C., and D. Wall (1993). Does washback exist? *Applied Linguistics* 14(2): 115–29.

Allwright, R. (1977). Language learning through communication practice. *ELT Documents* 76(3): 2–14. Reprinted 1979 in C. J. Brumfit and K. Johnson (Eds.), *The communicative approach to language teaching*, 167–82. Oxford: Oxford University Press.

Allwright, R., and A. Waters (Eds.) (1994). *Language in aid projects: Toward the year 2000*. Lancaster: Centre for Research in Language Education, Lancaster University.

Anderson, A., and T. Lynch (1988). *Listening*. Oxford: Oxford University Press.

Aoki, T. (1984). Towards a reconceptualization of curriculum implementation. In D. Hopkins and M. Wideen (Eds.), *Alternative perspectives on school improvement*, 107–18. Philadelphia: Falmer Press.

Aruchanalam, A., and P. Menon (1990). Suitability of the KBSR English Language Syllabus in Selected Urban Primary Schools in Malaysia. Vote F Project Report. Kuala Lumpur: Pusat Bahasa University of Malaysia.

195

# References

Bailey, K. M. (1983). Competitiveness and anxiety in adult second language learning: Looking at and through the diary studies. In H. W. Seliger and M. H. Long (Eds.), *Classroom oriented research in second language acquisition,* 67–103. Rowley, Mass.: Newbury House.

———. (1990). The use of diary studies in teacher education programs. In J. C. Richards and D. Nunan (Eds.), *Second language teacher education,* 215–26. Cambridge: Cambridge University Press.

———. (1992). The processes of innovation in language teacher development: What, why and how teachers change. In J. Flowerdew, M. Brock, and S. Hsia (Eds.), *Perspectives on second language teacher education,* 253–81. Hong Kong: City Polytechnic of Hong Kong.

Bailey, K. M., and R. Ochsner (1983). A methodological review of the diary studies: Windmill tilting or social science? In K. M. Bailey, M. H. Long, and S. Peck (Eds.), *Second language acquisition studies,* 188–97. Rowley, Mass.: Newbury House.

Baldridge, J. V., and T. E. Deal (1983). The basics of change in educational organizations. In J. V. Baldridge and T. E. Deal (Eds.), *The dynamics of organizational change in education,* 1–11. Berkeley, Cal.: McCutchan.

Banbrook, L., and P. Skehan (1990). Classrooms and display questions. In C. Brumfit and R. Mitchell (Eds.), *Research in the language classroom,* 141–52. ELT Documents 133. London: Modern English Publications/British Council.

Baumgardner, R. J., D. Chamberlain, A. T. Dharmapriya, and B. W. Staley (1986). ESP for engineers: Two approaches. In M. L. Tickoo (Ed.), *Language across the curriculum,* 93–104. Singapore: SEAMEO-RELC.

Beretta, A. (1989). Attention to form or meaning? Error treatment in the Bangalore Project. *TESOL Quarterly* 23: 283–303.

———. (1990). Implementation of the Bangalore Project. *Applied Linguistics* 11(4): 321–37.

———. (1992a). What can be learned from the Bangalore evaluation. In C. Alderson and A. Beretta (Eds.), *Evaluating second language education,* 250–71. Cambridge: Cambridge University Press.

———. (1992b). Evaluation of language education: An overview. In C. Alderson and A. Beretta (Eds.), *Evaluating second language education,* 5–24. Cambridge: Cambridge University Press.

Blair, R. W. (1982). *Innovative approaches to language teaching.* Rowley, Mass.: Newbury House.

Bottomley, Y., J. Dalton, and C. Corbel (1994). *From proficiency to competencies.* Sydney: National Centre for English Language Teaching Research.

Bowers, R. (1980a). War stories and romances: Interchanging experience in ELT. In E. Smyth (Ed.), *Projects in materials design,* 71–81. ELT Documents Special. London: British Council.

———. (1980b). The background of students from the Indian sub-continent. *Study modes and academic development of overseas students,* 104–13. ELT Documents 109. London: British Council.

———. (1983). Project planning and performance. In C. J. Brumfit (Ed.), *Language teaching projects for the third world,* 99–120. ELT Documents 116. London: British Council.

————. (Ed.) (1987). *Language teacher education: An integrated programme for ELT teacher training.* ELT Documents 125. London: Modern English Publications/British Council.

Boyle, H. (Ed.) (1987). *Dunford House seminar report, 1987.* London: British Council.

Breen, M. P. (1984). Process syllabuses for the language classroom. In C. J. Brumfit (Ed.), *General English syllabus design,* 47–60. ELT Documents 118. Oxford: Pergamon/British Council.

————. (1985). Authenticity in the language classroom. *Applied Linguistics* 6(1): 60–70.

————. (1987). Learner contributions to task design. In C. N. Candlin and D. F. Murphy (Eds.), *Language learning tasks,* 23–46. Lancaster Practical Papers in English Language Education 7. Hemel Hempstead: Prentice Hall International.

Breen, M. P., and C. N. Candlin (1980). The essentials of a communicative curriculum. *Applied Linguistics* 1(2): 89–111.

Brickell, H. M. (1969). Appraising the effects of innovation in local schools. In R. W. Tyler (Ed.), *Educational evaluation: New roles, new means,* 284–304. Chicago: National Society for the Study of Education.

Brindley, G. (1984). *Needs analysis and objective-setting in the Adult Migrant Education Program.* Sydney: Adult Migrant Education Service.

Brindley, G., and S. Hood (1991). Curriculum innovation in adult ESL. In G. Brindley (Ed.), *The second language curriculum in action,* 232–48. Sydney: National Centre for English Language Teaching Research, Macquarie University.

Brock, C. (1986). The effect of referential questions on ESL classroom discourse. *TESOL Quarterly* 20: 47–60.

Brown, G., and G. Yule (1983). *Teaching the spoken language.* Cambridge: Cambridge University Press.

Brumfit, C. J. (1981). National syllabuses revisited: A response. *Applied Linguistics* 2(1): 90–2.

————. (1984). The Bangalore procedural syllabus. *ELT Journal* (38)4: 233–41.

————. (1991). Problems in defining instructional methodologies. In K. de Boot, R. B. Ginsberg, and C. Kramsch (Eds.), *Foreign language research in crosscultural perspective,* 133–44. Amsterdam: Benjamins.

————. (Ed.) (1983). *Language teaching projects in the Third World.* ELT Documents 116. Oxford: Pergamon.

Budd, R., and T. Wright (1992). Putting a process syllabus into practice. In D. Nunan (Ed.), *Collaborative language learning and teaching,* 208–29. Cambridge: Cambridge University Press.

Burns, A., and G. Brindley (Eds.) (1994). *Prospect* 9(2). Entire issue on competency-based training. Sydney: National Centre for English Language Teaching Research.

Burns, A., and S. Hood (1995). *Teachers' voices: Exploring course design in a changing curriculum.* Sydney: National Centre for English Language Teaching Research, Macquarie University.

Candlin, C. N. (1984a). Syllabus design as a critical process. In C. J. Brumfit (Ed.), *General English syllabus design,* 29–46. ELT Documents 118. Oxford: Pergamon/British Council.

197

————. (1984b). Applying a systems approach to curriculum innovation in the public sector. In J. A. S Read (Ed.), *Trends in language syllabus design,* 151–79. Singapore: Singapore University Press for SEAMEO-RELC.

————. (1987). Towards task-based language learning. In C. N. Candlin and D. F. Murphy (Eds.), *Language learning tasks,* 5–22. Lancaster Practical Papers in English Language Education 7. Hemel Hempstead: Prentice Hall.

Candlin, C. N., C. J. Bruton, J. H. Leather, and E. G. Woods (1981). Designing modular materials for communicative language learning; an example: Doctor–patient communication skills. In L. Selinker, E. Tarone, and V. Hanzeli (Eds.), *English for academic and technical purposes,* 105–33. Rowley, Mass.: Newbury House.

Cazden, C. B. (1988). *Classroom discourse: The language of teaching and learning.* Portsmouth, N.H.: Heinemann.

Celani, M. A., J. L. Holmes, R. C. G. Ramos, and M. R. Scott (1988). *The Brazilian ESP project: An evaluation.* São Paulo: Editorada PUC-SP.

Chin, R., and K. D. Benne (1976). General strategies for effecting changes in human systems. In W. G. Bennis, K. D. Benne, R. Chin, and K. E. Corey (Eds.), *The planning of change,* 3rd ed., 22–45. New York: Holt, Rinehart and Winston.

Chinitz, L. (1995). The effect of group dynamics and task design on learner participation in small group work. EIL 312 term paper, Urbana-Champaign: University of Illinois.

Clarke, D. F. (1991). The negotiated syllabus: What is it and how is it likely to work? *Applied Linguistics* 12(1): 13–28.

Cohen, D. K., and L. Manion (1985). *Research methods in education,* 2nd ed. London: Croom Helm.

Cooper, R. L. (1982). A framework for the study of language spread. In R. L. Cooper (Ed.), *Language spread: Studies in diffusion and social change,* 5–36. Bloomington: Indiana University Press and Washington, D.C.: Center for Applied Linguistics.

————. (1989). *Language planning and social change.* Cambridge: Cambridge University Press.

Cracknell, B. E., and J. E. Rednall (1986). *Defining objectives and measuring performance in aid projects and programmes.* London: Overseas Development Administration.

Crocker, A. (1984). Method as input and product of LSP course design. In J. Swales and H. Mustafa (Eds.), *English for specific purposes in the Arab world,* 129–50. Birmingham: University of Aston in Birmingham.

Crookes, G. (1986). Task classification: A cross-disciplinary review. Technical Report #4. Honolulu: Center for Second Language Classroom Research, Social Science Research Institute, University of Hawaii at Manoa.

————. (1991). Second language speech production research: A methodologically-oriented overview. *Studies in Second Language Acquisition* 13(2): 113–32.

————. (1992). Theory format and SLA theory. *Studies in Second Language Acquisition* 14(4): 425–49.

————. (1993). Action research for second language teachers: Going beyond teacher research. *Applied Linguistics* 14(2): 130–44.

Cumming, A. (1993). Teachers' curriculum planning and accommodations of innovations: Three case studies of adult ESL instruction. *TESL Canada Journal* 11(1): 30–52.

DeCosmo, R. D., J. S. Parker, and M. A. Heverly (1991). Total quality management goes to community college. In L. A. Sherr and D. J. Teeter (Eds.), *Total quality management in higher education,* 13–26. New Directions for Institutional Research 71. San Francisco: Jossey-Bass.

Dendrinos, B. (1992). *The EFL textbook and ideology.* Athens, N.C.: Grivas Publications.

Dewey, J. (1910). *How we think.* Boston, Mass.: Heath.

Deyes, A. (1988). A framework for the design of English language projects. Paper presented at the 22nd annual TESOL convention, March 8–13, Chicago.

Doughty, C., and T. Pica (1986). "Information gap" tasks: Do they facilitate second language acquisition? *TESOL Quarterly* 20: 305–25.

Dow, I. I., R. V. Whitehead, and R. L. Wright (1984). *Curriculum implementation: A framework for action.* Alexandria, Va.: ERIC.

Duff, P., and M. Early (1996). In S. Gass and J. Schachter (Eds.), *Issues in conducting classroom research.* Hillsdale, N.J.: Erlbaum.

Ellison, L., and B. Davies (1990). Planning in education management. In B. Davies, L. Ellison, A. Osborne, and J. West-Burnhan (Eds.), *Education management for the 1990s,* 31–44. London: Longman.

Everard, B. E., and G. Morris (1990). *Effective school management,* 2nd ed. London: Paul Chapman.

Eykin, L. B. (1987). Confessions of a high school language teacher, or "Why I never (used to) read *Foreign Language Annals." Foreign Language Annals* 20(2): 265–6.

Freeman, D. (1992) Language teacher education, emerging discourse, and change in classroom practice. In J. Flowerdew, M. Brock, and S. Hsia (Eds.), *Perspectives on second language teacher education,* 1–21. Hong Kong: City Polytechnic of Hong Kong.

Freire, P. (1976). *Pedagogy of the oppressed.* New York: Continuum.

Fullan, M. (1982a). *The meaning of educational change.* New York: Teachers College Press.

———. (1982b). Research into educational innovation. In H. L. Gray (Ed.), *The management of educational institutions,* 245–62. Lewes, Sussex: Falmer Press.

———. (1989). Linking classrooms and school improvement. Address at the annual meeting of the American Educational Research Association, March 27, San Francisco.

———. (1993). *Change forces: Probing the depths of educational reform.* London: Falmer Press.

Fullan, M., and A. Pomfret (1977). Research on curriculum and instruction implementation. *Review of Educational Research* 47(2): 335–93.

Goswami, D., and P. R. Stillman (Eds.) (1987). *Reclaiming the classroom: Teacher research as an agency of change.* Upper Montclair, N.J.: Boynton/Cook.

Goulet, D. (1971). *The cruel choice.* New York: Academic Press.

Gross, N., J. B. Giacquinta, and M. Bernstein (1971). *Implementing organizational innovations.* New York: Basic Books.

Havelock, R. G. (1971). The utilization of educational research and development. *British Journal of Educational Technology* 2(2): 84–97.

———. (1973). *The change agent's guide to innovation in education.* Englewood Cliffs, N.J.: Educational Technology Publications.

Hawkins, B. (1985). Is an "appropriate" response always so appropriate? In S. Gass and C. Madden (Eds.), *Input in second language acquisition*, 162–78. Rowley, Mass.: Newbury House.

Heller, H. (1982). Management development for headteachers. In H. L. Gray (Ed.), *The management of educational institutions*, 219–44. Lewes, Sussex: Falmer Press.

Henrichsen, L. E. (1989). *Diffusion of innovations in English language teaching: The ELEC effort in Japan, 1956–1968.* New York: Greenwood Press.

Hilton, J., and R. D. Webber (1993). Language as a cross-cutting issue. Paper presented at the AIT/RELC Conference on Language Programs in Development Projects, Asian Institute of Technology, April 23–4, Bangkok, Thailand.

Holliday, A. (1992a). Tissue rejection and informal orders in ELT projects: Collecting the right information. *Applied Linguistics* 13(4): 403–24.

———. (1992b). Intercompetence: Sources of conflict between local and expatriate ELT personnel. *System* 20(2): 223–34.

———. (1994a). *Appropriate methodology and social context.* Cambridge: Cambridge University Press.

———. (1994b). The house of TESEP and the communicative approach: The special needs of state English language education. *ELT Journal* 48(1): 3–11.

———. (1995a). Handing over the project: An exercise in restraint. *System* 23(3): 57–68.

———. (1995b). A post-communicative era? Method versus social context. In R. Budd (Ed.), *Appropriate methodology: From classroom methods to classroom processes*, 147–57. Special issue of *Journal of TESOL France.*

———. (1995c). Assessing language needs within an institutional context: An ethnographic approach. *English for Specific Purposes* 14(2): 115–26.

Holliday, A., and T. Cooke (1982). An ecological approach to ESP. In A. Waters (Ed.), *Issues in ESP*, 124–43. Lancaster Practical Papers in English Language Education 5. Oxford: Pergamon Press.

Howatt, A. P. R. (1984). *A history of English language teaching.* Oxford: Oxford University Press.

Huberman, A. M. (1973). *Understanding change in education: An introduction.* Paris: Organization for Economic Co-operation and Development.

Hutchin, J. R. (1992). An evaluation of innovative curriculum development. Unpublished master's thesis, University of Illinois at Urbana-Champaign.

Hutchinson, T., and A. Waters (1987). *English for specific purposes: A learning-centred approach.* Cambridge: Cambridge University Press.

Illich, I. (1970). *Deschooling society.* New York: Harper and Row.

Jéquier, N. (1976). The major policy issues. In N. Jéquier (Ed.), *Appropriate technology: Problems and promises*, 16–112. Paris: Organization for Economic Co-operation and Development.

Johnson, K. (1982a). Five principles in a communicative exercise type. In K.

Johnson (Ed.), *Communicative syllabus design and methodology*, 163–75. Oxford: Pergamon.

———. (1982b). The procedural syllabus. In K. Johnson (Ed.), *Communicative syllabus design and methodology*, 135–44. Oxford: Pergamon.

Kachru, B. B. (1985). Standards, codification and sociolinguistic realism: The English language in the outer circle. In R. Quirk and H. G. Widdowson (Eds.), *English in the world*, 11–30. Cambridge: Cambridge University Press British Council.

Kasper, G. (1985). Repair in foreign language teaching. *Studies in Second Language Acquisition* 7(2): 200–15.

Kelly, P. (1980). From innovation to adaptability: The changing perspective of curriculum development. In M. Galton (Ed.), *Curriculum change: The lessons of a decade*, 65–80. Leicester: Leicester University Press.

Kennedy, C. (1982). Language planning. *Language Teaching* 15(3): 264–84.

———. (1987). Innovating for a change: Teacher development and innovation. *ELT Journal* 41(3): 163–70.

———. (1988). Evaluation of the management of change in ELT projects. *Applied Linguistics* 9(4): 329–42.

———. (1994). Language in aid projects: An overview. In D. Allwright and A. Waters (Eds.), *Language in aid projects: Toward the year 2000, 9–14*. Lancaster: Centre for Research in Language Education, Lancaster University.

Kiniry, M., and E. Strenski (1985). Sequencing expository writing: A recursive approach. *College Composition and Communication* 36(2): 191–202.

Kouraogo, P. (1987). EFL curriculum renewal and INSET in difficult circumstances. *ELT Journal* 41(3): 171–78.

Krashen, S. D. (1981). *Second language acquisition and second language learning*. Oxford: Pergamon.

———. (1982). *Principles and practice in second language acquisition*. Oxford: Pergamon.

———. (1985). *The Input Hypothesis: Issues and implications*. New York: Longman.

Krashen, S. D., and T. D. Terrell (1983). *The natural approach*. Hayward: Cal.: Alemany Press.

Kroeber, A. L. (1923). *Anthropology*. New York: Harcourt Brace.

———. (1937). Diffusionism. In E. R. A. Seligman and A. Johnson (Eds.), *The encyclopedia of the social sciences*, Vol. 3, 139–42. New York: Macmillan.

Kumaravadivelu, B. (1991). Language learning tasks: Teacher intention and learner interpretation. *ELT Journal* 45: 98–107.

———. (1993a). Maximizing learning potential in the communicative classroom. *ELT Journal* 47(1): 12–21.

———. (1993b). The name of the task and the task of naming: Methodological aspects of task-based pedagogy. In G. Crookes and S. M. Gass (Eds.), *Tasks in a pedagogical context: integrating theory and practice, 69–96*. Clevedon, Avon: Multilingual Matters.

Lai, J. (1995). Don't judge a book by its cover: A teacher's perceptions and misperceptions about a student. *IDEAL* 8: 73–91.

Lambright, W. H., and P. Flynn (1980). The role of local bureaucracy-centered coalitions in technology transfer to the city. In J. A. Agnew (Ed.), *Inno-*

*vation research and public policy*, 243–82. Syracuse Geographical Series
5. Syracuse, N.Y.: Syracuse University Press.

Language in Development Forum. N.d. World Wide Web site. URL: http://
deil.lang.uiuc.edu/ldf/

Larsen-Freeman, D. (1983). Training teachers or educating a teacher. In J. E.
Alatis, H. H. Stern, and P. Strevens (Eds.), *Georgetown University round
table on language and linguistics*, 264–74. Washington, D.C.: Georgetown University Press.

Larsen-Freeman, D., and M. H. Long (1991). *An introduction to second language acquisition research*. London: Longman.

Lee, J. F., and W. VanPatten (1990). The question of language program direction is "academic." In S. S. Magnan (Ed.), *Challenges in the 1990s for
college foreign language programs*, 113–27. Boston: Heinle and Heinle.

Leech, G., and J. Svartvik (1975). *A communicative grammar of English*. London: Longman.

Levine, A. (1980). *Why innovation fails*. Albany: State University of New York
Press.

Long, M. H. (1981). Input, interaction and second language acquisition. Unpublished doctoral dissertation, University of California at Los Angeles.

———. (1985). A role for instruction in second language acquisition. In K.
Hyltenstam and M. Pienemann (Eds.), *Modelling and assessing second
language acquisition*, 77–100. Clevedon, Avon: Multilingual Matters.

———. (1989a). Task, group, and task-group interactions. *University of Hawaii Working Papers in ESL* 8(2): 1–26.

———. (1989b). Second language classroom research and teacher education.
In C. Brumfit and R. Mitchell (Eds.), *Research in the language classroom*
161–70. ELT Documents 133. London: Modern English Publications British Council.

———. (1990). The least a second language acquisition theory needs to explain. *TESOL Quarterly* 24(4): 649–66.

———. (1991). Focus on form: A design feature in language teaching methodology. In K. de Bot, R. B. Ginsberg, and C. Kramsch (Eds.), *Foreign
language research in perspective*, 39–51. Amsterdam: Benjamins.

———. (1993). Assessment strategies for second language acquisition theory.
*Applied Linguistics* 14(3): 225–49.

Long, M. H., L. Adams, M. McLean, and F. Castaños (1976). Doing things
with words: Verbal interaction in lockstep and small group classroom
situations. In J. F. Fanselow and R. Crymes (Eds.), *On TESOL '76*, 137–
53. Washington, D.C.: TESOL.

Long, M. H., and G. Crookes (1992). Three approaches to task-based syllabus
design. *TESOL Quarterly* 26(1): 27–56.

———. (1993). Units of analysis in syllabus design: The case for task. In G.
Crookes and S. M. Gass (Eds.), *Tasks in a pedagogical context: Integrating theory and practice*, 9–54. Clevedon, Avon: Multilingual Matters.

Long, M. H., and P. A. Porter (1985). Group work, interlanguage talk and
second language acquisition. *TESOL Quarterly* 19(2): 207–28.

Long, M. H., and C. J. Sato (1983). Classroom foreigner talk discourse: Forms
and functions of teachers' questions. In H. W. Seliger and M. H. Long
(Eds.), *Classroom oriented research in second language acquisition*, 268–
85. Rowley, Mass.: Newbury House.

Loschky, L., and R. Bley-Vroman (1993). Grammar and task-based methodology. In G. Crookes and S. M. Gass (Eds.), *Tasks and language learning: Integrating theory and practice*, 123–67. Clevedon, Avon: Multilingual Matters.

Loucks, S. F., B. W. Newlove, and G. E. Hall (1975). *Measuring levels of use: A manual for trainers, interviewers and raters*. Austin: Research and Development Center for Teacher Education, University of Texas at Austin.

Lynch, B. K. (1996). *Language program evaluation: Theory and practice*. Cambridge: Cambridge University Press.

MacDonald (1991). Critical introduction: From innovation to reform – A framework for analyzing change. In J. Rudduck, *Innovation and change*, 1–13. Milton Keynes: Open University Press.

Maley, A. (1984). Constraints-based syllabuses. In J. A. S. Read (Ed.), *Trends in language syllabus design*, 68–90. Singapore: SEAMEO-RELC.

Markee, N. P. P. (1986a). The importance of sociopolitical factors to communicative course design. *English for Specific Purposes* 5(1): 3–16.

———. (1986b). Toward an appropriate technology model of communicative course design. *English for Specific Purposes* 5(2): 161–72.

———. (1993a). The diffusion of innovation in language teaching. *Annual Review of Applied Linguistics* 13: 229–43.

———. (1993b). Symposium on *Linguistic imperialism*. Perspective 3. *World Englishes* 12(3): 347–51.

———. (1993c). Clarifying the need for language programs. In W. Savage (Ed.), *Language programs in development projects*, 117–24. Bangkok: Asian Institute of Technology/Regional English Language Centre.

———. (1993d). Sustaining learning. In W. Savage (Ed.), *Language programs in development projects*, 471–6. Bangkok: Asian Institute of Technology/Regional English Language Centre.

———. (1994a). Using electronic mail to promote curriculum development. *System* 22(3): 379–89.

———. (1994b). Curricular innovation: Issues and problems. *Applied Language Learning* 5(2): 1–30.

———. (1994c). Toward an ethnomethodological respecification of second language acquisition studies. In A. Cohen, S. Gass, and E. Tarone (Eds.), *Research methodology in second language acquisition*, 89–116. Hillsdale, N.J.: Erlbaum.

———. 1995. Teachers' answers to students' questions: Problematizing the problem of making meaning. *Issues in Applied Linguistics* 6(2):63–92.

———. (1996). Making second language classroom research work. In S. Gass and J. Schachter (Eds.), *Second language classroom research: Issues and opportunities*, 180–218. Hillsdale, N.J.: Erlbaum.

McDonough, J. (1986). English for academic purposes: A research base? *English for Specific Purposes* 5(1): 17–25.

———. (1994). A teacher looks at teachers' diaries. *ELT Journal* 48(1): 57–65.

McHoul, A. (1978). The organization of turns at formal talk in the classroom. *Language in Society* 19: 349–77.

Medgyes, P. (1988). Queries from a communicative teacher. *ELT Journal* 40(2): 107–12.

Miles, M. B. (1964). Educational innovation: The nature of the problem. In

M. B. Miles (Ed.), *Innovation in education,* 1–48. New York: Teachers College Press.

Milstein, M. M. (1982). Training internal change agents for schools. In H. L. Gray (Ed.), *The management of educational institutions,* 163–78. Lewes, Sussex: Falmer Press.

Mintzberg, H., D. Raisinghani, and A. Théoret (1976). The structure of "unstructured" decision processes. *Administrative Science Quarterly* 21(2): 246–75.

Mullins, L. L. (1985). *Management and organizational behaviour.* London: Pitman.

Munby, J. (1978). *Communicative syllabus design.* Cambridge: Cambridge University Press.

———. (1984). Communicative syllabus design: Principles and problems. In J. A. S. Read (Ed.), *Trends in language syllabus design,* 55–67. Singapore: SEAMEO-RELC.

Nababan, P. W. J. (1984). The threshold level for high school English in Indonesia. In J. A. S. Read (Ed.), *Trends in language syllabus design,* 183–92. Singapore: SEAMEO-RELC.

Nicholls, A. (1983). *Managing educational innovations.* London: Allen and Unwin.

Nicholls, J. (1993). *Exchange structure in the ESL classroom: Q-A-C and Q-CQ-A-C sequences in small group interaction,* 183–93. Pragmatics and Language Learning Monograph Series 4. Urbana-Champaign: University of Illinois, Division of English as an International Language.

Nunan, D. (1985). Content familiarity and the perception of textual relationships in second language reading. *RELC Journal* 16: 43–51.

———. (1988a). *The learner-centred curriculum.* Cambridge: Cambridge University Press.

———. (1988b). *Syllabus design.* Oxford: Oxford University Press.

———. (1989). *Designing tasks for the communicative classroom.* Cambridge: Cambridge University Press.

———. (1990). Action research in the language classroom. In J. C. Richards and D. Nunan (Eds.), *Second language teacher education,* 62–81. Cambridge: Cambridge University Press.

———. (1991). Communicative tasks and the language curriculum. *TESOL Quarterly* 25(2): 279–96.

———. (1993). Task-based syllabus design: Selecting, grading and sequencing tasks. In G. Crookes and S. M. Gass (Eds.), *Tasks in a pedagogical context: Integrating theory and practice,* 55–68. Clevedon, Avon: Multilingual Matters.

———. (1995). Contextual factors in determining appropriate language methodologies. In R. Budd (Ed.), *Appropriate methodology: From classroom methods to classroom processes,* 15–25. Special issue of *Journal of TESOL France.*

Palmer, H. E. (1921). *The principles of language study.* London: Harrap. Republished 1964 by Oxford University Press.

Paulston, C. B. (1981). Notional syllabuses revisited: Some comments. *Applied Linguistics* 2(1): 93–5.

Pelz, D. C. (1985). Innovation complexity and the sequence of innovating stages. *Knowledge: Creation, Diffusion, Utilization* 6(3): 261–91.

Pennycook, A. (1989). The concept of method, interested knowledge and the politics of language teaching. *TESOL Quarterly* 23(4): 589–618.

———. (1990). Critical pedagogy and second language education. *System* 18(3): 303–14.

———. (1994). *The cultural politics of English as an international language.* Harlow, Essex: Longman.

Phillipson, R. (1992). *Linguistic imperialism.* Oxford: Oxford University Press.

Pica, T. (1987). Second language acquisition, social interaction and the classroom. *Applied Linguistics* 8: 3–21.

Pica, T., R. Kanagy, and J. Falodun (1993). Choosing and using communication tasks for second language instruction. In G. Crookes and S. M. Gass (Eds.), *Tasks and language learning: Integrating theory and practice,* 9–34. Clevedon, Avon: Multilingual Matters.

Porter, P. A. (1986). How learners talk to each other: Input and interaction in task-centered discussions. In R. R. Day (Ed.), *Talking to learn,* 200–24. Rowley, Mass.: Newbury House.

Porter, P. A., L. M. Goldstein, J. Leatherman, and S. Conrad (1990). An ongoing dialogue: Learning logs for teacher preparation. In J. C. Richards and D. Nunan (Eds.), *Second language teacher education,* 227–40. Cambridge: Cambridge University Press.

Prabhu, N. S. (1984). Procedural syllabuses. In J. A. S. Read (Ed.), *Trends in language syllabus design,* 272–80. Singapore: SEAMEO-RELC.

———. (1985). Coping with the unknown in language pedagogy. In R. Quirk and H. G. Widdowson (Eds.), *English in the world,* 164–73. Cambridge: Cambridge University Press.

———. (1987). *Second language pedagogy.* Oxford: Oxford University Press.

Ramani, E. (1987). Theorizing from the classroom. *ELT Journal* 41(1): 3–11.

Ranta, L., et al. (1996). Involving teachers in second language acquisition research. In S. Gass and J. Schachter (Eds.), *Issues in conducting classroom research.* Hillsdale, N.J.: Erlbaum.

Richards, J. C. (1984). The secret life of methods. *TESOL Quarterly* 18(1): 7–23.

———. (1985). *The context of language teaching.* Cambridge: Cambridge University Press.

Richards, J. C., and C. Lockhart (1994). *Reflective teaching in second language classrooms.* Cambridge: Cambridge University Press.

Richards, J. C., J. Platt, and H. Webber (1985). *Longman dictionary of applied linguistics.* London: Longman.

Richards, J. C., and T. Rodgers (1986). *Approaches and methods in language teaching.* Cambridge: Cambridge University Press.

Richterich, R., and J-L. Chancerel (1977). *Identifying the needs of adults learning a foreign language.* Oxford: Pergamon.

Rogers, E. M. (1983). *The diffusion of innovations,* 3rd ed. London: Macmillan.

———. (1995). *The diffusion of innovations,* 4th ed. London: Macmillan/Free Press.

Rogers, E. M., and F. Shoemaker (1971). *Communication of innovations: A cross-cultural approach,* 2nd ed. New York: Free Press.

# References

Rondinelli, D. (1983). *Development projects as policy experiments*. London: Methuen.

————. (1987). *Development administration and US foreign policy*. Boulder: Rienner.

Rondinelli, D., J. Middleton, and A. M. Verspoor (1990). Planning educational reforms in developing countries. Durham: Duke University Press.

Rounds, P. L. (in press). The classroom-based researcher as fieldworker. In S. Gass and J. Schachter (Eds.), *Issues in conducting classroom research*. Hillsdale, N.J.: Erlbaum.

Rudduck, J. (1991). *Innovation and change*. Milton Keynes: Open University Press.

Samuda, V., and P. L. Rounds (1993). Critical episodes: Reference points for analyzing a task in action. In G. Crookes and S. M. Gass (Eds.), *Tasks in a pedagogical context: Integrating theory and practice*, 125–38. Clevedon, Avon: Multilingual Matters.

Savage, W. (1996). Language and development. In B. Kenny and W. Savage (Eds.), *Language and development: Teachers in a changing world*. London: Longman.

Schmuck, R. A. (1982). Organization development for the 1980s. In H. L. Gray (Ed.), *The management of educational institutions*, 139–62. Lewes, Sussex: Falmer Press.

Simon, R. I. (1982). Mysticism, management and Marx. In H. L. Gray (Ed.), *The management of educational institutions*, 63–85. Lewes, Sussex: Falmer Press.

Stenhouse, L. (1975). *An introduction to curriculum research and development*. London: Heinemann.

Stoller, F. L. (1992). Analysis of innovations in selected higher education intensive English programs: A focus on administrators' perceptions. Unpublished doctoral dissertation, Northern Arizona University.

————. (1994). The diffusion of innovations in intensive ESL programs. *Applied Linguistics* 15(3): 300–27.

————. (1995a). Managing intensive English program innovations. NAFSA Working paper #56. Sewickley, Penn.: NAFSA Publications.

————. (1995b). The diffusion of innovations in intensive ESL programs. *Innovative Higher Education* 19(3): 177–95.

Straker-Cooke, R. H. (1987). Introducing ELT curriculum change. In R. Bowers (Ed.), *Language teacher education: An integrated programme for ELT teacher training*, 17–32. ELT Documents 125. London: Modern English Publications British Council.

Swaffar, J. K., K. Arens, and M. Morgan (1982). Teacher classroom practices: Redefining method as task hierarchy. *Modern Languages Journal* 66: 24–33.

Swain, M. (1985). Communicative competence: Some roles of comprehensible input and comprehensible output in its development. In S. Gass and C. Madden (Eds.), *Input in second language acquisition*, 235–53. Rowley, Mass.: Newbury House.

————. (1995). Collaborative dialogue: Its contribution to second language learning. Plenary paper presented at the annual AAAL conference, March, Long Beach, Cal.

Swales, J. (1980). The educational environment and its relevance to ESP programme design. In E. Smyth (Ed.), *ELT documents special: Projects in materials design*, 61–70. London: The British Council.

―――. (1988). ESP and applied linguistics: Hopes for a brave new world. In M. L. Tickoo (Ed.), *ESP: State of the art*, 14–20. Anthology Series 21. Singapore: SEAMEO-RELC.

―――. (1989). Service English programme design and opportunity cost. In R. K. Johnson (Ed.), *The second language curriculum*, 79–90. Cambridge: Cambridge University Press.

Terrell, T. (1982). The Natural Approach to language teaching: An update. *Modern Language Journal* 66(2): 121–31.

Terrell, T., M. Andrade, J. Egasse, and E. M. Muñoz (1990). *Dos Mundos*, 2nd ed. New York: McGraw-Hill.

Tetenbaum, T. J., and T. A. Mulkeen (1986). Designing teacher education for the twenty-first century. *Journal of Higher Education* 57(6): 621–36.

Tickoo, M. L. (1996). Task-based teaching for acquisition-poor environments: Forward and away from Bangalore. In B. Kenny and W. Savage (Eds.), *Language and development: Teachers in a changing world*, 268–79. London: Longman.

Tollefson, J. W. (1988). Covert policy in the United States refugee program in South East Asia. *Language Problems and Language Planning* 12(1): 30–42.

―――. (1989). Educating for employment in programs for South East Asian refugees: A review of research. *TESOL Quarterly* 23(2): 337–43.

―――. (1991). *Planning language, planning inequality.* New York: Longman.

―――. (Ed.) (1995). *Power and inequality in language education.* Cambridge: Cambridge University Press.

Tomlinson, B. (1990). Managing change in Indonesian high schools. *ELT Journal* 44(1): 25–36.

van Lier, L. (1988). *The classroom and the language learner.* London: Longman.

Wall, D., and J. C. Alderson (1993). Examining washback: The Sri Lankan impact study. *Language Testing* 10(1): 41–69.

Webber, R., and T. Deyes (Eds.) (1986). *Appropriate methodology: Dunford House seminar report, 1986.* London: British Council.

White, R. V. (1987). Managing innovation. *ELT Journal* 41(3): 211–18.

―――. (1988). *The ELT curriculum: Design, innovation and management.* Oxford: Blackwell.

―――. (1993). Innovation in curriculum planning and program development. *Annual Review of Applied Linguistics* 13: 244–59.

White, R. V., M. Martin, M. Stimson, and R. Hodge (1991). *Management in English language teaching.* Cambridge: Cambridge University Press.

Widdowson, H. G. (1978). *Teaching language as communication.* Oxford: Oxford University Press.

―――. (1993). Innovation in teacher development. *Annual Review of Applied Linguistics* 13: 260–75.

Wilkins, D. A. (1976). *Notional syllabuses.* Oxford: Oxford University Press.

―――. (1981a). Notional syllabuses revisited. *Applied Linguistics* 2(1): 84–9.

207

## References

————. (1981b). Notional syllabuses revisited: A further reply. *Applied Linguistics* 2(1): 97–100.

Willing, K. (1988). *Learning styles in adult migrant education*. Adelaide: National Curriculum Resource Centre.

Young, R. (1992). A systems approach to curriculum innovation in intensive English programs. In R. Young (Ed.), *Southern Illinois working papers in linguistics and language teaching*, vol. 1, 75–94. Department of Linguistics, Southern Illinois University at Carbondale.

Zaltman, G., and R. Duncan (1977). *Strategies for planned change*. New York: Wiley.

# Name index

# Subject index*

*Page references to tables and figures are followed by the letter *t*.

213

Printed in the United Kingdom
by Lightning Source UK Ltd.
92956